SACRAMENTS
Celebrating + Living + Believing

HARCOURT RELIGION HIGH SCHOOL

Harcourt Religion Publishers

www.harcourtreligion.com

Copyright © 2008 by Harcourt Religion Publishers

All rights reserved. No part of this publication may be reproduced or transmitted in any form or by any means, electronic or mechanical, including photocopy, recording, or any information storage and retrieval system, without permission in writing from the publisher.

Requests for permission ot make copies of any part of the work should be addressed to School Permission and Copyrights, Harcourt, Inc., 6277 Sea Harbor Drive, Orlando, Florida 32887-6777. Fax: 407-345-2418.

HARCOURT and the Harcourt Logo are trademarks of Harcourt, Inc., registered in the United States of America and/or other jurisdictions.

For permission to reprint copyrighted material, grateful acknowledgment is made to the following sources:

Costello Publishing Company, Inc., Northport, NY: From *Vatican Council II, The Basic Sixteen Documents,* edited by Rev. Austin Flannery, O.P. Text copyright © 1996 by Reverend Austin Flannery, O.P.

Division of Christian Education of the National Council of the Churches of Christ in the U.S.A.: Scripture quotations from the *New Revised Standard Version Bible: Catholic Edition.* Text copyright © 1993 and 1989 by the Division of Christian Education of the National Council of the Churches of Christ in the U.S.A.

International Commission on English in the Liturgy: From the English translation of *Rite of Baptism for Children.* Translation © 1969 by International Committee on English in the Liturgy, Inc. From the English translation of *Rite of Christian Initiation of Adults.* Translation © 1985 by International Committee on English in the Liturgy, Inc. From the English translation of *Rite of Confirmation (Second Edition).* Translation © 1975 by International Committee on English in the Liturgy, Inc. From the English translation of *Rite of Marriage.* Translation © 1969 by International Committee on English in the Liturgy, Inc. From the English translation of *Rites of Ordination of a Bishop, of Priests, and of Deacons.* Translation © 2000, 2002 by International Committee on English in the Liturgy, Inc. From the English translation of *The Liturgy of the Hours.* Translation copyright © 1974 by International Committee on English in the Liturgy, Inc. From the English translation of *Pastoral Care of the Sick: Rites of Anointing and Viaticum.* Translation © 1982 by International Committee on English in the Liturgy, Inc. From the English translation of *Rite of Penance.* Translation © 1974 by International Committee on English in the Liturgy, Inc. From the English translation of *The Roman Missal.* Translation © 1973 by International Committee on English in the Liturgy, Inc.

Libreria Editrice Vaticana: From *Dogmatic Constitution on Devine Revelation, Sacred Council,* and *Stay With Us, Lord* at www.vatican.va.

OCP Publications, 5536 NE Hassalo, Portland, OR 97213: Lyrics from "Come, O Holy Spirit." Lyrics © 1980 by OCP Publications.

Oxford University Press, on behalf of the British Province of the Society of Jesus, www.oup.com: From "God's Grandeur" in *Poems of Gerard Manley Hopkins* by Gerard Manley Hopkins. Published by Oxford University Press, 1970.

Penguin Books Ltd.: From *Saint Augustine: Confessions,* translated with an Introduction by R. S. Pine-Coffin. Translation copyright © 1961 by R. S. Pine-Coffin.

St. Anthony Messenger Press: From *Through the Year with Oscar Romero: Daily Meditations,* translated by Irene B. Hodgson, Ph. D. Translation copyright © 2005 by St. Anthony Messenger Press.

St. Pauls Publishing, UK: From *The Awe-Inspiring Rites of Initiation* by Edward Yarnold, S.J. Text © 1971 by St. Paul Publications.

United States Conference of Catholic Bishops, Inc., Washington, D.C.: From the *Catechism of the Catholic Church,* second edition. Text copyright © 2000 by Libreria Editrice Vaticana - United States Catholic Conference. From "Happy Are Those Who Are Called to His Supper." Text copyright © 2006 by United States Conference of Catholic Bishops. From *Stewardship: A Disciple's Response.* Text copyright © 2002 by United States Conference of Catholic Bishops.

Printed in the United States of America

ISBN 0-15-901884-6   ISBN 13: 978-0-15-901884-2

3 4 5 6 7 8 9 10   0877   11 10 09

Contents

Rituals are so much a part of our ordinary life that we usually are oblivious to them. They are like the air we breathe—essential for our survival, yet so familiar that we rarely take notice. Occasionally, if the wind is blowing fiercely, or if the breeze suddenly stops and there is a great stillness, or if we are sick with a chest cold, we may stop and take notice. We may be led to reflect on how essential the air around us is. But mostly we just take it for granted.

Rituals are like that. From infancy onward, we are immersed in a world of rituals. Bathing, feeding, and getting dressed are some of the earliest rituals a child experiences. In our families, we have little rituals we are so used to that we do not even think of them as such. We have ways of greeting our parents or siblings, ways of organizing life together in our homes, ways of accomplishing simple everyday tasks, and so forth. When guests arrive or relatives gather for festive occasions, we call on special rituals to mark the occasion. We greet them with hugs or hearty handshakes, provide food and drink, offer them a seat of honor or comfort, or do other familiar, stylized activities that represent rituals of hospitality and welcome. Oftentimes, it is only when we are exposed to other people's ways of acting under similar circumstances—for example, when visiting friends' homes or traveling in a foreign culture—that we become aware of the distinctive nature of our own ritual behaviors.

Rituals Reveal Values, Beliefs, and Identity

While most of our rituals are informal and happen without any conscious intent, we are also familiar with more formal, deliberate rituals that we adopt for specific purposes and occasions. When a new President of the United States is inaugurated, a whole repertoire of public rituals is enacted. On a more modest scale, when families celebrate births, weddings, or funerals, they usually have very definite ways of observing those important occasions—rituals that everyone is familiar with and that allow them to share the deeper meanings of the events taking place.

Because rituals are a universal feature of being human, they are wonderful objects of study if we wish to know more about a group, a society, or even an individual. That is why so many academic disciplines, for instance, sociology, psychology, and anthropology, are interested in and study rituals. Understanding the rituals of a people opens up a window into their core beliefs, values, and their unique identity as a nation or a culture. What matters most to any community is deeply embedded in the distinctive rituals that are used by its people, and the richness of a culture is opened up wonderfully when we look carefully at their rituals.

Rituals Tell Us about Ourselves

But another benefit we gain from studying about rituals is a better insight into ourselves. As we become more aware of the role that rituals have played in our lives, we come to appreciate better our own personal heritage, and how those rituals have formed us on deep, even unconscious, levels, and help make us who we are today. It may seem like an unlikely example, but few rituals gain as much attention in our society as the ones surrounding Super Bowl Sunday. Friends and families, those who root for favorite teams, hometowns, and even entire regions have distinctive ways of celebrating that annual extravaganza that is such a U. S. phenomenon, down to the greatly anticipated commercials that air for the first time during the game. It is as if the entire nation takes a day off to participate in a collective tailgate party!

Those who have studied our culture from the perspective of what the rituals on Super Bowl Sunday are saying about us often remark on the way we value teamwork, competition, and the cult of superheroes. They also note that ours is a society that thinks in terms of win-lose, rather than win-win. We admire strength, power, and vanquishing enemies more than we celebrate compromise, accommodation, or reverence for those who may be of noble intent but are physically weaker. Our rituals on Super Bowl Sunday make it clear that ours is a consumer society that values material success as much as, or more than, spiritual depth.

Reflecting on ritual highlights is an important way that our core beliefs and values are passed on to us from one generation to another. Rituals transmit attitudes about what is important and what isn't, what is right and wrong, and what is fair and unfair. Rituals embody in symbolic form the things that matter most to us, and they play a number of other roles vital to the organization and survival of any social group.

Most of all, we need to recognize that rituals are not just empty routine, nor are they mere habit: Rituals *mean* something; they are *meaningful* and *purposeful,* whether or not we recognize them as such. In fact, because they so often operate beneath the level of our reflective awareness, rituals are tremendously powerful in shaping not only our beliefs, attitudes, and values, but our behaviors as well.

Our Sacred Rituals—the Sacraments

The liturgical rituals the Church celebrates—our sacraments—are no exception to this universal understanding of how rituals function within human communities. Yes, they may celebrate mysteries beyond our ability to understand fully, because God is actually present and active in those sacred rites. But that does not remove from our sacramental rites the features that they have in common with other human rituals. Our sacraments, like other rituals, transmit to us the fundamental beliefs and values that our Catholic community of faith holds dear. They embody our beliefs and shape our attitudes, as well as call forth certain behaviors. Because they are about ultimate values and connect us to the presence of God in our midst, sacraments hold all the more weight and should touch us at even deeper levels than the other secular rituals in which we participate.

In this course you are going to have the opportunity to explore in depth and learn a great deal about the foundational rituals of our Catholic faith, the seven sacraments. You will learn about the human shape of those rites, their origins in Jesus and our early Judeo-Christian beginnings, the way they have evolved and developed over time, as well as how they are celebrated today. But the approach you will take is going to be quite different from that of a sociologist, anthropologist, or any of the other academic disciplines that make up the "human sciences." Both your starting point and your ending point in this book are going to be your faith in Jesus Christ, whom the Book of Revelation calls, "the Alpha and the Omega, the first and the last, the beginning and the end" (22:13), the source of our sacraments and their saving power.

An Invitation to Deepen Your Faith

As you learn more about each of the sacraments, you will be invited to deepen your own personal involvement in these sacred signs and symbols by which God involves himself in our human lives. You will discover how God the Holy Spirit works in mysterious and wonderful ways, calling us to be more and more open to the life of God that is within us. Unlike so many other academic courses that touch on subjects remote from your everyday experience, the things you will learn about in this course are going to have very personal implications for you. Just as Jesus in the Gospels challenged those who heard his words, demanding that they decide for or against him, so in learning about the sacraments you will be confronted with truths about which you cannot remain neutral.

The liturgy of the Church celebrates in many different ways a single truth: the Paschal Mystery of Jesus Christ. In doing so, we encounter the Lord Jesus in a manner that demands of us a wholehearted response. Jesus asked Peter, "Who do you say that I am?" and then awaited his response. So, too, as you study about the liturgy and the sacraments, Jesus is asking you to make a commitment, to come to a deeper and fuller faith—in him, and in the many different ways that he is present and can be encountered in the sacraments.

As you learn more about the sacraments you will also come to a more mature understanding of how meaningful and purposeful they are, and this in turn will call you to commit yourself to live more fully and actively as a disciple of Jesus Christ. This will happen because you will grow in your appreciation for the sacraments as mysteries of salvation, doorways into the divine, life-changing rituals that fill our lives with meaning and purpose.

How to Use This Book

Every chapter in this book will begin with a real-life story. These stories are "real" not in the sense that they describe actual people, but in the sense that the situations described in them are the kind that ordinary people really and truly live, day in and day out. Hopefully you will be able to identify with those stories, either as a situation in which you could imagine finding yourself, or as the sort of situation others might live that you can understand without difficulty.

In each of the seven chapters that look at a specific sacrament, the first two sections will help you to understand the actual ritual celebration of the sacrament under consideration: its historical origins and evolution, as well as how it is celebrated today. You will also be invited to consider what a person needs to do in order to be ready to celebrate that sacrament with the "full, conscious and active participation" called for by the Vatican Council's *Constitution on the Sacred Liturgy.*

In the third section of each of those chapters you will be challenged to connect the dots between what we celebrate in the liturgy and how we are supposed to live our lives in the world. Finally, in the fourth section you will explore more deeply what it is that the Church teaches about the meaning of the sacrament and how it connects to the larger mysteries of our faith.

At the end of this course, you will have learned a great deal about how we Roman Catholics celebrate the liturgies of the seven sacraments, and how those sacred rituals give meaning to our lives and guide us at every step of our life's journey. Even more importantly, you will have had the opportunity to grow in appreciation for the incredible gift of love that the sacraments represent. You will see them for what they are—signs of how much God the Father loves us, a unique way that Jesus Christ continues to live in our midst, and our ongoing experience of the Holy Spirit, who is breathing a spark of the divine into human hearts that long for life without end.

Features

FAITH ACTIVITY

Faith Activity Each chapter offers several "Faith Activities" that will take you beyond the textbook into other source materials, and into your own creativity. Good use of the Faith Activities will be one of the keys to learning to celebrate the sacraments. They will also help you to form your faith and to make connections between your daily life and your Catholic faith.

Group Talk Each chapter offers several "Group Talk" activities designed to help you and your classmates hold that part of the chapter up for discussion. The conversations are for small groups of three to six people. Don't worry! You don't have to reveal anything too serious about yourself. But discussing your ideas can help you to clarify what you believe, and listening to other people's ideas can enrich and sometimes challenge your thinking.

Connecting the Rite and Symbol to Everyday Life This feature follows sacramental charts and takes the elements and rites of each sacrament to lead you to make connections between the sacraments and your daily life. These help you to see how you live out the sacraments in various, everyday-life circumstances. These also lead you to see the impact of ritual on the way we look at society, our relationships, and our actions.

Quick Check Each section of the chapter concludes with a "Quick Check"—four questions intended to help you capture the major points you've considered in that section. These questions will also appear in a different format in the Study Guide, which concludes the Chapter Wrap-Up. If you can't answer one or more of them, go back and find the answer.

Person of Faith and Reflection Questions Each Chapter Wrap-Up begins by introducing you to one or more people of faith whose life personified the grace of the sacraments. You will also be given three "Reflection Questions" that focus on their lives and will lead you to deeper understanding of the sacraments. Answering these questions and reflecting upon them will help you see how the sacraments have been lived out in everyday lives.

Prayer Each chapter ends with a prayer celebration designed to immerse you in a mood of sacramental celebration. These prayer celebrations can be used in many ways. Perhaps your teacher will want to begin the chapter with one, instead of praying it at the end—or perhaps you'll use it both times. The prayers can be expanded by adding songs, more time for reflection and shared prayer, or time for intercessions for various needs.

You can also pray the chapter prayers alone, if you wish. Whether you use the prayers here, from other prayer sources, or simply prayers in your own words, praying often will help you in your celebrating and living the sacraments.

Study Guide The "Study Guide" consists of sixteen questions that correspond to the Quick Check questions and four Apply and Develop questions. These questions challenge you to summarize and apply what you've learned in the chapter, develop conclusions about what you believe, and to make connections between faith and life.

Study Guide
▶ **Check Understanding**
▶ **Apply and Develop**
▶ **Key Words**

The hour is coming, and is now here, when the true worshipers will worship the Father in spirit and truth, for the Father seeks such as these to worship him. God is spirit, and those who worship him must worship in spirit and truth.

John 4:23-24

UNDERSTANDING THE SACRAMENTS

CHAPTER GOALS

In this chapter, you will:

★ consider the different ways the term *sacrament* is used.

★ study how the Church as the Body of Christ is the fundamental sacrament of salvation and the Church's liturgy is our worship of the Father.

★ learn how every dimension of our lives and all of time are consecrated to God and made holy.

★ discover what you must do to participate in the sacraments with authenticity and integrity.

★ learn about the life of Saint Benedict.

Jim's Story

None of his friends—least of all his girlfriend—could believe his plans for a summer internship. "You're spending three months in a monastery?"

Jim was finishing his junior year at a prestigious Ivy League school on the East Coast, at the top of his class majoring in microbiology and molecular genetics. He had never been terribly religious. However, his background was thoroughly Catholic, and he had gone to Sunday Mass regularly through his high school years. But the bigger world of ideas he encountered at the university had made him question many of the teachings he had received as a child. In fact, he had gotten the reputation of being something of a rebel when it came to traditional religious ideas and practice.

Jim had been to church infrequently while away at college, and the last place he would have imagined himself finding a science internship was at an isolated Benedictine monastery in the Pacific Northwest. His research interest in genetically altered crops had put him in touch with one of the nation's largest agribusinesses, and they had assigned him to work in their "Saint Thomas Lab" for the summer.

The "Lab" turned out to be the Benedictine Monastery of Saint Thomas, founded nearly 30 years earlier by a priest named Father Peter. Father Peter also happened to be a Nobel Prize-winning scientist who had given up his life "in the world," joined the Benedictines, and eventually founded a new monastery on the Oregon coast. The monastery supported itself through an innovative agricultural research facility.

Father Peter's research into genetically engineered rice and wheat strains had won a Nobel Prize for breakthrough discoveries that had benefited millions of people living on the verge of starvation. Several of the two-dozen or so monks who lived in the monastery were also well-educated, highly specialized men who had been attracted by the holiness and personal charisma of Father Peter. Yet they could hold their own with many of the finest research scientists Jim had met at the university.

Jim was thrown into something for which he was quite unprepared. The combination of intellectual genius and deep faith that he encountered in the monks challenged him to look more deeply at his own spiritual ideas. Over the course of the summer, in long walks with Father Peter and other monks after work, Jim was able to voice his questions about God, faith, the Catholic Church, and many other religious ideas.

The fact that these men who were so obviously his intellectual superiors would dialogue with him on equal terms—that they took seriously his questions, and respected even his doubts and disagreements—moved Jim deeply and served to fuel his desire to think about his Catholic faith in more mature terms. The Benedictine tradition of the monastery was centered on the liturgy, and the way the monks followed a sacred rhythm of prayer and work every day struck Jim as particularly impressive. Only later did he learn about the Benedictine ideal of "*ora et labora*," prayer and work, and how influential Saint Benedict's vision had been on the Church's monastic tradition for nearly 1,500 years.

By the end of the summer Jim even found himself wondering when he could again spend time with the monks. He also wondered if Fr. Peter had friends on the East Coast whom he could talk to and perhaps even join at Mass. When he returned to the university in September his friends immediately recognized that something significant had happened to their friend.

GROUP TALK

1. How did Jim change in this story? Who and/or what contributed to that transformation?

2. What would you have asked the monks about the relationship between faith and life? Between prayer and work?

3. What role do faith and prayer have in your life—the choices you make, the things you do, the attitudes you have?

A Sacramental World

Keep in mind that although the characters, places, and events of the story of Jim and Father Peter are not historical in nature, they are important because they address real-life issues and situations through which God's plan for people unfolds. As the story continues, in the early weeks of his internship, Jim had asked Father Peter if he minded explaining to him how a brilliant scientist such as himself could flourish within a remote monastic community. The old abbot laughed, and said he'd be glad to, but first he wanted Jim to read two of his favorite texts. That evening, he handed Jim two freshly photocopied sheets of paper on which Father Peter had highlighted what he wanted Jim to read. The first was a page from chapter one of Saint Paul's Letter to the Romans. The following verses were highlighted in yellow.

For what can be known about God is plain to them, because God has shown it to them. Ever since the creation of the world his eternal power and divine nature, invisible though they are, have been understood and seen through the things he has made. So they are without excuse; for though they knew God, they did not honor him as God or give thanks to him, but they became futile in their thinking, and their senseless minds were darkened. Claiming to be wise, they became fools…

✝ Romans 1:19–22

The other was a poem by the Jesuit priest, Gerard Manley Hopkins, and the following lines were highlighted:

The world is charged with the grandeur of God.
It will flame out, like shining from shook foil;
It gathers to a greatness, like the ooze of oil
Crushed...

And for all this, nature is never spent;
There lives the dearest freshness deep down things;
And though the last lights off the black West went
Oh, morning, at the brown brink eastward, springs—
Because the Holy Ghost over the bent
World broods with warm breast and with ah! Bright wings.

Gerard Manley Hopkins, "God's Grandeur," *Poems of Gerard Manley Hopkins*

In the remainder of this section we will explore the Church's teachings that summarize what Father Peter explained to Jim in response to his curiosity about how the abbot had found God even in a remote monastery. In essence, the abbot told Jim how he was able to discover God in the beauty and wonder of creation, and how he found the fullest and most powerful expression of that beauty in the life of Jesus, the Son of God who revealed to him the Most Blessed Trinity at work in the world.

The Work of Creation

Human beings are more than a mere collection of molecules that have come together through a random process of evolutionary development. We know our existence as a species is part of a purposeful divine plan set in motion by the Creator of all things. Although it speaks in a poetic and theological rather than scientific fashion, the Book of Genesis describes the harmony of creation as a blessing from God who wished to share his life, goodness, and love with other beings. As creatures made in the divine image and likeness, only humans have an innate desire and inclination toward God. We search for meaning, we long for ultimate fulfillment, and our final happiness will be found in God alone.

In the passage quoted above from the Letter to the Romans, Saint Paul faults the pagan world for failing to recognize the Creator of all who stands behind the beauty and wonder of material creation. Church teaching emphasizes that we humans are capable of recognizing the hand of God at work in creation by reflecting on its order and its beauty. (See *CCC,* 32.) So, too, by reflection on our own existence we can recognize that man "bears in himself an eternal seed which cannot be reduced to sheer matter" (*Pastoral Constitution on the Church in the Modern World,* 18), and that we come from and are destined to find fulfillment in "a reality which is the first cause and final end of all things, a reality 'that everyone calls "God"'[1] (St. Thomas Aquinas, *Summa Theologica,* I: 2, 3)" (*CCC,* 34).

The lines quoted on the previous page from the Jesuit poet Gerard Manley Hopkins capture something of our deep Catholic sensibility to the way that the Creator is revealed in his creation. We see with spiritual eyes that behind and within creation itself, we can catch a glimpse of the infinite Mystery we call God. It is in this sense that material creation is sometimes spoken of as a sacrament of God, because it is a kind of sign that points beyond itself to a sacred dimension, calling us to encounter God himself.

The word sacrament is used in theological language in several senses, however. We must be aware of how the term is being used in order to understand just what is being suggested. Here, what we mean by calling creation a sacrament is that by carefully reflecting on material reality—and our human existence as part of that reality—a person can come to knowledge of God's existence. But we also recognize that our ability to arrive at a clear knowledge of God has been weakened by the way that sin and its many effects have adversely affected human reason.

FAITH ACTIVITY

A Sign of God We can learn something about God by meditating and reflecting on the world around us. Visit or think about some of your favorite nature spots or events. What do they reveal to you about who God is, what God does, how God calls you to be or live? Write your thoughts down, and go back to them after the conclusion of the chapter. What insights might you add? If you have any photos of these spots or events, see if your teacher would like you to prepare a PowerPoint presentation.

God More Fully Revealed

But God has not left us to our own halting, human efforts to find out about him and to discover how to reach our fulfillment in him. In their document on Divine Revelation, the bishops at the Second Vatican Council, which convened from 1962–1965 and was one of only three Church councils in the past 500 years, summed up this teaching this way.

> In His goodness and wisdom God chose to reveal Himself and to make known to us the hidden purpose of His will (see Eph. 1:9) by which through Christ, the Word made flesh, man might in the Holy Spirit have access to the Father and come to share in the divine nature (see Eph. 2:18: 2 Peter 1:4). Through this revelation, therefore, the invisible God (see Col. 1;15, 1 Tim. 1:17) out of the abundance of His love speaks to men as friends (see Ex. 33:11; John 15:14–15) and lives among them (see Bar. 3:38), so that He may invite and take them into fellowship with Himself.
>
> *Dogmatic Constitution on Divine Revelation, 2*

The mystery of the Most Holy Trinity is utterly beyond our human capacity to discover on our own, yet it has been revealed to us as the central truth of our Christian faith and our Christian life.

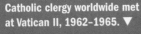

Catholic clergy worldwide met at Vatican II, 1962–1965. ▼

The Revelation of the Trinity was foreshadowed in the times of God's Chosen People as recorded in the Old Testament. But the Trinity's fullest and most definitive disclosure has come about in the person of Jesus Christ, the only son of the Father. Jesus is both true God and true man. We use the term Incarnation to refer to this mystery of the union of divine and human natures in the one person of the Word made flesh, Jesus Christ. The mystery of the Incarnation is the cornerstone upon which our Christian faith rests. Because he possesses two natures—one fully divine and the other fully human—Jesus Christ is able to be the one and only mediator between God and humans. By taking on human nature, Jesus shares his divinity with us, making it possible for us to become children of God.

We can come to knowledge of God only in and through our human nature. That is why it is so important for Jesus to be fully human and to communicate the Revelation of divine truth to us in a human fashion. By the whole of his human life—his teachings, his miracles, his prayer, his love for all people shown by the things he said and did—Jesus brought to us the fullness of Revelation. In this sense, Jesus has been called "the human face of God."

In this same sense we can say that Jesus is the sacrament of God the Father: He is the tangible image or sign of what is ultimately beyond all human understanding. Yet, as mediator between God and humans, he is an effective sign, one that truly connects us to God. Thus, we see that there is a second use of the term sacrament that indicates the richness of this concept.

Against the backdrop of the story of Jim and his dialogue with Father Peter, we have learned about how both creation and Jesus are sometimes described as sacraments that reveal God to us, pointing us beyond ourselves and connecting us to the realm of the sacred. In the next section we will explore more deeply the concept of sacrament in its more specific application to the Church and the seven major rituals by which the Church celebrates the mystery of God's saving action in our human lives.

Toward a Deeper Understanding

In telling Jim about how he felt himself called to the religious life, Father Peter explained how the movement of his own spiritual journey had progressed from a sense of God at work in creation, to his discovery of how powerfully one could experience the divine presence in a faith community. Father Peter explained that he had converted to Catholicism as a young man not long after finishing his post-graduate studies at UCLA. At the time, his faith was very fresh, very personal, but also very individual. He really had never felt part of a Christian community. It was God the Father and Jesus and the Gospels that had attracted him. He encountered a Benedictine community not far from his home at the time, and the power of their praying together utterly blew him away. The sense of peace they radiated—and the way their whole life was shaped by the rhythm of the community's prayers—spoke so powerfully to him that he had to find out more about that way of life. He was sensing more and more strongly in his heart that God was calling him to find his home in that sort of community.

A Sister of Saint Joseph of Carondelet, Los Angeles province, works with a child and his father. ▼

Discovering the Church as Sacrament

The *Catechism* describes the Church as "The universal sacrament of salvation" (*CCC*, 776). In their foundational document on the nature of the Church, the bishops at the Second Vatican Council said, "the Church is in Christ like a sacrament or as a sign and instrument" (*Dogmatic Constitution on the Church*, 1). They explained this teaching by saying that the Church's purpose is to be a sign or sacrament of the union that is meant to exist between humankind and God, as well as of the unity of the human race itself. It is important to know that the bishops were drawing on the traditional theological understanding that a sacrament brings about that which it signifies. Thus, they were saying that the Church is God's instrument to bring about that unity which she (the Church) signifies—the unity between humanity and God, as well as among all people. In this sense "the Church is both the means and the goal of God's plan" (*CCC*, 778).

Describing the Church as a sacrament helps us understand that the Church has both a visible and an invisible reality. She is both a hierarchical, ordered society with a historical presence and tangible, human aspects; and, she is also the Mystical Body of Christ, a spiritual reality that includes a divine aspect of her essential identity. We have seen above that Jesus Christ, who is both human and divine, can be called the sacrament of God who mediates God's salvation to us. Because the Church is the Body of Christ, it follows that she, too, has both a human and a divine aspect to her fundamental nature. As the bishops put it,

> [These two dimensions of the Church] form one complex reality which coalesces from a divine and a human element. For this reason . . . [the Church] is compared to the mystery of the incarnate Word.
>
> *Dogmatic Constitution on the Church, 8*

What Father Peter tried to communicate to Jim was his own discovery of how a community of ordinary human beings can be a place where one is connected to this larger mystery of divine presence, that is, to God. When we say that the community of the Church is the presence or sacrament of Christ on earth, we point to the fact that this is a very specific way that Jesus still lives in our midst. The Church is the way that Jesus continues to be present among us throughout time. Because he is the perfect link between humanity and divinity, his "body," the Church, is also the extension throughout time and space of that same linkage. Thus "all salvation comes from Christ the Head through the Church which is his Body" (Catechism, 846). Christ gave his first followers, and all in the Church since then, a missionary mandate to spread the Good News to people everywhere so that they could come to know his saving work through the Church. She is the sacrament of our communion with God, and she links us to the divine through the Holy Spirit—the Spirit of Jesus—who is the life's breath of the Church, the life principle of this "body" of believers.

GROUP TALK

1. Using your parish and school as examples, name some ways the Church is a visible reality. An invisible reality?

2. How do the various ministries and services within your parish model the way the Church is the Body of Christ to others?

3. All baptized members of the Church are signs of God's presence, love, and action in the world. How can you be a sign of God? How can your family be?

The Church's Worship The link between the human and divine that we recognize in the Incarnation of Jesus Christ and in his Body, the Church, are very significant because of the longing within every human heart for God. We are made for God, and, as Saint Augustine put it, our hearts are restless until they rest in God. God continually calls us to a relationship of prayer. Throughout salvation history we see prayer as back and forth dialogue between God and humans.

Created with free will, humans have the choice to respond to God and to seek him out. The human choice to sin ruptured the relationship of intimate love and unity with God that was the gift of creation, and we all experience the separation of humanity from God. So we long for reconciliation at the deepest level of our being. Thus, the truth that God has reached out to us, offering to us the opportunity to restore the harmony between him and us, and between creation and us, is Good News indeed!

The magnitude of the gift of **grace** given to us in the Redemption is the ultimate mystery of love. Grace does not take away our freedom. It does the opposite, responding to our desire to be free, making it possible for us to cooperate with God's life in us. How can we not try to respond by returning that love—to offer praise, to adore, and to thank and bless God the Father, who is the source of every blessing and has loved us in this astounding way? Once we come to know God in a personal way, we know that we have to respond to him in some significant way. But Jesus, the Son of God, is the only human who can offer to the Father a complete response, precisely because he is true God and true man, human *and* divine.

Jesus offers humanity's prayer of praise and thanks throughout all time, on behalf of every human person. In fact, Jesus our High Priest celebrates an unceasing heavenly liturgy, together with all of the saints in heaven. The liturgy is the Church's official public prayer. It is the prayer of the entire Communion of Saints and is one of the most important ways that we are joined to those who have gone before us in faith. It is because Jesus has shared his Spirit with us in the Church that we are drawn into that mystery of unceasing prayer, and it is as members of the Body of Christ—the Church—that we are able to join our prayer to his. Along with the Church's liturgy, Scripture and the theological virtues are sources of prayer.

The term *liturgy* is a combination of two Greek words that mean "the people's work." Indeed, this truly is the work of the People of God: to worship the Father who has blessed us in Christ Jesus and delivered us from sin and the tragic consequences of sin. There is a sense, however, in which not only the Church's official prayer but *everything* we do—work and prayer, joys and sorrows—can be offered to God as a kind of liturgy, an act of worship, just as Jesus offered everything he did up to the Father.

Liturgy is the core of the "people's work"—to bring our whole selves to God by offering up every aspect of our lives in service of his Kingdom. This is what Saint Paul was referring to when he told the early Christians "to present your bodies as a living sacrifice, holy and acceptable to God, which is your spiritual worship" (*Romans 12:1*). In the liturgy, the Holy Spirit gathers up the whole of our lives and brings them to God, together with the prayer of Jesus for all of humanity.

GROUP TALK

Theologians sometimes talk about a series of conversions one must undergo to arrive at a fully mature faith: first to God, then to Jesus, to the Church, to a life led by Gospel values, and so forth. Discuss what it means to deepen one's faith by gaining a new sense of how we can encounter God in the Church's liturgy, in the person of Jesus, and in all of creation.

Work of the Trinity While liturgy is certainly the work of the people, the *Catechism* also reminds us that it is the "work of the Holy Trinity" (*CCC*, Part Two, Section One, Article 1). This expression indicates that in the sacred liturgy something much more is involved than mere human activity. Liturgy has its source in God, the Father of all blessings, and it in turn is directed back to him as the one to whom all liturgical prayer is addressed. However, liturgical prayer is always also the prayer of God's Son, Jesus Christ, and it is always prayed in the power of the Holy Spirit. We are reminded of the Trinitarian character of all liturgical prayer each time

FAITH ACTIVITY

The Liturgy Read the *Catechism of the Catholic Church* to find out what *liturgy* means (1069-1070), how liturgy, prayer, and the Trinity relate (1073), and how the Holy Spirit and the Church cooperate in the liturgy (1091-1092). Discuss how you would explain why you participate in the Church's liturgy to another Christian seeking to understand it.

Instituted by Christ Through his action and ministry, Christ commanded his Apostles to continue his work; he gave his Church the sacraments. Read the following Scripture passages and identify to which sacrament it connects. 1 John 4:7–21, Acts 3:1–10, John 2:1–11, Luke 9:10–17, Mark 3:13–19, Matthew 10:5–7, John 20:22, John 20:23, John 8:1–11, John 3:1–5, Matthew 18:21–22, Matthew 15:29–31, Luke 9:6, Matthew 19:3–6, Acts 2:1–4, John 21:15–17, John 6:32–35.

the priest at Mass concludes the Eucharistic Prayer with the words, "Through him [Christ], with him, in him, in the unity of the Holy Spirit, all glory and honor is yours, almighty Father, for ever and ever."

The *Catechism* offers a concise summary of the nature of the work of the Holy Spirit in the Church's liturgy:

- preparing us to encounter the Lord there
- stirring up the gift of faith in our hearts by making us mindful of all that the Lord has done for us
- making Christ present in our midst
- making real the gift of our union with God—truly joining us together, not only with one another but with the whole Trinity.

The Seven Sacraments

The *Catechism* also has a marvelous way of expressing the action of the Holy Spirit in the seven sacraments—effective signs of grace instituted by Christ and entrusted to the Church by which divine life is shared with us through the work of the Holy Spirit. "In the liturgy the Holy Spirit is teacher of the faith of the People of God and artisan of 'God's masterpieces,' the sacraments of the New Covenant" (CCC, 1091). Christ gave us the sacraments so that, through the Holy Spirit's action in them, we would share in the divine life.

The seven sacraments are the way the foundational sacrament of the Church is localized in every time and place, and in every phase of a person's life. Each of the sacraments in its own way celebrates the life, death, Resurrection, and Ascension of Jesus—what we call his Paschal Mystery. These sacraments that accompany us from birth to death make a whole universe of meaning available to those who live the liturgy as the basic rhythm of their lives.

The rites of the sacraments are not empty signs. Given to us by the will of Christ himself, they are symbols filled with meaning and the holy presence of the divine. They don't simply point to something else (a sacred reality), they make that reality present; they bring about the grace they signify (new life, healing, forgiveness, membership, and so on). Each of the sacraments makes God's grace present, and "they bear fruit in those who receive them with the required dispositions" (CCC, 1131). Sacraments, in fact, give us a taste of the heavenly liturgy that is our common destiny. In the course of studying each of the sacraments, you will be invited to understand and appreciate more deeply the wonderful mystery of salvation that is ours and that we celebrate in the sacraments.

The phrase the *Catechism* uses, "God's masterpieces," to describe the sacraments offers a hint at what will be possible as you study carefully each of the sacraments in turn. Just as with any other form of a masterpiece—be it music, painting, poetry or any other art form—one must cultivate a certain knowledge and background in order to appreciate fully the genius involved. So, too, through your careful study of and reflection upon the sacred rituals by which the Church worships God, you will hopefully develop a greater understanding for the goodness of God who acts in our midst in such ordinary and extraordinary ways. "O taste and see that the LORD is good; happy are those who take refuge in him" (*Psalm 34:8*).

At the end of your course of study of the sacraments, you will be able to understand these "masterpieces" with a new depth that enlarges your appreciation significantly. However, before we narrow our focus to the liturgy's seven sacraments, we will consider in the next section some other important dimensions of the Church's life of prayer and worship.

Sacraments of Initiation
· Baptism
· Confirmation
· Eucharist

Sacraments of Healing
· Penance and Reconciliation
· Anointing of the Sick

Sacraments at the Service of Communion
· Holy Orders
· Matrimony

FAITH ACTIVITY

Symbolic Actions Make a list of symbolic gestures (for example, shaking hands with someone, turning your back on someone, waving, etc.). Next to each gesture, write what they mean in our culture. What message do the words or actions convey? Then make a list of some of the rituals and symbols used in the sacraments. What messages do they convey? Taking it a step further than everyday signs, how do they help make God present to us? For further research, find out what these signs mean in other cultures and what signs other cultures use as equivalents to those of our culture.

Quick Check

1. How is the Church a sacrament of God's presence and action in the world?
2. What is liturgy?
3. What are the sacraments?
4. What is the Paschal Mystery?

Unending Praise

We spoke in the previous section about the fact that Jesus our High Priest continually offers a heavenly liturgy on our behalf. Here on earth, the Church participates in that timeless liturgy by worshiping throughout all of time. The phrase the liturgical cycle, also known as the liturgical year, refers to the way that the Church strives to consecrate all time to God, thus making sacred every moment of our earthly existence.

The idea of dividing up the flow of time into distinct segments, each with its own character, is not original to the Christian tradition. Every culture in every age has had its ways of marking the passage of time. From the dawn of human history, the rhythms of nature have provided the basic framework for how people have experienced time's passing. The solar cycle of 24 hours and 365 days and the lunar cycle provided daily, monthly, and annual segments of time that could be measured in predictable ways. Many cultures adapted seasonal rhythms associated with these cycles to their religious beliefs, incorporating sacred rituals into the way the community observed the passage of time.

Our Jewish Heritage The ancient Jews were no exception to this pattern. They marked dawn and dusk every day with morning and evening prayer. Many of their feasts and

Jewish family celebrates Passover ▼

religious festivals were tied to the cycles of nature such as planting, harvesting, and so forth. One of the distinctive features of Jewish religious rituals, however, was the way they linked those originally nature-based festivals with actual historical events in which they had experienced God's saving grace and intervention on their behalf.

History, for the Jews, was not an endlessly cyclic repetition of patterns lacking ultimate meaning. Rather, history was a gradual unfolding of God's plan, filled with purposeful events that aimed at a final resolution in what came to be thought of as the messianic era. Festivals of Passover, Pentecost, and others—although they were still tied to seasonal rhythms—took on the character of historical commemorations of how God had acted in Jewish history. These commemorations also frequently came to be thought of as foreshadowing future events whose meanings could be found in historical recollection.

In addition, the concept of a memorial came to have special significance for the Jews. For, in a mysterious but real way, a memorial made present here and now the past events that were being commemorated. For example, the annual Passover meal connected those who celebrated it with the historical reality of God freeing the people from slavery. But, it also anticipated the messianic banquet, when God's final vindication of the people would be accomplished once and for all.

Prayer without Ceasing

The early Church inherited this Jewish framework for using religious ritual to support and celebrate faith. But the community also frequently transformed what she inherited and marked it with a distinctively Christian stamp. The Jewish custom of morning and evening prayer, for example, was incorporated seamlessly into Christian religious practice. In the early monastic communities, daily prayer evolved into a more elaborate way of marking the entire day with prayers every few hours. From these origins what we currently know of as the **Liturgy of the Hours** developed. In the Liturgy of the Hours today, the Church continues to place major emphasis on Morning Prayer and Evening Prayer, but other hours of the day are also identified as deserving of specific prayer.

At the time of the Second Vatican Council, the Liturgy of the Hours (also known as the "Office" or "Breviary") was regarded almost exclusively as the prayer of priests and monks. The Council's liturgical reform sought to restore this prayer to its original ownership by all of the faithful, but success in that regard has still been quite limited. More and more Catholics, however, are discovering some version of Morning Prayer and Evening Prayer based on the Liturgy of the Hours and adopting it as their basic form and rhythm of prayer.

FAITH ACTIVITY

Your Liturgy of Hours Make a schedule for a typical day in your life (for instance, wake up at 6:30 A.M., go to school at 8 A.M., and so on). Identify the rhythms of your days. What are the prayers you pray at these times? What prayers might you add to the times you have yet to accompany with prayer?

God the Holy Spirit calls us to pray at all times. He is the one who instructs the Church in the ways of prayer, inspiring us to new ways of expressing the key forms of prayer: blessing, petition, intercession, thanksgiving and praise.

Saint Paul says,

Likewise the Spirit helps us in our weakness; for we do not know how to pray as we ought, but that very Spirit intercedes with sighs too deep for words. And God, who searches the heart, knows what is the mind of the Spirit, because the Spirit intercedes for the saints according to the will of God.

✝ Romans 8:26–27

GROUP TALK

1. When are some times you pray? Why do you pray then?

2. What prayer time might you initiate with your family, or what are some ways your family prays already?

3. Have you ever experienced a powerful prayer experience within a community, perhaps a retreat, a school Mass, or a youth event? What was the experience like?

4. Are there particular places where you like to talk to God? What makes those places special?

5. In what ways can your class mark the day as sacred?

Sunday—the Lord's Day One of the most original ways that the early Church marked out time in a distinctive manner—and transformed an inherited Jewish tradition in the process—was the observance of Sunday as the Lord's Day. This observance of Sunday was to become, in the words of the *Constitution on the Sacred Liturgy,* "the foundation and kernel of the whole liturgical year" (106). Instead of continuing to make Saturday, the Sabbath, their primary weekly festival, the followers of Jesus met faithfully every Sunday to celebrate their sacred fellowship meal "in remembrance" of him, just as he had commanded at the Eucharist—the Last Supper. They did this despite the fact that Sunday was an ordinary workday, and their gatherings often had to be held in secret, lest they be discovered, persecuted, and even killed.

Sunday was chosen because it marked the day of the Lord's Resurrection, and it soon came to be thought of also as the day that foreshadowed his final return in glory at the end of time. Thus, the first Christians' Sunday observance looked back in remembrance but also looked forward in anticipation. The intersection of these two perspectives was the present moment, a sacred time when the followers of Jesus honored his command to gather and break bread in his memory. In doing so they recognized his presence in their midst, transforming their earthly reality into a sacred experience of his salvation. We still retain an expression of this viewpoint in the acclamation said after the Eucharistic words of institution: "Christ has died; Christ is risen; Christ will come again." The importance of Sunday in the Christian tradition flows from Jesus' command to celebrate the Eucharist until he comes in glory. It is because of this fact that the Church requires every Catholic to participate in Mass on Sundays.

The Annual Cycle of Feasts and Seasons Sunday was observed with sacred ritual right from the beginning, as we have noted. But the larger cycle of the liturgical year only took shape gradually over the course of several centuries. Early on, the annual commemoration of Easter emerged as an important time for Christians to celebrate in a special way their faith in the Resurrection. By the fourth century the sacraments of Christian initiation began to be celebrated more frequently, and eventually exclusively, at Easter, and this practice was the origin of a preparatory period of Lent, as well as a time to prolong the celebrations associated with new members being "born again" into the Christian family during the Easter Season.

FAITH ACTIVITY

Celebrating the Lord's Day With a partner, make a list of the ways that our culture makes it difficult to follow the ancient practice of keeping the Lord's Day holy by worship, rest, acts of social justice, and family time. Make another list of the ways that our culture supports the practice. Then create an Internet banner ad depicting the importance of honoring Sunday and encouraging Catholics to do so.

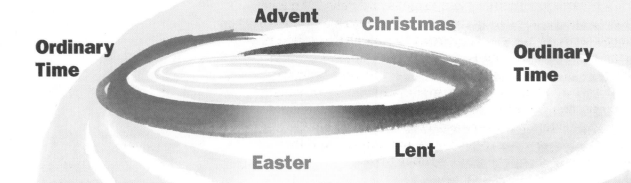

Ordinary Time · Advent · Christmas · Ordinary Time · Lent · Easter

Later on the celebration of the Lord's birth became a more important occasion and was prolonged for nearly two weeks of Christmas season, and it, too, eventually was given a preparatory time of Advent, parallel to Lent.

In between the four seasons of Lent-Easter and Advent-Christmas, the Church began to fill in the year's calendar with the feasts of Mary and the other saints to mark the anniversaries of their deaths, and in some cases, important events in their lives. This was also a way to ritualize the conviction that Christians on earth were still connected to those who had died and were with Jesus in heaven.

In this way, the entire cycle of the liturgical year gradually took shape and became the structure within which believers could claim the passage of time as a sacred experience of God's abiding presence in the Church. In the words of the *Constitution on the Sacred Liturgy*,

> [The liturgical year is the way that the Church] unfolds the whole mystery of Christ . . . Recalling thus the mysteries of redemption, the Church opens to the faithful the riches of her Lord's powers and merits, so that these are in some way made present for all time, and the faithful are enabled to lay hold upon them and become filled with saving grace.
>
> *Constitution on the Sacred Liturgy*, 102

Sacramental Prayer We have also been introduced in an earlier section to the nature of liturgy as embodied or "sacramental" prayer. The liturgy is human ritual, made up of human signs and symbols, and is the way that the Incarnate Christ now acts among his followers. The *Catechism* explains that in the time after Pentecost—what we call the era of the Church—Christ "acts through the sacraments in what the common Tradition of the East and the West calls 'the sacramental economy'; this is the communication . . . of the fruits of Christ's Paschal mystery in the celebration of the Church's 'sacramental' liturgy" (*CCC*, 1076).

Catholics are famous for our "smells and bells." We love incense and candles and prayers like novenas and the rosary and so forth. There is a whole reservoir of what is called popular devotions that nourish the faith of ordinary Catholics and draw them into the mystery of God in very ordinary, simple ways. Many of these symbols and rituals are called sacramentals, because they prepare us for the sacraments and they help us to make every aspect of our lives holy. However, they do not convey grace as the sacraments do, and they were given to us by the Church, not Christ.

Sacramentals can be simple rituals, such as making the Sign of the Cross with holy water; types of prayers, such as the Rosary, Stations of the Cross, or Benediction of the Blessed Sacrament; and, sacred objects, such as crucifixes, icons, rosaries, statues, holy water, blessed oil, ashes, and palms. The most important sacramentals are blessings, and Catholics bless everything, from babies to dogs to cars to buildings. Blessings are the Church's way of saying *everything* is part of God's world, and *everything* can be a source of praise and a reason for heartfelt prayer.

Sometimes in the past, popular devotions have bordered on superstition, and the Church from time to time has had to reform and renew the piety of the faithful, to avoid it degenerating into magical thinking. But for all of the simplicity of the Church's sacramentals, they have carried the faith of millions of ordinary believers through life's toughest times, as well as through moments of joy and happiness. They are God's *ordinary* way of being part of our lives, and they prepare us for the *extraordinary* encounter with God that we share in the sacraments.

✓ Quick Check

1. What is the Liturgy of the Hours?
2. Why is Sunday so important to Christians?
3. What is the liturgical cycle?
4. What is a sacramental?

GROUP TALK

1. With what sacramentals are you familiar?

2. Why do you think sacramentals are important to people's faith?

3. When do you or your family make use of sacramentals? Why do you do so?

4. What are some of the sacramentals used in the liturgy? Why are they used?

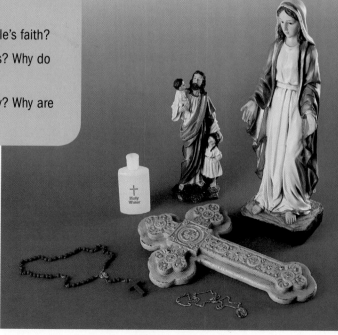

Worship in Spirit and in Truth

Authentic Participation

There are two very different worldviews that are common-place in today's American culture. On the one hand, scholars have described what they call a "postmodern" individual, someone who is not sure if there is anything such as ultimate truth, who expresses skepticism, or perhaps agnosticism, regarding the possibility of belief in God, and who looks on religious ritual as anything from quaint to foolish, but certainly not "meaningful."

On the other hand, one still encounters in many people what scholars describe as a "classical" worldview. The best of traditional Catholic thinking operates out of this framework. Such a person believes in ultimate truth and is convinced of the meaningfulness of life and its ultimate fulfillment in God. A person with a classical viewpoint can regard sacramental rituals not only as credible but also as filled with meaning and as sources of purpose and direction in life.

All of us encounter various expressions of these two quite different stances that one might take toward the sacramental life of the Church. Hopefully this course will help you shape your worldview in a way that opens up for you just how

Catholic Relief Services' Cyber Bridges project strives to form global youth leaders with under-standing of other cultures. ▼

meaningful the liturgy of the Church can be for a believer. As a citizen of a highly pluralistic society, you will have to be able to explain your faith and your religious practice to those who are merely curious, as well as to those who may be aggressively negative. Most importantly, you will need to live your faith with an inner sense of integrity, to know its teachings and to understand its practices and customs.

The question of integrity is particularly important when it comes to the issue of your participation in the Church's liturgical life and the celebration of her sacraments:

- You may have already celebrated all of the Sacraments of Initiation.

- The Sacraments of Healing are also familiar to you as well—certainly Penance and Reconciliation, and perhaps even Anointing of the Sick for yourself or someone close to you.

- In the years ahead, you will possibly experience one of what the Church calls Sacraments at the Service of Communion, Matrimony and Holy Orders.

- On an ongoing basis, the Eucharist should be a regular part of your life.

- You probably celebrate to some degree the rhythms of the Church's liturgical year—her seasons and the feasts of the saints and other holy days.

Thus, as a Catholic, your life takes place within a sacramental and liturgical world that speaks to you of ultimate meaning and ultimate value. For your participation in this sacramental life to be done with integrity, some things are required of you.

GROUP TALK

Discuss the following in small groups:

1. Which sacraments of the Church have you received in your life thus far?

2. If you can, recall the actual celebration. What were you thinking and feeling during the liturgical celebration? What did you think and feel after?

3. How has each one made a difference in your life of faith?

The Demands of Integrity

Faith First of all, you need to have a living faith. The Church requires us to have faith—to believe—before we can participate in the sacraments. If a person goes through the rituals of the sacraments without any real belief in their power or without believing that God is present in the rites, then such participation will be empty and without effect.

At the heart of our participation in the liturgy is an expectation that we are true believers, that we have turned our lives over to God as followers of Christ Jesus, and that we see in the sacraments a genuine moment of encounter with the Lord. Sacraments presume faith on the part of those who celebrate them, and without faith one only goes through the motions. This does not mean that God is absent from sacrament, as if God's presence depended on our worthiness or level of faith. But it does mean that in order for the sacraments to be fruitful, to have an effect in our lives, we must be properly disposed and open to the grace that God offers in them.

This is the reason why the bishops at the Second Vatican Council insisted that in the reform of the liturgical rites a greater place be given to Sacred Scripture. Faith is stirred up and nourished by the proclamation of God's word, and each of the revised rites of the sacraments now has a Liturgy of the Word which comes before the actual celebration of the sacrament. The word of God proclaimed as part of each sacramental ritual helps us to have the proper dispositions for each of the sacraments.

The question of what constitutes the "proper dispositions" for the sacraments is enormously important, and you will consider that topic in each of the chapters that follows. The second section of each chapter will help you to consider the dispositions that are required in order for the sacrament to bear fruit in the life of one who receives it.

Knowledge and Understanding The second essential element that must be present for you to celebrate the sacraments with integrity is a level of knowledge and understanding of the sacraments appropriate to your age and educational level. In every other area of your education, the breadth and sophistication of your knowledge is already considerable. In literature, social studies, math, the sciences, sports and entertainment, and the arts, you and your peers have already achieved an impressive mastery.

It would be disastrous to enter your young adult years with a knowledge of your faith and its practice in the sacraments that remained "frozen" at the level of your elementary school understanding. The Catholic Church has a 2,000-year history of celebration and prayerful reflection on the way that we encounter God in the liturgy and the sacraments. Brilliant thinkers of every age have subjected their faith experience to the rigors of disciplined, critical thought as they attempted to understand more fully the scope of God's involvement in human history in and through the Church.

The early Christian believers referred to what we today call sacraments by using the Greek term *mysterion*. The "mysteries" in question were the mysteries of Christ's life, death, and Resurrection as celebrated in what we now call the sacraments. They were not mysteries in the sense that they were unsolvable riddles or impenetrable and totally unknowable realities. Rather, Christians called them mysteries because the richness of their meanings is literally inexhaustible.

We will never be able to know and understand everything there is to know about the sacraments and how we encounter God there with his saving graces. But, if our faith is to be mature, and if we are to participate in the sacraments with integrity, we must always be growing in our understanding of these spiritual realities.

In the chapters that follow you will study in depth each of the seven sacraments. You will learn about how they were once celebrated, how they are celebrated now, and what the Church teaches about each sacrament in particular. Along with the explanations of the Church's doctrines, you will be invited to enter personally and spiritually into what the sacraments mean for your own life of faith and for the redemption of the world.

FAITH ACTIVITY

What Does It Take? Each of the sacraments requires certain things of us if we are to celebrate them with integrity and authenticity. In a group, make a chart identifying for each sacrament what you think is the single most important requirement for participating in it with integrity. Then spend some time personally reflecting on how you can do this in your own participation in the sacraments.

Quick Check

1. Why is faith essential for authentic participation in the sacraments?
2. What is the importance of Sacred Scripture in the celebration of the sacraments?
3. Why is knowledge and understanding important for authentic participation in the sacraments?
4. Why is a commitment to live a life of conversion important for authentic participation in the sacraments?

Life of Conversion Celebrating with authenticity and integrity has a third dimension, in addition to the two described above. That is why each chapter that follows will also have a section focused on making life connections. Every sacrament requires a commitment to live the specifics of our Christian life in a particular way. Integrity requires that there be a connection between what we celebrate in the sacred ritual and how we attempt to live our lives. Our lives of worship are intimately connected to our moral lives. The liturgy, most especially the grace of the sacraments, gives direction, strength, and maturity to our moral lives. Likewise, living a good and moral life leads us to the liturgy and is a form of praise and worship. Our spiritual and moral lives have their goal in the joy of life forever with God in heaven. If someone were to go to confession with no intention of changing his or her sinful ways, for example, the hypocrisy of such an action would render the absolution meaningless and devoid of its intended effect. Similarly, if one were to go through a marriage ceremony with no intention of a lifelong, faithful commitment to an exclusive relationship, the marriage would be invalid and such an individual would receive none of the graces of the sacrament. These are obviously rare and scandalous possibilities. Often when we celebrate a sacrament, we may forget how important it is that we have the sincere intention of translating its graces into the way we live our lives.

Integrity and authenticity do not mean a person has to guarantee holiness—this is not possible—or one hundred percent success in living every virtue possible. Rather, what is required is simply a sincere effort to live out our Christian life in accordance with the meaning of the particular sacrament that we are celebrating.

GROUP TALK

Each of the sacraments also implies certain behaviors in our lives if we are to celebrate them with integrity and authenticity. In a group, discuss the following.

1. For each sacrament, what do you think is the single most important way we are to live if we connect liturgy and life?

2. How would people's experience of family, school, work, and the broader community be different if people lived out the sacraments in these ways?

The Saint John's Bible

After the collapse of the ancient Roman Empire, during the period of history sometimes called the "Dark Ages," the lamp of learning was kept alive in Western civilization thanks in large part to monastic communities that became centers of study and scholarship. One of the most important tasks of many monastic communities came to be the copying of ancient manuscripts to preserve the heritage of ages past. In the *scriptoria,* as they were called, the monks saw it as their religious vocation to meticulously copy ancient texts with their quill pens and handmade inks. Chief among the texts that they copied were the Church's sacred writings, especially the writings of the Fathers of the Church and the Bible itself. From this practical task of preservation emerged the practice of making copies of the Scriptures in large, lavishly illuminated volumes that were used primarily within the monastic communities themselves. Some of our most precious works of art from the medieval period are to be found in those volumes of illuminated Bibles. The invention of moveable type printing presses and the publication of the Gutenberg Bible in the mid-15th century ended the era of illuminated manuscript Bibles.

At the turn of the third millennium, in a bold homage to their monastic tradition, the Benedictine Abbey of Saint John's in Collegeville, Minnesota, commissioned the production of the first complete, illuminated manuscript Bible in nearly five hundred years. Scheduled for completion in 2008, the work is destined to become a landmark in the history of this magnificent art form that goes back many, many centuries. The Saint John's Bible has been produced by six professional scribes in a *scriptorium* in Wales, England, under the direction of Donald Jackson, one of the world's foremost calligraphers. Written and illustrated entirely by hand, the approximately 1,000 pages of this remarkable volume represent a blending of modern technology and ancient craftsmanship.

The product of computer design and layout, as well as e-mail collaboration on both sides of the Atlantic, the actual book has also been produced following rigorous standards unchanged since medieval times. Computers were used to size the text and define line breaks for each page, as well as to guide the layout of pages and determine placement of the 160 illuminations found in the seven volumes of the project. The scribes used quill pens crafted in the *scriptorium,* natural handmade inks, and hand-ground pigments on carefully prepared vellum pages, just as their ancient predecessors would have done. Gold and silver leaf was used to gild the pages, and the illuminations represent a blending of ancient and modern techniques and imagery that is nothing short of spectacular. The illuminations reflect Scripture from a contemporary perspective that reflects a multicultural world and humanity's great strides in science and technology. The English translation that is used is the popular ecumenical version called the New Revised Standard Version (NRSV), the same translation used in this textbook.

▲ **Genesis 1:25–2:4,** *The Garden of Eden*

Saints Benedict and Scholastica

Saint Benedict (c. 480–547) Nearly all that we know about Saint Benedict comes from the Rule which he wrote for the monastic community he founded at Monte Cassino and from the story of his life written by Pope Gregory the Great approximately fifty years after Benedict's death. Gregory, following the literary style of his time, intermingled pious legends with historical data, but we have sufficient, reliable information to sketch the outlines of Benedict's life.

Benedict was born, together with a twin sister, Scholastica, around A.D. 480 to a noble family in Nursia, Umbria, northeast of Rome. Early in his teenage years he was sent along with a nurse/governess to receive a classical education in Rome. However, he was so scandalized by the immorality that he encountered in the city that he fled to a mountain retreat in Subiaco, southeast of Rome, where he lived as a hermit for three years under the tutelage of a monk by the name of Romanus.

It was there in Subiaco that he was discovered by a group of monks who begged him to become their spiritual leader. He initially refused, explaining to the monks that he would be too strict for them. They eventually prevailed, but before long found his manner of governing their lives so strict and intolerable that they plotted to kill him. He withdrew from them and soon found other monks more willing to follow his leadership. With these followers he established twelve communities of monks, with twelve members each, who lived together under his direction. However, the jealousy and attacks of another monk in the area soon convinced Benedict to leave Subiaco completely.

It was at that point—around 529—when Benedict went to Monte Cassino, approximately eighty miles southeast of Rome. There, atop a massive rock

promontory, he tore down a pagan shrine to Apollo and founded what was to become the mother community of the worldwide Benedictine Order. His holiness and wisdom had already earned him considerable renown, and people came to him from Rome and the surrounding countryside seeking his spiritual advice and asking to form a monastic community around him. This time, instead of establishing a series of smaller, scattered communities, he gathered together in one place all of those who wished to share his monastic way of life. It was in this context that he wrote his famous Rule, a document regulating and guiding the monastic community at Monte Cassino, but subsequently followed or imitated by monastic communities worldwide. Many still follow its basic outlines to this day.

The Rule which Benedict established is a practical guide that structures the lives of the community members and offers sound advice for how to help his followers grow in holiness. It directs that the day be divided into periods devoted to communal liturgical prayer—the Divine Office, about four hours a day, the reading and study of Scripture—*lectio divina,* about five hours per day, six hours of manual labor, one hour for eating, and eight hours for sleeping. This rhythm of life is an intermingling of prayer and work, *ora et labora,* that achieves a healthy balance and integrates all of a monk's life around the service and praise of God. Benedict directed that in the course of a month the entire Book of the Psalms was to be recited in the Divine Office. One of the lasting heritages that Benedict left to his followers across the centuries was a particular love of Scripture as the source of one's spiritual life, and a commitment to the liturgy as the framework within which one lives out the details of day-to-day existence.

Saint Scholastica (c. 480–543) Not a great deal is known about Benedict's family relationships, or his sister Scholastica, but clearly she was close to him throughout his life. She followed him to Monte Cassino and settled near his monastery, became the head of a convent herself, and was allowed to visit with her brother only one day a year.

Pope Gregory tells a quaint tale of their last visit in 543, just days before she died, when Benedict was preparing to return to the monastery for the evening after a day's visit. When he refused to stay longer at her request, she bowed her head and prayed to God. Immediately, such a violent thunderstorm broke out that Benedict and his companions were forced to spend the night there. The two talked throughout the night, recounts Pope Gregory's biography, "discoursing of the joys of heaven."

Reportedly, Saint Benedict had a vision of Saint Scholastica's soul leaving her body when she died. It was in the form of a dove and flew up to heaven. Benedict had her body buried in his own tomb. Four years later, on March 21, 547, Benedict himself died. He was buried beneath the high altar in the monastery, in the same tomb where his sister was interred.

The Rule of Saint Benedict spread from his original monastery throughout Western monasteries during the sixth century, and it began being applied to nuns by the seventh. So, of course, Saints Benedict and Scholastica are now patrons of these orders.

REFLECT

1. How do Saints Benedict and Scholastica's lives and teachings relate to worship and the sacraments?

2. What challenge does the Benedictine motto, "pray and work," present to us?

3. How can you use structure in your life to more devoutly worship God?

Prayer

The Liturgy of Hours exhorts us to follow the example of Saint Benedict:

> And so, girded with faith and the performance of good works; let us follow in the paths by the guidance of the Gospel; then we shall deserve to see him *who has called us into his kingdom.* If we wish to attain a dwelling-place in his kingdom we shall not reach it unless we hasten there by our good deeds.

Leader: He lived a holy life; Benedict, blessed in name and in grace.

Let us pray.

All: God our Father,
You made Saint Benedict an outstanding guide
to teach men how to live in your service.
Grant that by preferring your love to
everything else,
we may walk in the way of your commandments.
We ask this through our Lord Jesus Christ,
your Son,
who lives and reigns with you and the
Holy Spirit,
one God, for ever and ever.
Amen.

Study Guide

▶Check Understanding

1. Identify what is unique about humans in God's creation and what this means for human existence.

2. Explain what it means to say that creation is a kind of sacrament of God's presence in the world.

3. Define Incarnation and explain its significance to knowing God.

4. Explain what it means to say that Jesus is the sacrament of God the Father.

5. Describe how the Church is a sacrament of God's presence and action in the world.

6. Explain what the liturgy is and what the term means.

7. Define sacrament in the sense of the seven sacraments.

8. Discuss the Paschal Mystery and its significance to the celebration of the sacraments.

9. Tell why the Liturgy of the Hours helps the Church pray unceasingly.

10. Recall the significance of Sunday as a day to gather for worship.

11. Describe what the liturgical cycle, with its feasts and seasons, celebrates.

12. Define sacramental.

13. Summarize why faith is essential for authentic participation in the sacraments.

14. Explain the significance of Sacred Scripture in the celebration of the sacraments.

15. Identify why knowledge and understanding are important for authentic participation in the sacraments.

16. Tell why a commitment to live a life of conversion is important for authentic participation in the sacraments.

▶Apply and Develop

17. The term *sacrament* in Catholic theology has a very precise meaning and a much broader application. Write a brief essay describing and illustrating the different ways that the term is used in the Catholic Church.

18. Each of the Persons of the Trinity—Father, Son, and Holy Spirit—has a distinctive role to play in the liturgy. Point out what their respective roles are and what these imply for our relationship with each Person.

19. Our secular society has its annual rhythms that define time in a certain way, such as the academic year, the fiscal year, and so forth. It even has its rhythm of national holidays, annual sporting events, and other observances. Compare and contrast the meaning and celebration of these with our religious seasons and feasts that are based on the Church's liturgy.

20. Differentiate between the two worldviews described in this chapter. How does one support faith and the other disregard faith? Refer to what is required for participating in the sacraments authentically and with integrity.

▶Key Words

See pages noted for contextual explanations of these important faith terms.

grace (p. 18)

Incarnation (p. 15)

liturgy (p. 19)

Liturgy of the Hours (p. 23)

Paschal Mystery (p. 20)

sacrament (p. 13)

sacramentals (p. 27)

worship (p. 19)

And Jesus came and said to them, "All authority in heaven and on earth has been given to me. Go therefore and make disciples of all nations, baptizing them in the name of the Father and of the Son and of the Holy Spirit, and teaching them to obey everything that I have commanded you. And remember, I am with you always, to the end of the age."

Matthew 28:18-20

BAPTISM

CHAPTER 2

CHAPTER GOALS

In this chapter, you will:

* learn how Baptism is celebrated and how the Church's baptismal rituals have evolved over time.

* study the relationship between faith and Baptism.

* explore the implications of the Church's teaching that Baptism gives us a share in Christ's identity as priest, prophet, and king.

* consider how the Church has deepened her understanding about Baptism and forgiveness of sin.

* learn about the life of Saint Augustine.

Maria's Story

Maria's parents arrived in this country as immigrants from El Salvador when she was only a toddler. They had rarely been able to go to Mass in their war-torn native land. With no Spanish-speaking community near their new home, it never occurred to them to take Maria to be baptized. So she grew up with a vague "Catholic" identity, but completely uninvolved in the Church. Now fifteen, Maria was inspired by the example of her best friend, Carol, an active member of her parish's youth group and a regular at Sunday Mass. At Carol's urging, Maria talked to the parish priest and was shocked to learn that as an unbaptized person, she actually was not yet a Catholic. Her surprise deepened when the pastor explained that in order to become a Catholic she would have to participate in a spiritual formation process that could last up to two years.

Thus began a dramatic journey of conversion for Maria. She gradually discovered more about her Catholic roots and explored the stories of Jesus in the Gospels. She grew excited at all that she was finding out about the Catholic way of life and about what it means to be a follower of Jesus. Maria participated in the Saturday morning precatechumenate inquiry sessions for several months, exploring the most basic information about God, the Bible, and the Catholic Church. She saw that her questions were similar to the questions of other young people in the process with her, and she grew more and more attracted to what she was learning.

When Maria celebrated the Rite of Acceptance into the catechumenate on a cold January morning, Carol was at her side as her sponsor. They began to go to Mass together every Sunday. Afterwards they met with other teens and adults in a group that studied and discussed the Sunday readings. It was there that Maria found out the difference between a catechumen (someone who is unbaptized) and a candidate (an already baptized person seeking to join the Catholic Church and complete initiation through Confirmation and Eucharist).

The following year, on the First Sunday of Lent, Maria went to the cathedral where hundreds of catechumens and candidates from parishes throughout the diocese gathered to celebrate the Rite of Election. The bishop who presided at that celebration listened as everyone's name was called out. He told them of the importance of Lent as a time to make final preparations for their full initiation into the Catholic Church.

Maria's initiation at the Easter Vigil was an intense experience that she knew would remain vivid in her memory for the rest of her life. When it was her turn to be baptized—plunged under the water three times as the priest said aloud the name of the Trinity—she felt as if she were literally being born again to a new life. Carol helped her change into dry clothes and put on her baptismal robe, and then she returned to the waiting assembly to celebrate Confirmation. As the sweet-smelling oil of chrism flowed over her head, Maria wept with joy, remembering what she had been taught about the Holy Spirit, and how the same Spirit that came on the Apostles now filled her heart, too. Later, when she answered "Amen" to the Body of Christ offered at Communion, a calmness descended upon her. She remembered how one of her catechists had quoted Saint Augustine to her, teaching that *she* was also saying "Amen" to the fact that now she was part of the Body of Christ.

FAITH ACTIVITY

Your Baptism Create a mural or storyboard to show the symbols of your Baptism—the baptismal record or certificate, candle, white garment, water, baptismal font, and worship aid. Share your storyboard with your friends and family, and keep it with your memorabilia.

The Church Celebrates New Life

Maria and her parents at first were surprised to learn how long it would take her to be prepared for Baptism. They, like many Catholics, did not know that the public rituals and lengthy preparation were not new to the Church. In actuality, the rituals and preparation were a return to the ancient practice of the early centuries, a return brought about by the renewal of the Church's sacramental rituals by the Second Vatican Council in the 1960s.

Changing Forms, but an Unchanging Truth

The New Testament gives only the briefest descriptions of how the first generation of believers incorporated new members into the Christian community through a simple water rite and laying on of hands with prayer for the Spirit—usually described as occurring almost immediately after a person pledged faith in Jesus (*cf. Acts 2:41; 8:13–38; 10:44–48*). However, we know from scholars who have studied the early history of the Church and her evolving liturgical forms, that within a century or two of the New Testament era, the Church had developed a much more elaborate and lengthy process for initiating new members. To prepare new converts to live lives of committed discipleship, the Church developed a gradual way of forming them in faith. This formation involved a combination of instruction, mentoring, rich use of symbol and ritual, and strong social bonds with members of the Christian community. This process, called the **catechumenate**, flourished through the early centuries of the Church, until there were fewer and fewer adults seeking Baptism.

Infants and children, from earliest times, had always been initiated along with their parents as part of believing households. Eventually, however, those to be baptized were almost exclusively children. As that transition took place, the formation in Christian faith previously given prior to Baptism (during the catechumenate) became part of lifelong formation offered after baptismal initiation. The rituals that had previously been spread out over a number of years during the catechumenate were adapted and compressed into a single

FAITH ACTIVITY

Spiritual Gifts We have been given spiritual gifts to further the Church's mission to preach the Good News of God's Kingdom. Interview two or three Catholic friends or family members about the spiritual gifts each has been given. Discover how each might already be using these gifts and explore ways to use them in the school, parish, home, or community.

Temple of Jupiter and Baptistry of Saint John in Split: Interior with Baptismal Font ▼

Baptism 41

ceremony, much as we know it today in the Rite of Baptism for Children. In the Eastern Rite, the custom of celebrating all three Sacraments of Initiation (Baptism, Chrismation, Eucharist) at the same time was never changed, even with infants. To this day in that tradition, infants are baptized, confirmed, and administered Holy Communion in a single ceremony. However, in the tradition of the West, Confirmation and Eucharist were separated from infant Baptism and celebrated at a later age, when the child was more aware.

Today, as a result of the reforms of Vatican II, the Church has separate rituals for the Baptism of infants and young children, as well as a more elaborate catechumenal process for adults and children of catechetical age. However, the rite used in baptizing infants and young children includes in one liturgy the key symbols that have long been used in the more elaborate catechumenal process that includes several stages and liturgies. The next section of this chapter will explore in greater detail the catechumenate.

The outline of the chart below follows the Rite of Baptism for Children. The Rite of Baptism ideally takes place within the Sunday Mass. If done this way, the Liturgy of the Eucharist would follow the explanatory rites at the bottom of the chart.

Celebrating the Sacrament	
Ritual Actions/Symbols	**Toward a Deeper Understanding**
RECEPTION	
Reception of those to be baptized **Naming**	· The reception takes place at the entrance or doorway of the church. At the threshold, those seeking Baptism are invited into the church where they will bless themselves with the waters of Baptism for years to come. · The parents are asked what name they have given their child. · The name that a person is given is the name called by God: "The name one receives is a name for eternity. In the kingdom, the mysterious and unique character of each person marked with God's name will shine forth in splendor" (*CCC*, 2159). · Catechumens are asked their names during the Rite of Acceptance into the Order of Catechumens, the first of several rites they will participate in.
Questions to parents/ catechumens	· The parents or catechumens are asked what they ask of the Church; the parents are asked if they are ready to undertake raising their child in the faith. · The celebrant is greeting the parents or the catechumen, who publicly state their intentions and commitments. · Catechumens are asked their names during the Rite of Acceptance into the Order of Catechumens, the first of several rites they will participate in.
Questions to the godparents/ sponsors	· These questions emphasize the fact that all members of the Christian community, in their respective ways, share responsibility for forming the faith of those to be initiated.

Chart continued on next page

Ritual Actions/Symbols	Toward a Deeper Understanding
Signing with the Cross	The cross reminds us that the Paschal Mystery of Jesus is at the heart of what it means to be made one of his disciples. · The pledge of the Church culminates in the signing with the cross. This is one of the most ancient and provocative symbols associated with Baptism. · The forehead of infants is traced with a cross by the celebrant, parents, godparents, and others gathered. · Catechumens may have their entire forehead and all their senses traced (eyes, ears, hands, and so on).
LITURGY OF THE WORD	
LITURGY OF THE WORD	As in all sacraments, we first encounter the Word of God before we celebrate the sacramental rite. We celebrate God's initiative and our attempt to respond. · Parents of the infants are invited to hear God's word so they may have faith. Baptism and the rest of the initiation are dependent upon the faith and commitment of the adult believers. · The Church invites catechumens to hear God's word in order to come to faith.
Litany of Saints	· Asking the saints to pray for those to be baptized reminds us that Baptism makes one a member of the communion of saints. We are initiated into a Church that is larger than any local parish. · Baptism incorporates us into the Body of Christ that extends to every time and place.
Prayer of exorcism **Anointing with oil of catechumens**	In the lengthy process of adult initiation, the three minor rites can be differentiated from each other and provide separate, complementary meanings. In the compact rite of baptizing children, the minor rites preceding Baptism itself have been condensed into two elements. · In the prayers of exorcism, the Church asks that the one to be baptized be freed from evil and filled with new life. · The anointing with the oil of catechumens is used to mark the person as one called by God and filled with the power of God. This is a minor, optional rite with adult catechumens. In Baptism for children, this anointing marks a transition and conclusion to the Liturgy of the Word.
Procession to the site of Baptism	· Processions are important symbols and intend to invoke the Christian journey of pilgrim people. We are led by God into the Church to hear the word and respond. · The procession benefits the entire assembly, drawing them to the water. It marks a clear and decisive shift to another set of rites.
CELEBRATION OF THE SACRAMENT	
Blessing and invocation over the waters	· This prayer is a prayer of thanksgiving and remembrance of God's action in history and how often he used water to bring salvation to his people. God is petitioned to continue the legacy of saving action.

Chart continued on next page

Ritual Actions/Symbols	Toward a Deeper Understanding
Renunciation of Sin and Profession of Faith	· These promises include both a renunciation of sin and a profession of belief. They show that conversion is both a turning away from sin and a turning toward God. When infants and young children are baptized, parents make these promises.
Baptism	· In the Roman Rite the preferred way of baptizing is by immersion, because it is a fuller, more expressive symbol of dying and rising with Christ. However, a three-fold pouring of water is also permitted. · Either way, the water ritual is accompanied by the Trinitarian formula, "I baptize you in the name of the Father, and of the Son, and of the Holy Spirit."
EXPLANATORY RITES	
Anointing with Chrism	· Infants are anointed immediately after Baptism with chrism. This anointing on the crown of the head with perfumed oil symbolizes this child of God is becoming like Christ; he or she is "a priest, prophet, and king" anointing. · Catechumens at the Vigil wait until the Sacrament of Confirmation that follows before receiving the laying of hands and chrism.
Clothing with white garment	· The putting on of the white garment means the person drops the old distinctions, and now "puts on Christ." The baptized are "clothing" themselves with new ways of living.
Lighted candle	The candle is lighted from the Paschal Candle, which symbolizes the light of Christ that has illuminated the mind and heart of the newly initiated.
Ephphetha, or Prayer over ears & mouth [optional]	· This ritual calls on Christ to touch the infants' ears to hear God's word and open their mouth in praise of God.

Connecting the Rite and Symbol to Everyday Life

RECEPTION

· What is the meaning behind your name? How was it chosen for you?

LITURGY OF THE WORD

· How are you challenged by Scripture readings during Mass, in class, in your own prayer?

· In your community, who are most in need of God's strengthening power and favor?

· What meaning does journey have in your life? In what ways do you notice God as leading your journey?

CELEBRATION OF THE SACRAMENT

· The importance of water in the baptismal liturgy is highlighted—cleansing, purifying. How do you respect the gift of water?

EXPLANATORY RITES

· How do clothes say who you are? What do you want your clothes to say about you? What kind of clothes do you wear to the Sunday liturgy?

· How can your school or parish become the light of Christ to your local community?

A Unity of Vision

The development of the rituals of Christian Initiation offers an excellent example of the way the Church has been faithful to the command of Christ in his institution of the sacraments. The Church has preserved the essential elements of each sacrament (for example, the water rite of immersion or pouring on the head, together with the invocation of the Trinity), yet still has exercised flexibility by adapting certain rituals to changing historical and pastoral circumstances.

In the current ritual for Christian Initiation, a variety of rites may be used, reflecting the Church's long and rich history of adapting to meet changing circumstances. The catechumenate has been restored for anyone who has reached the age of reason. It includes processes that allow for many variations depending on age, circumstances, and so forth. For those initiated as infants and young children, there is a Rite of Baptism for Children. The sacraments of Confirmation and Eucharist are received later, sometimes in a single celebration and sometimes separately, years apart.

In all of these ways of celebrating Christian Initiation, a single, unchanging vision remains of what it means to be incorporated into the Body of Christ through these sacramental rituals, regardless of the timing or sequence with which they are celebrated.

That unity of vision includes the following understandings regarding the effects of Baptism:

- Baptism is always the first sacrament of the Christian life, since it grants forgiveness of Original Sin and personal sin and is thus a person's spiritual birth to a new life as God's adopted child.

- In Baptism, one is joined to the Body of Christ with an indelible spiritual sign or "character" imprinted on the soul (which is why Baptism is celebrated only once, never repeated).

- Baptism makes a person a member of the Church.

- A baptized person is "consecrated for worship" by being joined to the one priesthood of Christ.

- Baptism effects a real change in the person, making him or her different than before being baptized.

- The grace of Baptism brings the person into a new relationship with the Trinity—Father, Son, and Holy Spirit; they receive the theological virtues of faith, hope, and charity, which make it possible to believe in, hope in, and love God.

- All three sacramental rites (Baptism, Confirmation, Eucharist) are necessary for complete initiation.

FAITH ACTIVITY

Raising Children Parents are the first teachers of the faith for their children. Make a list of recommendations for parents that will help them in raising their child in the faith.

✓ Quick Check

1. How did the early Church prepare for and celebrate Baptism?
2. What are the major differences in the way the Sacraments of Initiation are celebrated in the East and West?
3. What are some of the ritual actions and symbols in the Sacrament of Baptism and what do they signify?
4. What are the effects of Baptism?

A Journey of Faith

The restoration of the catechumenate following the Second Vatican Council was initially envisioned as a way to meet the needs of missionaries who worked in nations whose population was predominantly non-Christian, evangelizing people with very little knowledge of the Christian message. However, in a wonderful surprise that must surely be the work of the Holy Spirit, the Rite of Christian Initiation of Adults (RCIA) has proven to be an important force for renewal in our country and many other places where Christianity already is flourishing. One reason for the positive impact of the RCIA is its focus on the importance of conversion and the spiritual journey of faith. *Conversion* is a sincere change of mind, heart, and desire to turn away from sin and turn toward God. Conversion implies a new way of relating to God in such a way that one also relates differently to other people. Conversion is a matter of living a just life through reaching out to everyone and sharing with those in need.

Baptism is a sacrament of conversion, as well as membership into a community that supports and encourages that conversion. For many "cradle Catholics" that process of conversion happens so gradually—as part of an ongoing formation in faith throughout their lives—that it is sometimes difficult to identify any specific moments of decision related to their Catholic faith. For other Catholics, to be Catholic is part of their family heritage or ethnic identity, without much emphasis on religious meaning or practice. The restored catechumenate reminds all of us in the Catholic Church how fundamental conversion is to discipleship, and how closely conversion is linked to our celebration of the sacraments in general and Baptism in particular. The summary chart of the catechumenal process on the next page offers an overview of how the restored catechumenate supports and calls forth a deep conversion in those who are preparing to be baptized.

Overview of the Catechumenate Process

Period	Purpose	Rituals During the Period	When
Precatechumenate (Inquiry)	To awaken initial faith and make first introductions to the Christian community through sharing of personal stories and stories of the Church's Tradition.	No specific rituals assigned	Available year-round: duration is determined by individual circumstances
Major Liturgy: Rite of Acceptance into the Order of Catechumens			Whenever a candidate is ready
Catechumenate (Formation)	To develop a mature faith through a formation process that includes catechesis, life in community, liturgical participation, and apostolic service.	· Celebrations of the Word · Blessings · Anointings · Exorcisms	Available year-round: Recommended duration is a minimum of one full year, but it is sometimes shorter.
Major Liturgy: Rite of Election			First Sunday of Lent
Purification and Enlightenment (Spiritual Retreat)	To deepen conversion and make final spiritual preparation for full initiation. A time to eliminate what is weak and sinful and to affirm what is good and holy.	· Scrutinies on 3rd, 4th, and 5th Sundays of Lent · Presentations of the Creed and the Lord's Prayer	Lent (40 days)
Major Liturgy: Baptism, Confirmation, and Eucharist			Easter Vigil
Mystagogy (Post-baptismal Instruction)	Deepening of sacramental life with emphasis on the Gospel, Eucharist, and service to others. Integrate new identity as full member of the community.	· Sunday Masses of the Easter Season	Easter Season (50 days)

GROUP TALK

1. How has Jesus been made known to you? Do you have a desire to change your life and to enter into a relationship with Jesus Christ?

2. How is your membership in the Church similar or different to other organizations that you belong to?

The story of Maria's conversion that introduced this chapter provided a brief glimpse into what it takes for a person of catechetical age to be baptized today and to live as a disciple of Jesus Christ in the Catholic Church. When people first begin the catechumenal process, they may not be particularly spiritual. Generally, inquirers are not living wicked lives by any means, but may not have had a significant place in their lives for God or the Church, and perhaps little desire to direct their lives toward a higher purpose. They may know something about the story of Jesus, but there is often a minimal relationship with him. Jesus is more like any other historical figure from the past than the Son of God that they feel is present to them here and now. As they begin to learn more about the message and the life of Jesus, however, inquirers experience stirrings of a real, personal faith that makes a claim on their lives.

The symbols and rituals that are part of the catechumenate process make what catechumens are learning "come alive" in a very powerful way. Over the period of many months and sometimes even years, faith matures, conversion deepens, and catechumens find themselves developing a stronger and stronger sense of belonging—not only to Christ, but to the Church as well. The relationship with their sponsors is always a key element in catechumens feeling more at home in a particular community. As time goes on and catechumens become more involved in the life of the local parish, that sense of belonging only grows stronger and deeper.

During the extended period of time they spend in spiritual formation, catechumens come to understand that faith is not some "once and for all" kind of event. Rather, as they see their faith gradually grow stronger, they, as many Catholics do, realize the nature of the spiritual journey—a developing and growing relationship with God the Father in Jesus Christ that lasts a lifetime. In theological terms the word **justification** is used to refer to God's gracious action that frees humans from sin and bestows God's righteousness through their belief in Jesus Christ. (See *CCC*, Glossary.) Justification involves God's free gift of grace and our willingness to accept it. Through this gift of grace, we turn away from sin and turn toward God. This grace of being justified joins us to the Paschal Mystery of Jesus—the work of redemption through his Passion, death, Resurrection, and Ascension—in a special way because we actually share in Christ's life, thanks to the Holy Spirit within us.

FAITH ACTIVITY

Map Your Journey While each of us has a unique journey, we are never on the road alone. Create a visual representation of your faith journey thus far, and where you hope it will lead. Indicate important moments or stops along the way, where your path may have taken a turn. Who has accompanied you at different stages? What goals do you have for yourself as a disciple of Christ? How might your life as his follower look in 5 years? 10 years?

Those words—*justification, grace, Paschal Mystery, sin,* and *forgiveness*—can seem very remote and abstract when a catechumen first hears them. But once the process of Christian initiation is completed, catechumens are usually able to connect those words to a real experience of faith—their own faith—that is celebrated in an unforgettable manner at the Easter Vigil in the sacraments of Baptism, Confirmation, and Eucharist.

Faith and Baptism

For many Catholics, when asked what the word *faith* means, the answer would be a set of beliefs, the "truths of the faith" taught in formal classes or preached about during Sunday Mass. But a more penetrating understanding of the notion of faith presents it as a relationship, or to use the biblical word, a *covenant* between the believer and God. A covenant is a solemn promise or agreement between humans or between God and humans. The Church teaches that through the Sacrament of Baptism one is born into the "People of God of the New Covenant" (*CCC*, 1267), and thus it is necessary for salvation. But that teaching recognizes that sometimes there are circumstances when, even without the water rite of the sacrament, a person can be saved by God's grace—as long as there is a relationship with Christ in faith, however implied it might be. Two expressions that have been traditionally used to capture this insight were "Baptism of blood" and "Baptism of desire." The ancient Church used the first expression during the time of persecutions to refer to the martyrs—many of them still unbaptized catechumens—who shed their blood for the faith because of their belief in Jesus Christ. Their Baptism was in their own blood, and no one doubted that they were saved from their sins by Jesus in whom they had put their faith.

The second expression, "Baptism of desire," applies to people who die before receiving Baptism. If they explicitly desire its reception, are sorry for their sins, and practice acts of justice, their desire to be baptized and their good actions enable them to be saved.

People of goodwill, who follow their conscience, without knowing of the Gospel of Christ or his Church, may nonetheless be saved if they sincerely seek the truth and follow God's will as they know it. It may be the case, for example, that many people know "about" the Gospel and the Church, without really "knowing" in a way that effectively reveals the Gospel's truth and goodness. For countless people, the message of the Gospels has been so distorted, either by the way it is presented or the way it is lived by Christians, that those people of goodwill may be unable to recognize it as an authentic revelation of God. It is always a great sadness when this occurs. It reminds us of the importance of each Christian living faith authentically and willingly sharing it with others in a way that invites them to discover the truth of the Gospel.

▲ **Portrait of Saints Perpetua and Felicity**

In God's love and providence, the Church teaches that such people of goodwill can be saved without benefit of Baptism. This was an important topic discussed in several places in the documents of Vatican II (*Dogmatic Constitution on the Church* 16, *Pastoral Constitution on the Church in the Modern World* 22, *Decree on the Church's Missionary Activity* 7). It is clear that the bishops wished to continue to teach that faith and Baptism remain the necessary way to salvation offered by Jesus. But they also wished to point out that, as the *Catechism* says, "[God] *is not bound by his sacraments*" (*CCC*, 1257) when it comes to his offer of salvation to every human person. So he can open the way to heaven for people of goodwill even without the sacramental ritual.

The Church's teaching that God offers salvation to every human person is also the reason why we do not despair when a baby dies before Baptism. In fact, the *Catechism* offers very consoling words of reassurance that we must entrust such children to the mercy of God, remembering Jesus' love for children and his desire that all people be saved. (See *CCC*, 1261.) In the liturgy we pray for the salvation of children who die before Baptism as a sign of our hope on their behalf. The prayer of the Church (called in Latin the *lex orandi*, meaning "law of prayer") is a reliable guide to what the Church believes (called in Latin *lex credendi*, meaning "law of belief"). So, we find great reassurance in the fact that the liturgy encourages us to be optimistic about the eternal fate of such little ones who have gone to God prematurely.

Baptism at All Ages

Because of the obvious linkage between faith and Baptism, some Protestant denominations do not share our viewpoint that children should be baptized in their infancy. They feel

that an explicit profession of faith, such as Maria made in her baptismal promises at the Easter Vigil, is a necessary requirement for Baptism. The Catholic Church, however, has always taught that faith is a free gift (grace) just as much as it is a human response to God's grace, an act of the community as much as an individual act. For that reason, from the earliest times, the Church has celebrated Baptism with infants who are thereby joined to the faith of the Church and granted true freedom as a child of God.

Faith is still seen as an important ingredient in Baptism of infants. We see this in the fact that the official rite says the Baptism of infants should be delayed if the parents who bring the child show no signs of faith and appear unlikely to raise the child as a Christian. The concern is that Baptism is not to be understood as a mere formula, as if the water rite alone suffices to enable a child to grow up as a believer. Instead, the emphasis in the rite used for infants is on the faith of the parents and godparents. Both parents and godparents are questioned in the rite about their faith and are asked to make the baptismal promises in their own names as well as on behalf of the child they present for Baptism. The believing parents and godparents also represent the faith of the larger community, the Church, to whose faith and fellowship the infant is being joined through the sacrament.

GROUP TALK

1. How did you learn as a child to keep promises? Think of a time when you said yes to something, but only later realized the depth of its implications. How did this realization affect the way you viewed your promise?

2. How do you see yourself living out your baptismal promise every day?

Because Baptism is so important for our salvation, the Church has made it possible for it to be administered by someone other than a deacon, priest, or bishop. In fact, Baptism is the only sacrament that does not require the presence of an ordained minister in order to be validly celebrated. The essential rite of the sacrament is quite simple: water must be used, and the water must flow over the person (generally the person's head) while the traditional formula invoking the name of the Trinity is used.

> [Name], I baptize you in the name of the Father, and of the Son, and of the Holy Spirit.

Rite of Baptism for Children, 60

The person baptizing must have the intention of baptizing according to the mind of the Church, even if the person's understanding of what that means is minimal. In the case of adults or anyone over the age of reason, in order for the sacrament to be valid, the person being baptized must have the necessary faith and desire to be baptized. Baptism by someone other than an ordained minister is limited to emergency situations when no ordained person is available, such as danger of death in a hospital. But regardless of other details, as long as the essential rite is performed correctly and with the proper intention, the Baptism is a valid one.

We have considered some aspects of what is required for a person to be baptized. But we also know that Baptism is only a beginning—the start of a lifelong journey of discipleship.

Quick Check

1. What are the stages and rites of RCIA and why are they important for the conversion process?
2. What do the terms *justification*, *grace*, and *faith* mean?
3. What is meant by Baptism of blood and Baptism of desire?
4. What is the essential Rite of Baptism?

Rituals Are about Commitments

All of the important rituals that we participate in have consequences. When a public official takes an oath of office, whether he or she is the President of the United States, a police officer, or someone in the armed forces, that individual makes a public commitment to accept certain responsibilities and play a specific role in our society. An oath of office is a public ritual, and it has both personal and public implications. When two people get married, even if it is a simple civil marriage before a Justice of the Peace, they take part in a public ritual that changes who they are in the eyes of society. From then on, they have legal obligations and social expectations different from what they had been before they participated in the ritual.

So it is with Baptism. In addition to being a sacrament of the Church, it is also a public ritual. Both in terms of its spiritual meanings and its public dimension, the ritual of Baptism changes people, gives them new roles and responsibilities, and makes them different than they were prior to the ritual celebration. But how are we to know what these commitments are? How do we make explicit what often is rather implicit in the ritual itself? First, we go to the rite itself—the words that are spoken and the symbols and ritual actions that take place. Second, we look at the experience of those before us who have participated in the ritual, and we learn much from their example about what may be only vaguely clear to us in the moment of the rite.

GROUP TALK

What do we mean by "public" ritual as opposed to a private ritual? Why is it necessary for Baptism to be a public ritual?

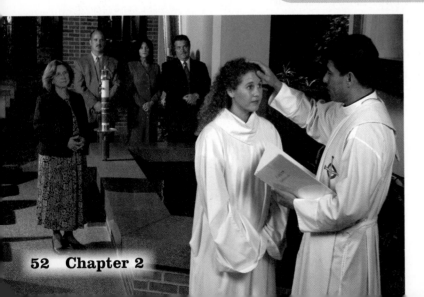

Priest, Prophet, and King

An important part of the ritual of Baptism occurs immediately following the water ritual, just before the minister anoints the newly baptized infant with sacred chrism. He says to the newly baptized:

> The God of power and Father of our Lord Jesus Christ has freed you from sin and brought you to new life through water and the Holy Spirit. He now anoints you with the chrism of salvation, so that, united with his people, you may remain for ever a member of Christ who is Priest, Prophet, and King.
>
> *Rite of Christian Initiation for Adults*, 228

What does it mean to live as a consecrated member of Christ's Body, given a share in his three-fold ministry as priest, prophet, and king? What does that look like in the life of a baptized disciple of Jesus Christ?

Priest The Church teaches that by Baptism into Christ, a person now shares in what is called the "common priesthood of the faithful" of all believers. This priesthood is different—in essence and not just degree—from the ministerial priesthood of the ordained. It is nonetheless a real and true sharing in the priesthood of Christ. Through Baptism, all Christians share in the saving work of Christ, the supreme high priest. By virtue of baptized persons' status as members of the "priestly people," it is their right and responsibility to join with Christ in offering worship to God the Father. That is why the bishops at the Second Vatican Council taught in the *Constitution on the Sacred Liturgy* that the faithful have both a right and obligation "to which they are bound by reason of their baptism" to join in the worship of the liturgy in their "full, conscious and active part" (14).

What are some ways teenagers can live out their priestly consecration from Baptism? One important way is through their attitude toward liturgical worship and the way they participate in Sunday Mass. Participation is so much more than simply being there physically. By Baptism, we are a priestly people, able to share in Jesus' own prayer to the Father on behalf of the world. Our presence matters, as do our prayers and offerings. Our participation is more than a mere obligation; it is a joyful opportunity to offer ourselves to God, as well as all the good and bad things that have happened since the last time we gathered.

Through our priestly anointing at Baptism, we are called to a life of holiness. The bishops at the Vatican Council, in their teaching about the nature of the Church, included a special chapter about the call to holiness, which they said was directed to all the baptized, not just to priests and consecrated religious. Because of our Baptism, God the Father calls each of us to become more like his Son, Jesus. As we follow Christ's example, we grow closer to the person God created us to be—someone who loves and acts in his image. God calls each of us to be as good a person as we possibly can, so that we can live up to the gift of new life given us in Baptism. We can only grow more like God if we get to know him, through those around us, through the Scriptures, and by spending time with him in prayer. The grace of the baptismal anointing helps us develop a habit of daily prayer. We can pray in many different ways, offering prayers for others and ourselves, sharing our joys and fears, with or without words. Jesus told his disciples to "pray constantly," and he himself taught us the words of the Lord's Prayer. We should not let a day go by without reverently and fervently saying the Lord's Prayer, just as Jesus commanded.

The term *priest* is rooted in the Latin word *pontifex*, meaning, "one who builds a bridge." As priestly people, we strive to make everything and everyone we touch holy. We are called to work toward reconciliation and the common good. Because we are consecrated in Baptism, we are called to make the world holy.

Mother Theresa addressed the United Nations. ▼

Prophet In addition to helping us reflect on our priestly identity, the words that accompany our baptismal anointing remind us that we share in the mission of Christ the prophet. Our prophetic mission does not usually have anything to do with predicting the future. Instead, being a prophet means doing two things: (1) *listen* to God's word, and (2) *speak* God's word. The idea of being a prophetic person can be frightening, especially since the prophetic people we hear about are those we admire but know we could never match for holiness. Stories of people such as Blessed Mother Teresa of Calcutta or Archbishop Oscar Romero of El Salvador inspire us, but also intimidate us. The real breakthrough, however, comes when we realize that the heart of the prophetic vocation is within our reach.

We must simply be people who listen to God's word, who develop a habit of reading and praying the Scriptures, and who listen carefully to its proclamation as we try to apply its meaning to our lives. These are challenging but doable steps toward claiming our role as God's prophets.

Once we have heard God's word, the second element of the prophetic vocation is to proclaim it to others. This, too, can seem intimidating until we recognize how we can proclaim God's word in very ordinary ways. Saint Francis used to tell his friars: *"Preach the Gospel always. If necessary, use words!"* All we have to do is just try to live every day the best we can, and that is all God wants. We can be God's prophets and "preach the Gospel" just by trying to give a good example to others— it's as simple as that!

King The prayers of the baptismal rite explicitly connect the newly baptized with Christ—Priest, Prophet, and King. This latter title, King, is a paradoxical one. When Pilate asked Jesus if he was a king, his answer was enigmatic and elusive. In Jesus' time the term *king* often implied power and prestige. Jesus' kingship is not of this kind. Rather, his kingdom is one of service.

The early Christian community proclaimed the Risen Christ as King and Ruler of heaven and earth. His rule is not about power but serving the needs of others. In a baptismal passage found in the First Letter of Peter (2:9), the author uses the term "royal" in describing the dignity that his early Christian readers should feel because of their Baptism. But how would we explain what it means to share in the work of Christ the King in this day and age?

In answering this question it helps to remember the many passages in the Old Testament that describe God's anointed as a shepherd king, entrusted with the care of the flock, so dedicated to their safety that he is willing to lay down his life to keep them safe. The Gospels show that Jesus understood his own ministry in these terms. He is a servant-king, a shepherd who is willing to die so that we might live. More importantly, as the glorious one who reigns over heaven and earth, Jesus invites us to help build his kingdom on earth by opening our hearts to conversion and working for justice and love of our neighbor.

Our Baptism commits us to personal and social change. We first seek to overcome that which keeps us from loving God and living by his ways. This leads to a freedom that allows us to share in Christ's work of transformation of the world. We pray, "Thy Kingdom come." But we quickly ask that God's will be done "on earth as it is in heaven." That is the key to how we share in Christ's role as king: we work with him to see to it that God's will prevails right here, right now, on earth as surely as it does in heaven. We do this by worshiping God and serving our neighbor. We still long for the full coming of

FAITH ACTIVITY

A Living Witness Write an essay about a person you feel is true to their baptismal identity by the way he or she lives out his or her share in Christ's role as "priest, prophet and king." Choose someone you actually know. You might want to include pictures or spend time interviewing the person.

God's reign of peace and justice, to be sure. But in the meantime our baptismal anointing equips us to be agents of transformation, leaven to transform the dough, lights set on a hilltop shining in the darkness. We the baptized are a "royal" nation of God's chosen ones, and we received that consecration in Baptism so that we can work more wholeheartedly to bring to fulfillment the reign of God here on earth.

In simple, ordinary terms, this means that every time we work toward making a more just, peaceful, and compassionate world, we are fulfilling our baptismal call to share in Christ's royal work. Every time we stand in solidarity with the poor, suffering, and marginalized members of society, we are active agents of the loving Shepherd King who feeds his flock and pastures them in green fields. Every time we tend the earth and God's creation with care, preserving the environment for future generations, we cooperate in God's ongoing work of creation. In so doing, we anticipate the coming Day of the Lord, when all will become as God wants it to be "on earth as it is in heaven." These actions are all based on the principles of Catholic social teaching. By living out these teachings, we show our royal dignity in concrete, practical ways that exercise the gifts of our Baptism and make us part of that "royal nation" that carries on Jesus' work throughout history until he comes again in glory.

GROUP TALK

With a partner, respond to these sentence starters:

· I reach out to others with the gracious heart of Jesus whenever I...

· Whenever I remember that God has chosen and anointed me, the difference it makes is...

· I am able to be a servant leader rather than lording power over people when...

A Member of Christ and His Body

The prayer quoted on page 53 that accompanies the postbaptismal anointing with chrism contains the phrase, "united with his people, you may remain for ever a member of Christ." These words suggest another consequence of the baptismal ritual—membership in the Church, the Body of Christ. God has chosen to save us as a People, not just as isolated individuals. By being joined to the Body of Christ, the Church, we experience baptismal grace as entrance into a community of believers. One of the responsibilities flowing from the union that we share in Christ involves a commitment on our part to become an active member of a particular community.

Baptism makes us members of the entire communion of saints throughout every time and place. It joins us to the Church universal, putting us in communion with Catholics everywhere around the globe. But we live in very specific places, and as baptized people we navigate our spiritual journey in our local parish community where we develop relationships with others who support and nourish our faith. It is there that we, in turn, can offer support and nourishment to others. As baptized members of the Body of Christ, we are called to care about the other members of our local faith community, and to help build up that community by joining in various ministries and mission-oriented efforts as our time and circumstances permit.

"Belonging" to Christ through Baptism implies a process of "belonging" to a specific faith community. That is why Catholics are expected to support their parish through gifts of time, talent, and treasure—why we are invited to volunteer to help build up the parish in various ways, and why it is often through our local parish that we give of ourselves to larger communities of need. The result of this awareness is a desire to become actively involved in the life of a parish community. There we discover firsthand that one of the outcomes of "belonging" is a life of service, with both hard work and many rewarding joys.

In the next section we will explore more deeply how the Church's reflection on the experience of Christian Initiation over many centuries has helped to shape her teachings about the meaning and effects of Baptism. What the Church believes comes to us as revealed truth, inspired by the Holy Spirit and taught by the popes and bishops. These doctrines were distilled by countless generations of faithful Catholics who based their beliefs on Scripture, the Church's living Tradition, and their own lived experience of Baptism. Over the centuries, saints and theologians refined and deepened our understandings of God's revealed truths. The Church's magisterium (the Church's living teaching office of the bishops in union with the Pope) has the responsibility to interpret authentically God's Word whether in Sacred Scripture or Sacred Tradition. (See CCC, Glossary.) Under its guidance, many of these understandings have been formulated in careful ways and taught as the official beliefs of the Catholic Church.

FAITH ACTIVITY

Responsibilities Work in pairs to draw up a list of what you think are the five most important responsibilities an adult assumes as a baptized Christian. Then compare your lists and explain to one another the reasons for your choice of priorities.

Quick Check

1. What do *common priesthood of the faithful* and the *ministerial priesthood* mean?
2. How does the post-baptismal anointing with chrism mark the newly baptized?
3. What does it mean to share in Christ's role as priest, prophet, and king?
4. How does Baptism relate to the communion of saints?

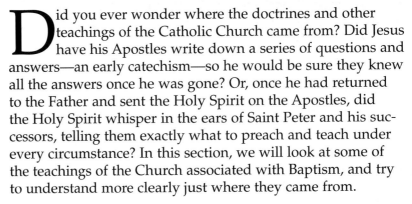

Faith Seeking Understanding

D id you ever wonder where the doctrines and other teachings of the Catholic Church came from? Did Jesus have his Apostles write down a series of questions and answers—an early catechism—so he would be sure they knew all the answers once he was gone? Or, once he had returned to the Father and sent the Holy Spirit on the Apostles, did the Holy Spirit whisper in the ears of Saint Peter and his successors, telling them exactly what to preach and teach under every circumstance? In this section, we will look at some of the teachings of the Church associated with Baptism, and try to understand more clearly just where they came from.

An ancient definition of theology is captured in the phrase, "faith seeking understanding." This phrase also summarizes the process by which believers across the centuries have pondered the meaning of what God has revealed to the Church and how we respond in faith. The Church, directed by the magisterium, has gradually developed a language to capture and pass on to subsequent generations the revealed truths of the faith. The term Tradition is often used to describe the living transmission of the Gospel's message and basic Catholic beliefs. Believers in every age seek to understand and apply God's Revelation in Scripture and Tradition. The process of clarifying Catholic belief is guided by the continuing presence and work of the Holy Spirit in the Church. Through the teaching ministry of the bishops, as successors of the Apostles, the process of reflection, discernment, and clarification has developed over time.

GROUP TALK

Theology has been described as "faith seeking understanding." What aspects of your faith do you feel you want/need a deeper understanding of? Discuss how you might go about reaching that deeper understanding.

Forgiveness

In the section that explains the meaning of the phrase from the Creed, "I believe in the forgiveness of sins," the *Catechism of the Catholic Church* states, "Baptism is the first and chief sacrament of the forgiveness of sins: it unites us to Christ . . . and gives us the Holy Spirit (985)."

To understand better the meaning of Tradition, let's trace the faith experiences of believers over the centuries that are part of the *Catechism's* brief summary statement of Catholic doctrine.

The New Testament Era Near the beginning of Mark's Gospel, the entire message of Jesus' preaching is summarized in these words, "The time is fulfilled, and the kingdom of God has come near; repent, and believe in the good news" (*Mark 1:15*).

Jesus delivered this message after his own baptism by John the Baptist. We know from Scripture that the ritual bath described in the ministry of John the Baptist was an expressive gesture of repentance; it was not the sacrament as we know it. Because he was free from sin, Jesus had no need to change or to make a change of heart publicly. However, he stood with those for whom he came. In his baptism, we learn about Jesus' unique relationship with the Father and the Holy Spirit.

The ritual bath of Baptism in the early Church and today differs from the baptism of John. Christian Baptism is a sacrament of the New Covenant. It effects what it symbolizes because of the power of the Holy Spirit at work in it. For the Christian community there is no longer any need to repeat ablutions, or washings, over and over as the Jews of Jesus' time did. Christian Baptism accomplishes forgiveness of sins in a definitive way, just as Jesus pronounced forgiveness during his earthly ministry.

Jesus preached repentance, calling people to a conversion of heart and mind, urging them to turn from their sinful ways and to turn back to God. In some ways his message mirrored that of John the Baptist. However, Jesus went the next step. He not only called for repentance, he granted forgiveness and healing, something only God can do. For those who accepted this call, he offered forgiveness and healing from sin. Nearly every page of the Gospels includes some story of how Jesus reached out to sinners, eating with them, urging them to abandon their sinful ways, and offering them healing if only they would become his disciples.

The New Testament also records how Jesus instructed his Apostles to continue his ministry of healing and forgiveness after he was gone. Both Matthew 28:19 and John 20:23 record the command of the Risen Lord to baptize and forgive sins. In addition, many stories in the Acts of the Apostles describe how the early Church followed that command from the beginning.

FAITH ACTIVITY

The Baptism of Jesus Find out more about what John the Baptist taught about his baptism of repentance and discover what is unique about Christ's baptism. Read Matthew 3, Mark 1:1–11, Luke 3:1–22, and John 1:19–34. Compare and contrast the stories, identifying three truths of faith you've learned.

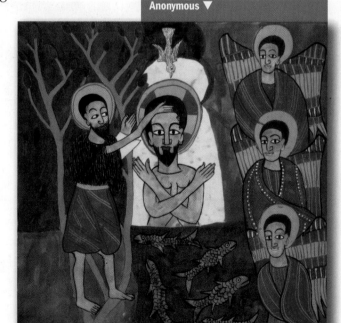

"John the Baptist baptising Christ in the River Jordan," Anonymous ▼

The Church's belief in the forgiveness of sins linked to Baptism is so radical and comprehensive that Saint Paul and the author of the Gospel of John describe Baptism in terms of being born again. It is a rebirth. The faith and experience of the early Christians are described in the passage previously quoted from the *Catechism*.

The Post-Scriptural Era Understanding the full scope of Baptism's forgiveness did not happen all at once in the history of the Church. One of the greatest bishops and theologians during the period known as the Patristic Era (roughly, the second through sixth centuries) was Saint Augustine of Hippo. He, more than any other single figure of his day, expressed in powerful fashion the developing understanding of the Church regarding sin, forgiveness, and Baptism.

Augustine tells us in his autobiographical *Confessions* that he was preoccupied with the question of evil. "But still I sought, 'Whence is evil?' and found no answer" (*Confessions* 7, 7, 11). But by reflecting on Scripture and his own experience of conversion and Baptism, Augustine better understood the mystery of sin and forgiveness. Taking as his starting point the Book of Genesis' biblical account of creation and the fall of the first humans, Augustine pointed out that the sin of our first parents (which he called the Original Sin) lost—not only for Adam and Eve but for all of their descendants—the "paradise" that God had intended. That paradise was a state of holiness and justice, a harmony within the human person, between God and humans, between man and woman, and between humankind and all creation.

The sinful rebellion of our first parents resulted in all of their descendants suffering the consequences. Deprived of

original justice and holiness, humanity's wounded nature was forevermore inclined toward evil, and all people would experience ignorance, suffering, and death. Every human person born after the sin of Adam and Eve, Augustine taught, was destined to be born into this fallen state, unable without God's help to rise above the power of sin that weakened all humanity. To understand Augustine's description of Original Sin, it helps to remember that he spoke of it as a state of being that we inherit by virtue of our being members of the human race, rather than a guilt we are responsible for because of a deliberate choice on our part. Original Sin is different from personal sin, because it is a *state* we *inherit*, while personal sin is an *act* we freely *commit*.

Despite the difference between the two, Augustine linked our need to be freed from the state of Original Sin to our need for redemption from the personal sins we commit. We cannot overcome either one on our own without God's grace. Without it, we are helpless, deprived of that intimacy with God that the Creator intended in the beginning. That is why God the Father sent Jesus, to save us from our sins—both from the state of Original Sin and from the personal sins we have committed. For Augustine, salvation consists in our being restored to intimacy with God—an intimacy that surpasses all human expectations because it offers us a share of God's own divine life.

Augustine teaches about the crucial role Baptism plays in the drama of our salvation. It frees us from Original and personal sin. Baptism joins us to Christ, makes us Temples of the Holy Spirit, and so inserts us into the mysterious life of the Blessed Trinity itself. Catholic theological language calls this share in God's life sanctifying grace, and it is the fundamental effect of Baptism. It is *grace* because it is God's pure gift to us, something we could never earn or deserve. It is *sanctifying* because it makes us holy by giving us a real share in God's own holiness. The *Catechism* refers to this in the remarkable expression "the . . . *deifying grace* received in Baptism" (*CCC*, 1999). Little wonder that this extraordinary gift should prompt Saint Paul to say, "where sin increased, grace abounded all the more," (*Romans 5:20*); and at the Easter Vigil, on the night when the Church everywhere celebrates Baptism, we sing, "O happy fault, O necessary sin of Adam, which gained for us so great a Redeemer!"

In the teaching of Augustine linking Original Sin, personal sin, redemption, and Baptism, we have an excellent example of how the Church's constant reflection on the faith and experience of believers results in deeper and deeper understanding of the mystery of salvation. In the centuries after Augustine, the magisterium chose to give recognition to much of his teachings as part of the Church's official doctrine. The relationship between Augustine's teaching, the belief of the broader faith community, and the authoritative teaching of the Church's magisterium shows how Tradition is a living, dynamic experience of the Holy Spirit's ongoing activity within the Church.

Each generation of believers continues to ponder the mystery of sin and the wondrous reality of God's forgiveness. Each generation "stands on the shoulders of giants" and can recognize how God's grace unfolds throughout history and in our own personal lives. Aspects of our faith that one generation may be aware of but not fully appreciate may be thrown into bright relief in another generation, as faith continues to seek understanding.

A Contemporary Emphasis

We close this section with one example of how recent teaching on the sacraments has focused attention on a particular aspect of the Church's faith that is especially helpful to believers today. Contemporary theology highlights a very ancient notion—that of the Paschal Mystery—as a way of inviting deeper reflection on how our participation in the sacraments draws us into the mystery of the life of the Blessed Trinity.

For many centuries, emphasis was placed on Jesus' death on the cross as a key way of understanding how we were redeemed. Catholic piety encouraged our identification with Jesus on the cross and many explanations of the sacraments held up the cross as the means of our redemption. All of that was—and is—certainly true. But contemporary theology has recognized that the Resurrection was just as important as the death of Jesus in the story of our salvation. The Paschal Mystery embraces both the dying and the rising of Jesus, and so it seems to be a more balanced and more complete way of understanding how Jesus won salvation for us.

One consequence of this emphasis is that Baptism is now explained not just as a share in the death of Jesus. It is also seen as a share in his risen life. This more balanced approach is very ancient. It is found very explicitly in Saint Paul's teaching on Baptism in his Letter to the Romans.

Do you not know that all of us who have been baptized into Christ Jesus were baptized into his death? Therefore we have been buried with him by baptism into death, so that, just as Christ was raised from the dead by the glory of the Father, so we too might walk in newness of life. For if we have been united with him in a death like his, we will certainly be united with him in a resurrection like his…. So you also must consider yourselves dead to sin and alive to God in Christ Jesus."

 Romans 6:3–5, 11

A similar emphasis on new life in the Church's understanding of Baptism in contemporary terms is found in an excerpt from the Roman Ritual's *General Introduction to Christian Initiation*. This is an important pastoral and theological document that offers an overview of how to understand all of the sacraments of Christian Initiation—Baptism, Confirmation, and Eucharist. The excerpts below from that document deal specifically with Baptism. They summarize much of what is important to know about that sacrament. These passages also illustrate the contemporary emphasis of the Church on how the sacraments offer salvation by giving us a share in the Paschal Mystery of Christ.

▲ Deacon holding Paschal candle with priests and congregants in Easter procession.

Quick Check

1. What is Original Sin?
2. What are the consequences of Original Sin for all humans?
3. What is sanctifying grace?
4. What does the Paschal Mystery have to do with Baptism?

Christian Initiation, General Introduction

1. In the sacraments of Christian initiation we are freed from the power of darkness and joined to Christ's death, burial, and resurrection. We receive the Spirit of filial adoption and are part of the entire people of God in the celebration of the memorial of the Lord's death and resurrection.

2. Baptism incorporates us into Christ and forms us into God's people. This first sacrament pardons all our sins, rescues us from the power of darkness, and brings us to the dignity of adopted children, a new creation through water and the Holy Spirit. Hence we are called and are indeed the children of God . . . .

3. Baptism, the door to life and to the kingdom of God, is the first sacrament of the New Law, which Christ offered to all, that they might have eternal life. He later entrusted this sacrament and the Gospel to his Church, when he told his apostles: 'Go, make disciples of all nations, and baptize them in the name of the Father, and of the Son, and of the Holy Spirit.' Baptism is therefore, above all, the sacrament of that faith by which, enlightened by the grace of the Holy Spirit, we respond to the Gospel of Christ . . . .

4. Further, baptism is the sacrament by which its recipients are incorporated into the Church and are built up together in the Spirit into a house where God lives, into a holy nation and a royal priesthood. Baptism is a sacramental bond of unity linking all who have been signed by it . . . .

5. Baptism, the cleansing with water by the power of the living word, washes away every stain of sin, original and personal, and makes us sharers in God's own life and his adopted children. As proclaimed in the prayers for the blessing of water, baptism is a cleansing water of rebirth that makes us God's children born from on high. The blessed Trinity is invoked over those who are to be baptized, so that all who are signed in this name are consecrated to the Trinity and enter into communion with the Father, the Son, and the Holy Spirit . . . .

6. Far superior to the purifications of the Old Law, baptism produces these effects by the power of the mystery of the Lord's passion and resurrection. Those who are baptized are united to Christ in a death like his; buried with him in death, they are given life again with him, and with him they rise again. For baptism recalls and makes present the paschal mystery itself, because in baptism we pass from the death of sin into life.

Christian Initiation, General Introduction

❯Person of Faith

Saint Augustine of Hippo (A.D. 354–430)

Saint Augustine influenced in very significant ways the Church's understanding of the Sacrament of Baptism at a crucial period in its early history, when there were numerous controversies about the faith of the Church. He is also a fascinating individual, whose life story and whose spiritual journey still resonate with people today.

Augustine was born on November 13, 354, in the northern African city of Tagaste (now Souk-Ahras) to a devout Christian mother (Monica) and a pagan father (Patricius, who later converted to Christianity before he died in 371). His mother enrolled him in the catechumenate as a child and gave him a Christian education, but Augustine was never baptized. Later in life, in his famous spiritual autobiography, the *Confessions,* he reminisced about the seeds of faith planted during his infancy, and how he had always kept the name of his Savior in the depths of his heart.

Augustine's intellectual brilliance was recognized early on, and at the age of 16 his father sent him for studies in Carthage. Sadly, the young boy soon gave himself over to pursuing pleasures of the flesh more than his studies, and two years later he fathered an illegitimate child, whom he named Adeodatus. He was to remain in an illegitimate liaison with the child's mother for the next fifteen years. Three years after arriving in Carthage, he fell under the spell of the Manicheans, a heretical sect whose exotic claims to truth held him spellbound for nearly a decade.

In 383, at the age of twenty-nine, Augustine left Africa for Italy, and soon landed a prestigious position in Milan, renowned at the time as a center of sophisticated philosophical learning. His search for truth and the deeper meaning of life was carried out primarily through philosophical inquiries,

SAINT AUGUSTINE BISHOP OF HIPPO

but at a deeper level his soul was undergoing a restless spiritual search, which he was to chronicle later in his *Confessions.* Augustine's mother Monica soon joined him in Milan and prevailed upon him to leave the woman with whom he had been living, so that she could arrange a marriage with a more socially acceptable young woman. His fiancée was too young to marry at that point, and in the interim Augustine began an illicit relationship with yet another woman. He later reported, in a famous quote, that his prayer at this time was to ask God for the gift of chastity, "but not yet." His struggle with the pleasures of the flesh had, in fact, tormented him for years. It was only following his conversion to Christianity that he was finally able to make a commitment to chastity—in fact to celibacy.

During his time in Milan, Augustine came under the influence of the very learned and holy bishop, Ambrose, whom he admired greatly. The story of his conversion tells how in September 386, he heard a child saying, "take up and read" and so picked up the Bible and opened to Romans 13:13–14, where he read: "Let us live honorably as in the day, not in reveling and drunkenness, not in debauchery and licentiousness, not in quarrelling and jealousy. Instead, put on the Lord Jesus Christ, and make no provision for the flesh, to gratify its desires." The story makes it seem that his conversion was quite sudden, but in fact it was the culmination of years of spiritual torment and searching, as the *Confessions* so eloquently describes. This event did, however, serve as the catalyst for his decision to be baptized. In Lent of 387 he enrolled in the catechumenal instructions and was baptized by Ambrose that same year at Easter, along with his son Adeodatus. The following year, while returning home to Africa with his son and his mother, Monica died in the port of Ostia, outside of Rome. The death of his son Adeodatus a short time later left him completely without family.

Several years later, while in Hippo visiting a friend, the people of the town begged the bishop, Valerius, to ordain Augustine. Reluctantly, he accepted and was ordained a priest in 391. Five years later, at the age of forty-two, he was consecrated a bishop and succeeded Valerius in the See of Hippo, where he was to minister for the next thirty-four years until his death on August 28, 430.

During the more than three decades that Augustine served as bishop of Hippo, many heresies and misunderstandings about various important doctrinal questions afflicted the Church. He dedicated his life to preserving and defending the truth of the Gospel. He was a brilliant and enormously influential theologian, but he was also a bishop who pastored his people, preaching very practical sermons as easily as he wrote complicated theological

treatises. His teachings on the mystery of Baptism helped to clarify and deepen the Church's understanding of this foundational sacrament. And his leadership in developing how the catechumenate in Hippo prepared converts for Baptism was both pastoral and practical.

REFLECT

1. Why is Saint Augustine an appropriate person to read about in connection with the Sacrament of Baptism?

2. Do you know of any people who have had dramatic conversions such as Augustine's? Explain your understanding of the process of conversion.

3. What are some types of struggles people your age face? How can faith and the sacraments help?

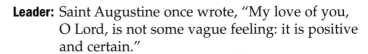

Prayer

Leader: Saint Augustine once wrote, "My love of you, O Lord, is not some vague feeling: it is positive and certain."

All: Lead us to new life that comes from believing in you, O Lord.

Leader: Let us silently reflect on the words of Saint Augustine.

Let me know you, for you are the God who knows me;
let me recognize you as you have recognized me.[1]
You are the power of my soul;
come into it and make it fit for yourself,
so that you may have it and hold it *without stain or wrinkle.*[2]
This is my hope;
this is why I speak as I do;
this is the hope that brings me joy,
when my joy is in what is to save me.
Amen.

Study Guide

▶Check Understanding

1. Highlight similarities and differences between how Maria came to membership in the Church and how the earliest Christians (those described in the Acts of the Apostles) were baptized.

2. Identify the major differences in the way the Sacraments of Initiation are celebrated in the East and West.

3. Outline the major symbols in the Sacrament of Baptism and what they signify.

4. List the effects of Baptism.

5. Summarize the catechumenal process that prepares a person for Baptism and how it supports/encourages a process of conversion.

6. Explain the terms *justification*, *grace*, and *faith*.

7. Describe what is meant by Baptism of blood and Baptism of desire.

8. Describe the essential Rite of Baptism.

9. Distinguish between the common priesthood of the faithful and the ministerial priesthood.

10. Describe what the post-baptismal anointing with chrism says about belonging.

11. Expand upon what it means to share in Christ's role as priest, prophet, and king.

12. Tell how Baptism relates to the communion of saints.

13. Define Original Sin.

14. Summarize the consequences of Original Sin for all humans.

15. Restate the explanation of sanctifying grace and then describe it in your own words.

16. Explain what the Paschal Mystery has to do with Baptism.

▶Apply and Develop

17. Illustrate how the Rite of Baptism for Children and the Rite of Christian Initiation of Adults both include the major ritual actions and symbols of the Sacrament of Baptism.

18. Examine the significant role that parents, godparents, and the entire community have in the Baptism of infants and young children.

19. Write a brief essay illustrating three specific issues where the conflict between Catholic social teaching and our nation's values is obvious, indicating how you see your Baptism calling you to take a countercultural stand.

20. Create a presentation, visual representation, short story, or play that depicts how Baptism is a rebirth and new life in Christ, not just at the moment of Baptism, but in the years that follow.

▶Key Words

See pages noted for contextual explanations of these important faith terms.

catechumenate (p. 41)

Catholic social teaching (p. 56)

character (p. 42)

common priesthood
  of the faithful (p. 53)

justification (p. 48)

lex credendi (p. 50)

lex orandi (p. 50)

magisterium (p. 57)

ministerial priesthood
  of the ordained (p. 53)

mystagogy (p. 47)

Original Sin (p. 60)

paradise (p. 60)

sacred chrism (p. 53)

sanctifying grace (p. 61)

Tradition (p. 58)

[In Christ] you . . . were marked with the seal of the promised Holy Spirit; this is the pledge of our inheritance. . . .

Ephesians 1:13, 14

3

CONFIRMATION

CHAPTER GOALS

In this chapter, you will:

★ consider Christ's institution of the sacrament and how the Church's rituals of Confirmation have evolved over time.

★ explore how Confirmation is celebrated, what is required to receive the sacrament fruitfully, and how one goes about preparing to do so.

★ study the transformation that occurs in one who is confirmed and how that change unfolds in a person's life through the seven Gifts of the Holy Spirit.

★ learn how the Church has deepened her understanding of the effects of Confirmation in a person's life.

★ learn about the life of Saint Cyril of Jerusalem.

69

Adam and Teresa's Story

Adam had not been a very enthusiastic Catholic throughout junior high school. His faith was more routine and habit than anything he thought much about. But some friends got him involved in his parish's youth ministry program the summer before his sophomore year. Adam had experienced a kind of "awakening" as he met new friends who helped him come to a new appreciation of his Catholic faith. He enrolled in the parish's preparation process for Confirmation along with others in his sophomore class. He was lucky enough to have a catechist who made many aspects of his spiritual journey "come alive" in a way he never thought possible. His Catholic heritage began to make more and more sense to him, and he realized that it gave him a grounding in life that other friends he knew lacked. As a result, when the time came for him to be confirmed, he approached the celebration with a genuine eagerness and a real desire to make a recommitment to his Catholic faith in a more mature way than he had ever done before.

Shortly after his Confirmation, the family moved to another state after Adam's father received a job transfer. When his parents registered in their new parish, they also made arrangements for Adam's little sister Teresa to be prepared for her First Communion. "We'll prepare her not only for First Communion, but also for her Confirmation," the parish secretary explained. "What?" exclaimed Teresa's mother, dumbfounded. "You mean they confirm eight-year-olds in this parish?" "Yes," the secretary explained, "lots of folks who come here from other dioceses are surprised by that, but this diocese has been confirming children at their First Communion for more than ten years now."

When Teresa's parents spoke to the parish's director of religious education, they shared their confusion. They said, "We've always understood that Confirmation was a sacrament of maturity in the faith, a time to make a more adult commitment. How can you possibly confirm children who are just making their First Communion?" The DRE gave them some materials that explained why the local diocese had shifted the age of Confirmation out of eighth grade and placed it at the time of First Communion. "It's called 'Restored Order,'" she explained, and then she told them some of the history of Confirmation that they had never heard before: that Confirmation was originally celebrated between Baptism and First Eucharist, and that many dioceses today are returning to this more ancient practice. In fact, she explained further, today in the United States, bishops have the option of celebrating Confirmation for young people in their diocese anywhere between the ages of seven and sixteen. In some places, a "restored order" practice places Confirmation at the time of First Eucharist. In many other places the sacrament is delayed until later in high school, while in most dioceses it is celebrated in the eighth grade.

Teresa was delighted with this surprising opportunity, and she asked her big brother Adam to be her sponsor and help her prepare for both her Confirmation and her First Communion. When the day came for the celebration, the entire family was very pleasantly surprised at how natural it seemed to celebrate these two Sacraments of Initiation (Confirmation and First Eucharist) together. The bishop preached a wonderful homily about how the sacraments of Baptism, Confirmation, and Eucharist all "fit together" in making us—regardless of our age—disciples of Jesus, and the family barely remembered how surprised they originally had been at the idea.

GROUP TALK

Reflect on your experience of the Celebration of the Sacrament of Confirmation.

- Are you familiar with the restored order of Baptism and Confirmation?
- What are the advantages and disadvantages of restored order—that is receiving Confirmation prior to First Eucharist—and of receiving Confirmation as an adolescent, some years after receiving First Eucharist?

The Church Celebrates the Gift of the Holy Spirit

Pope Benedict's 2007 Synodal Apostolic Exhortation stated that the variations in the order of the Sacraments of Initiation, "are not properly of the dogmatic order, but are pastoral in character" (*Sacrament of Love*, 19). The variety of pastoral practices regarding the age of Confirmation surprised the parents of Adam and Teresa, as it does many people today. But understanding Confirmation as a sacrament of Christian Initiation helps us to grasp its significance. In the official document (called an Apostolic Constitution) promulgating the new Rite of Confirmation that was revised after Vatican II, Pope Paul VI offered a theology of the sacrament that highlights the Gift of the Holy Spirit. He points out the following:

- The Holy Father traces in the origins of the sacrament in the ministry of Jesus, recalling the many ways that the Gospels show how the Holy Spirit was with him to bring his mission as the Messiah to fulfillment. The Spirit descended upon Jesus when John baptized him, and the Spirit remained with him. Christ understood his mission and knew himself to be the Anointed One on whom the Spirit of the Lord rested. (See *Luke 4:17–21*.)

- On numerous occasions Jesus promised his disciples that he would send them the Spirit. (See *Luke 12:12; 24:49; John 14:16; 15:26; Acts 1:8*.) The fulfillment of that promise is recorded extensively in the Acts of the Apostles, beginning with Pentecost and extending to the ministry of the Apostles. (See, especially, *Acts 2*.)

- The New Testament also records how the early Christian community continued to confer the gift of the Spirit on the newly baptized, especially through the laying on of hands, which Pope Paul VI says "is rightly recognized by reason of Catholic tradition as the beginning of the sacrament of Confirmation, which in a certain way perpetuates the grace of Pentecost in the Church" (*Apostolic Constitution on the Sacrament of Confirmation*). (See *Hebrews 6:2*.)

FAITH ACTIVITY

Scripture Search Read the various passages that include Jesus' promise to send the Holy Spirit. What can we learn about the Spirit from Jesus' words? Make a list of adjectives, phrases, and titles that describe the Spirit. Then in small groups discuss how Jesus fulfilled his promise. What were the signs of the Holy Spirit's presence in the early Church? How does he act in the lives of Catholics today?

Changing Forms but an Unchanging Gift

In the Apostolic Constitution introducing the new Rite of Confirmation, Pope Paul VI wrote, "From ancient times the conferring of the Gift of the Holy Spirit has been carried out in the Church through various rites. These rites have undergone many changes in the East and the West, but always keeping as their meaning the conferring of the Holy Spirit" (*Apostolic Constitution on the Sacrament of Confirmation*).

As we saw in the previous chapter, in the early centuries, the Church routinely celebrated all three Sacraments of Initiation in a single ceremony. Initially, there was no effort to distinguish the three separate sacraments, since all three of them were part of a single ritual experience. In fact, in the Eastern Rite Church still today, Confirmation (or "chrismation," as it is called) is always celebrated immediately following Baptism and leads directly to the celebration of the Eucharist. This unbroken practice is a powerful reminder to the larger Church of the profound unity that exists among all three Sacraments of Christian Initiation.

In the Church of the West, liturgical customs took a different turn, and the roots of the different ages at which Adam and his sister Teresa were confirmed are found in varied practices observed in the Roman rite for many centuries. In different eras and in different places, both the order of the sacraments (Baptism-Confirmation-Eucharist or Baptism-Eucharist-Confirmation) and the age of those who received them (in infancy, at the age of discretion, in early adolescence) varied enormously. What did not change, however, were the essential elements of the rite, namely the laying on of hands by which the anointing is done, the anointing on the forehead with chrism, and the words accompanying the anointing.

GROUP TALK

1. What is the practice in your diocese regarding the preparation for and the reception of Confirmation?

2. What do you know and what questions do you have about how and when your parents or other family members were confirmed?

A New, Old Formula One of the more significant aspects of the new rite promulgated after Vatican II was the change made in the essential formula that accompanies the anointing. These words that had been used for many centuries: "I sign you with the sign of the cross and I confirm you with the chrism of salvation in the name of the Father, and of the Son, and of the Holy Spirit" (*Apostolic Constitution on the Sacrament of Confirmation*). Pope Paul VI reverted to an even more ancient formula, based on the words still used in the Byzantine liturgy (the liturgy of one of the Eastern Catholic Churches) today.

> "N., be sealed with the Gift of the Holy Spirit."

Rite of Confirmation, 27

In his Apostolic Constitution, Pope Paul VI says specifically that the gesture of laying on of hands before the anointing with chrism "is still to be regarded as very important, even if it is not of the essence of the sacramental rite: it contributes to the complete perfection of the rite and to a more thorough understanding of the sacrament." This laying on of hands that accompanies the bishop's prayer for the sevenfold Gifts of the Holy Spirit from the anointing "in a certain way represents the apostolic laying on of hands." However, the Pope determined that "the Sacrament of Confirmation is conferred through the anointing with chrism on the forehead, which is done by the laying on of the hand, and through the words: Be sealed with the Gift of the Holy Spirit" (*Apostolic Constitution on the Sacrament of Confirmation*). The **Eastern Churches** use a similar rite that includes the anointing with chrism and the proper formula. The Eastern Churches also call *chrism* by the term *myron*.

In this section, we followed the story of Adam and Teresa's Confirmations and learned about the varied history of how the Church has celebrated over the centuries the Gift of the Holy Spirit in this ancient sacramental ritual. In the section that follows, we will explore more deeply what it means to celebrate Confirmation today in a way that the *Constitution on the Sacred Liturgy* refers to as their "full, conscious and active part" (14).

Quick Check

1. What are some of the differences in the way Confirmation was celebrated across the centuries?
2. What can we learn from the New Testament about the role of the Spirit in the ministry of Jesus and in the ministry of the early Church?
3. What were some of the significant changes made by Pope Paul VI when he promulgated the new Rite of Confirmation after Vatican II?
4. How are the Confirmation practices of Eastern Catholic Churches and the Roman Catholic Church different?

Eastern Catholic Churches

We have alluded to the fact that the way the Sacraments of Initiation are celebrated in Eastern Rite Churches differs somewhat from our Western practice in the Roman Church. It is important to keep in mind that all of these Churches, both East and West, are authentic Christian Churches deriving from the earliest centuries and share a fundamentally common faith and worship. They have preserved sacramental and liturgical practices whose validity we recognize, and they embody deep spiritual traditions of great value.

Tragic divisions over the centuries resulted in separation of many Churches in the East from communion with Rome. Now only twenty-one of the Eastern Catholic Churches have *sui iuris* ("of its own right") status in the Catholic Church. (See page 250 for a list of these Churches.) The three largest are the Ukrainian Catholic Church, the Syro-Malabar Catholic Church of India, and the Maronite Catholic Church. The Byzantine Rite is perhaps the more familiar of these to Roman Catholics.

In all of these Eastern Churches, the three Sacraments of Christian Initiation are always celebrated together in the same celebration, even with infants. The sacrament we call Confirmation is known as *chrismation* and is conferred by the one who baptizes, namely the priest. In the celebration, those being confirmed are anointed not only on the forehead but also on the eyes, nose, ears, lips, chest, back, hands, and feet.

▲ Saint George's Cathedral, Lviv, Ukraine

Despite the rich diversity of ritual traditions, there is a unanimous understanding that the chrismation rite confers the Gift of the Holy Spirit on the newly baptized and "seals" or completes the grace of Baptism. In all of these traditions, another very important element is that each year (usually during Lent) the patriarch or senior bishop consecrates the chrism, which is seen as a symbol that the newly initiated is a member of the larger Church. The chrism is a mixture of olive oil, wine, balsam, and as many as 40 different aromatic spices.

Much as our Roman tradition has a highly developed piety surrounding the Real Presence of Christ in the Eucharist, Eastern Catholic Churches reverence the presence of the Holy Spirit in the consecrated chrism.

FAITH ACTIVITY

Learn More about Diversity Find out if there are any Eastern Catholic Churches in your area. As a class, research the possibility of a trip to visit the Church and meet with some of the staff there. Create a list of questions you have about the Sacrament of Confirmation specifically and the ways the community worships in general. If you visit the church building, pay close attention where the baptismal font and oils are located.

What Does the Rite Require?

The Introduction to the *Rite of Confirmation* (12), lists requirements for one who wishes to receive the sacrament:

- Candidates must already be baptized.

- Those who have reached the age of reason must be in the state of grace.

- They must be properly instructed.

- They must be capable of renewing their baptismal promises.

The *Catechism* adds two further criteria for readiness:

- Candidates must have the intention of receiving the sacrament.

- They must be ready to assume the responsibilities of being a disciple and witness to Christ, both in the Church and in the world.

The directive in the *Rite of Confirmation* that says a person must be properly instructed before celebrating the sacrament has resulted in various programs aimed specifically at preparing candidates for this sacrament. In such programs those to be confirmed learn about the meaning and effects of the sacrament, its connection to the other sacraments of Christian Initiation, and how it is celebrated today. In addition, these programs teach candidates what the Church believes about the Holy Spirit's work in their lives to draw them more deeply into the life of God. Some participation in social outreach and justice activities is often required for older candidates as well. Some of these sacrament preparation programs are concentrated in a few months' time, while others extend over a period of a year or two. Some are integrated into a parish's regular religious education curriculum, while others are "stand alone" programs apart from the regular classes.

Readiness In the pages that follow, we will explore more deeply just what it means to be "ready" to celebrate the Sacrament of Confirmation. In doing this, we will understand better why Teresa was just as likely a candidate for the sacrament as was her older, more mature brother. One way of looking at this question of "readiness" is to ask what is required for a person to take

part in the liturgy of Confirmation with their "full, conscious and active part." The *Constitution on the Sacred Liturgy* says that this kind of participation is "the paramount concern" (14), and so it seems appropriate to think about the question of readiness in these terms.

What does the liturgy of Confirmation—its ritual actions, its symbols, its prayers, and Scripture texts—require of a person who grasps their real meaning and makes a commitment to live out those meanings in a deliberate manner as a disciple of Jesus Christ? The chart on the next pages may help us understand the Rite of Confirmation and its claim on those who are confirmed. It's important to note that to show its connection to the other Sacraments of Initiation, the celebration of Confirmation normally occurs within a Mass.

GROUP TALK

Each candidate for Confirmation has a sponsor who supports the candidate during the preparation period, presents the candidate to receive the sacrament, and will help them in the future to live out their baptismal promises. Sponsors must be fully initiated Catholics with spiritual maturity and good standing in the Church.

1. What qualities do you think a sponsor should possess?

2. If you have already been confirmed or are preparing for the sacrament, what led you to choose your sponsor?

3. Is being a sponsor something you would like to do in the future? Why or why not?

Preparing to Receive the Gift

As we focus on what is required from a candidate for Confirmation in order to be "ready" to receive the sacrament, it is extremely important that we keep in mind the balance that is always necessary between God's divine initiative and our human response. We can never "earn" God's grace. By definition, grace is a free gift of God, not anything to which we can lay claim as if by right. It is always God who takes the initiative and who acts first on our behalf. Even our ability to respond to his invitation is a work of the Spirit's goodness within us. Some sacrament preparation programs put so much emphasis on what the candidates must "do" in order to be ready for the sacrament that it can easily seem that they can "earn" the right to God's gifts of grace. Rather, the better way to understand our efforts to prepare ourselves to celebrate the sacraments is to remember the example of Mary, Mother of God, the first disciple: It is how we learn to *be* rather than what we *do* that makes us ready to meet God.

of Confirmation	Key Symbol(s), Action(s), or Texts	Toward a Deeper Understanding
wal of Baptismal ises	The bishop asks the candidates the same questions that are posed to those seeking to be baptized.	· This echoes the baptismal liturgy and is a reminder that Confirmation is the completion of Baptism. · The response "I do" from the candidates is their answer to the preceding instruction of the bishop, as well as their personal reaffirmation of the commitment to discipleship initiated at their Baptism. · They commit themselves to reject evil, and to profess and live the faith as members of the Catholic Church.
ng on of Hands	The bishop invites the community present to join him in prayer for the Gift of the Holy Spirit to come upon the candidates. A time of silent prayer follows. The bishop extends his hands and prays, recalling the candidates' Baptism and asking for the sevenfold Gifts of the Spirit.	· This is a powerful reminder that the bishop's prayer is part of the prayer of the whole Church, assembled here as the Body of Christ. · This evokes the apostolic gesture described in the New Testament for the conferral of the Holy Spirit. · The presence of the bishop in their midst serves to broaden the candidates' vision to include the diocesan Church, and the universal Church. · The baptized faithful who are present exercise their common priesthood by joining their prayers to those of the bishop. · Candidates should be prayerfully open to receive from God an increase in the grace of the Holy Spirit. They are receptive, and not passive.
inting with Chrism	This is the essential rite of the Sacrament of Confirmation. The bishop anoints each candidate with chrism, making the Sign of the Cross on the forehead of each candidate while saying the sacramental formula, "Be sealed with the Gift of the Holy Spirit." The bishop offers the ancient ritual exchange of peace that Saint Paul called a "holy kiss."	· The words of the formula spoken by the bishop recall Saint Paul's text in Ephesians 1:13 that describe our sealing with the Spirit as a pledge of our future inheritance. · The sign of peace was a traditional gesture in the ancient Church that prepared for the Eucharist. · Candidates remain prayerfully open to receive an increase in the grace of the Holy Spirit. · The response of the newly confirmed to the bishop is highly suggestive: the first words from their mouths after being confirmed are words of peace.

Chart continued on next page

Celebrating the Sacrament

Rite of Confirmation	Key Symbol(s), Action(s), or Texts	Toward a Deeper Underst...
LITURGY OF THE WORD		
	Proclamation of Scripture from the Lectionary	· God's living word speaks in a rich array of teachin Holy Spirit and the trans brings. · Candidates more fully p their ability to listen with mind open to God's call willingness to be instruc to live as a fully initiatec transformed by God's gr · They have an awareness word has an impact not ually, but for the commu
CELEBRATION OF THE SACRAMENT		
Presentation of the Candidates	A representative of the community testifies to the readiness of the candidates. Each may be called by name (optional).	· This action indicates ob candidates to come to t with proper dispositions · Calling by name in bibli symbolizes being choser by God. · Candidates "present the before the bishop as a s willingness to accept Go to live a life of disciples
Homily or Instruction	The rite calls for the bishop to speak of the effects of the sacrament and the responsibilities the candidates undertake as a result of their Confirmation.	· This kind of liturgical "ins a sign of the Church's m candidates. · She expects them to live responsibilities that will fully initiated disciples. · Candidates will be famili these responsibilities fro preparation, and from se living them out. · They must pay attention understand as deeply as gift of God they are to re what is expected of them

Chart continu

Rite of Confirmation	Key Symbol(s), Action(s), or Texts	Toward a Deeper Understanding
General Intercessions	The prayer of the faithful who are gathered follows the usual format.	· This is a reminder that the Church embodied in this community offers her support for those newly confirmed not only that day, but in the future. · The newly confirmed join with the rest of the assembly in this exercise of their common priesthood in the general intercessions.
LITURGY OF THE EUCHARIST		
	Bread and wine consecrated. The Body of Christ broken and shared. The Blood of Christ poured out and shared.	· The rite encourages communion under both kinds as an expression of the fuller share in divine life that the newly confirmed experience. · They join the assembly in praying the Our Father. This is especially meaningful to the newly confirmed, as the Holy Spirit prays in us and through us, allowing us to address God as "Abba, Father." · The newly confirmed participate in the Eucharist as a recognition that this is the culmination of their initiation into life in Christ and his Church.
Blessing	A special blessing is prayed over the people.	This is a response of gratitude to God and acceptance of the mission of the Gospel.

Connecting the Rite and Symbol to Everyday Life

Quietly reflect on the following questions. Record your thoughts in your notebook.

· Who are the people who know you best? What testimony can they give to your life as a disciple?

· What evidence can you give from your life that what "I do" is what "I believe"?

· Having received the Holy Spirit, what gifts can you offer back to God Sunday after Sunday?

Mary could do nothing on her own to accomplish the miracle of the Incarnation, yet she was eminently prepared by God the Holy Spirit for the gift she was to receive. To be sure, there was an irreplaceable part that she and she alone had to play, and that was *her consent* (her "fiat") *to God's gift*. Without Mary's willingness to allow God's action in her life, the Incarnation would not have taken place in her. Surely, Mary had been "preparing" over her lifetime to receive the grace of God by choosing to live humbly, prayerfully, with concern for her neighbor, and so forth. She exercised all of her human powers to grow in virtue so as to be ready to accept the gift of God. But when all was said and done, Mary simply allowed herself to be filled with the Holy Spirit so that his divine plan for her would be successful.

GROUP TALK

Mary had been "preparing" over her lifetime to receive the grace of God. Reflect on your life.

· What are ways that you have been "preparing" to receive the grace of God?

· Name some people in your family, parish, school, or broader community who serve as good role models for welcoming God into their lives.

· How do they "prepare" to receive God's life and love and to ultimately share them?

Developing Virtue Candidates for Confirmation—Adam and Teresa, for example—prepare themselves in much the same way. Both Adam and Teresa worked in their respective ways to develop **virtues**—qualities and habits of goodness—so that they would be properly disposed to accept God's call and his grace when the moment came that they were asked to be present for the divine gift. For example, every celebration of Confirmation begins with a Liturgy of the Word, a proclamation of the Scriptures in which God speaks to his people words of love and invitation. In order for Adam and Teresa to be ready to "hear" God's word during their Confirmation, they had to practice daily the discipline of *listening* to the Lord's voice, not only in the Scriptures, but also in the events of daily life and in the experience of those around them.

They did that, first of all, as they learned to listen to their parents. They needed to learn to listen to each other and to God in a way that would benefit the whole family, not just themselves. Teresa had the habit of being easily distracted and often did not really pay attention when her mother asked her to do certain things. She had to learn greater focus and self-discipline in order to put aside whatever she was doing when one of her parents spoke to her. She had to "practice" paying attention in Mass, remembering that it was God speaking in the Bible no matter who was reading it. Adam had to learn how to read the Bible on his own as part of his prayer, learning to listen to God's word in a new way that involved paying attention to what was echoing in his heart after he read a passage and sat silently thinking about its meaning.

Some people may think that "preparing" is just about getting ready for a liturgy that is over in an hour or so. But in reality, preparing to receive a sacrament is about getting ready to live the rest of one's life in a whole new way, a deeper and more Spirit-filled way.

The *Code of Canon Law* and the *Roman Ritual* say that a candidate for Confirmation must be in the state of grace. But that is a bareminimum way of approaching readiness. How much more is required, for example, in order to participate in the rejection of evil that is part of the baptismal promises made during the Confirmation liturgy? What does it mean to foster a keen awareness of the implications of saying "I do" as the bishop asks, "Do you reject Satan, and all his works, and all his empty promises?" For Teresa, it meant she had to think about being nicer to her classmate who always got on her nerves. It meant overcoming her selfishness and being willing to share more generously—her toys, her time, and so forth. For Adam, it meant that he came to realize he was rejecting much of what the culture around him considered "cool"—drugs, pre-marital sex, abuse of alcohol and tobacco, and so forth. Adult candidates for Confirmation often struggle with even more complex ways that they must reject Satan's empty promises: forgoing selfish ambition in their careers, avoiding the everyday consumerism of a materialistic culture of greed, becoming more ethical in their workplace, making sacrifices for their family, and so forth.

In the next section we will look more closely at the effects of the Sacrament of Confirmation in the everyday lives of those who receive it. We will explore how a person defined anew by God's grace in the Sacrament of Confirmation lives life differently because of the Gift of the Holy Spirit that he or she has received.

FAITH ACTIVITY

Living Out Promises Choose four situations people your age face with friends, parents, classmates, or people they don't know very well. For each situation, list what temptations might arise. How could that temptation represent an empty promise that leads away from God and the "I Do" of our baptismal promises? Describe what a person could do to "say no" to that temptation.

✔ Quick Check

1. What are the minimum requirements for a person to be confirmed?
2. What are the main parts of the Rite of Confirmation?
3. What is the meaning of the symbols of laying on of hands and anointing with chrism?
4. What is a virtue?

Transformed by the Holy Spirit

The account of Pentecost in the Acts of the Apostles makes it clear that the Apostles were changed dramatically when they were filled with the Holy Spirit.

When the day of Pentecost had come, they were all together in one place. And suddenly from heaven there came a sound like the rush of a violent wind, and it filled the entire house where they were sitting. Divided tongues, as of fire, appeared among them, and a tongue rested on each of them. All of them were filled with the Holy Spirit and began to speak in other languages, as the Spirit gave them ability.

✝ Acts 2:1–4

From frightened they became fearless; from those who denied the Lord they became heralds of his Gospel. In subsequent chapters of the Acts, story after story recounts the radical transformation of other disciples as well, all who had received the Gift of the Holy Spirit. The story of the conversion of Saint Paul on the road to Damascus and his subsequent life as an Apostle of the Good News is perhaps the best-known and most dramatic example of this kind of transformation. It is no exaggeration to say that one of the most compelling "proofs" of the presence and action of the Spirit in the early Church was the way that these dramatic conversion stories were manifested in the lives of the followers of Jesus.

GROUP TALK

1. What are some signs of the Holy Spirit's presence and action in the Church today?

2. How might people experience dramatic conversions in contemporary culture? How might these be similar to and different from the early Church?

3. Who are some people in your life who help you see the Holy Spirit's action in your life?

The Anointed One The books of the Old Testament do not contain an explicit understanding of the doctrine of the Blessed Trinity. But they do speak of the "spirit of Yahweh" at work in the world, often coming close to personifying the notion of "spirit" in a manner that foreshadows the New Testament's subsequent Revelation of the mystery of the Trinity. An example of this is found in the Book of Isaiah, where the prophet announces the coming of the Messiah— the Lord's Anointed One—who will bring peace and justice to the world. In a famous prophecy announcing the coming of the Messiah in chapter eleven, Isaiah describes the Lord's Anointed One in these words.

> *A shoot shall come out from the stock of Jesse,*
>   *and a branch shall grow out of his roots.*
>
> *The spirit of the LORD shall rest on him,*
>   *the spirit of wisdom and understanding,*
>   *the spirit of counsel and might,*
>   *the spirit of knowledge and the fear of the LORD.*
>
> *His delight shall be in the fear of the LORD.*

 Isaiah 11:1-3

In this passage, Isaiah foretells the coming of one who will be transformed by the gift of a divine spirit resting upon him—a spirit that will make the Anointed One capable of delivering the nation from all its afflictions. Other similar texts throughout the Old Testament speak of individuals being transformed by the divine presence. Jesus himself applied another messianic prophecy of Isaiah to himself, describing his own sense of being filled with the Spirit and being sent on a mission from his Father. Saint Luke sets the scene in chapter four of his Gospel by saying, "Then Jesus, filled with the power of the Spirit, returned to Galilee . . . " (*Luke 4:14*); and a few verses later, "[Jesus] unrolled the scroll and found the place where it was written: 'The Spirit of the Lord is upon me, because he has anointed me to bring good news to the poor. He has sent me'" (*Luke 4:17–18*).

GROUP TALK

Luke 4:11-22 describes the mission of Jesus Christ. Matthew 28:16-20, Luke 24:44-49, and Acts 1:8 give insight into the mission of the disciples. Read all these passages, then discuss the following.

1. What mission did Jesus Christ send his disciples to participate in?

2. Does your school or parish have a mission statement? How does it reflect the mission of Jesus Christ?

3. What would you include in a mission statement for your class on how you can continue the work of Christ in your school?

Filled with the Spirit

The experience of being filled, or engulfed by, the presence of the Holy Spirit is at the heart of our Christian faith. The experience of just such a transformation—one that believers have often described as having the Holy Spirit poured out upon them—is what the sacraments are all about. The dramatic stories of life-changing encounters with the divine that are found in the pages of the New Testament mirror what subsequent generations have experienced in their sacred rituals. Saint Luke, for example, tells the story of the two disciples on the road to Emmaus in a way that his readers would recognize as paralleling their own experience of celebrating the liturgy of the Lord's Supper. (See *Luke 24:13–35*.)

For more than two millennia now, believers have testified how their lives have been transformed by the Gift of the Holy Spirit that they received in the sacraments of the Church, especially in Baptism and Confirmation. It is little wonder that the Church has given voice to these experiences of transformation by using words and imagery from both the Old and New Testament. One such example is the incorporation of the imagery from Isaiah 11:1–3 into the liturgy of Confirmation. The laying on of hands is one of the oldest Christian symbols associated with the invocation of the Holy Spirit and consecration for mission. As the bishop extends his hands over the candidates just prior to anointing them with chrism, he prays:

> All-powerful God, Father of our Lord Jesus Christ,
> by water and the Holy Spirit you freed your sons and
> daughters from sin and gave them new life.
> Send your Holy Spirit upon them
> to be their Helper and Guide.
> Give them the spirit of wisdom and understanding,
> the spirit of right judgment and courage,
> the spirit of knowledge and reverence.
> Fill them with the spirit of wonder and awe in your presence.
> We ask this through Christ our Lord.
>
> *Rite of Confirmation*, 25

Tradition has named these the seven **Gifts of the Holy Spirit**, permanent dispositions that move us to respond to the guidance of the Spirit (*United States Catholic Catechism for Adults*, p. 513). These Gifts make it possible for us to deepen these seven innate tendencies into lived habits of virtue. The seven Gifts of the Holy Spirit are wisdom, understanding, counsel, fortitude, knowledge, piety, and fear of the Lord.

These Gifts of the Holy Spirit—called permanent dispositions—are the ways that Christians across the centuries have come to name their experience of being transformed by God's grace in Confirmation. At the end of the last section, we described this transformation as being "a person defined anew by God's grace in the Sacrament of Confirmation."

An indication of the decisive nature of Confirmation is the fact that it is a non-repeatable sacrament, received only once in a lifetime. Tradition speaks of receiving a *seal* or *character* on the soul—just as is the case at Baptism. This implies that God has intervened in this person's life in a definitive fashion, transforming that person by grace through the Gift of his Holy Spirit. We emerge from the ritual sealed by God's grace. The born-anew experience of our Baptism is deepened, the Holy Spirit penetrating ever more deeply into the core of our being, rooting in our hearts "permanent dispositions"—inclinations to do good rather than evil, inclinations that manifest themselves over time as virtues.

Most of us won't experience the kind of sudden, compressed transformation that is described in conversion stories recorded in the New Testament. For us, that transformation usually unfolds more gradually, almost imperceptibly, over the course of a lifetime. But frequently we are able to recognize moments when we "put on the Lord Jesus Christ" (*Romans 13:14*) more fully, in a particularly intense encounter with divine grace. Celebrating Confirmation is for many people that kind of moment. What follows Confirmation, then, is an unfolding of the graces of the sacrament—the Gifts of the Holy Spirit—and is generally termed a process of growing in virtue.

FAITH ACTIVITY

The Gifts for Today Read the daily news for your town or city. Have each person in your group choose an article and name the Gift of the Holy Spirit that is obviously evident in the story or that is most needed to make it a positive, spirit-filled story. Discuss what a spirit-filled world would be like. Close with a prayer for the transformation of your community.

The Seven Gifts of the Holy Spirit

Those who approach Confirmation come already as "children of the light" (*Ephesians 5:8*), blessed in their Baptism with the Gift of the Holy Spirit. Because of their faith-filled openness and desire to grow even more in love of God, the celebration of Confirmation deepens their initiation, pouring out in full measure the Gift of the Holy Spirit into their hearts (see *Romans 5:5*). Those confirmed are given the seven Gifts of the Holy Spirit to help them grow by cooperating with God's grace in their lives in various ways.

The following points suggest and illustrate some of the possible ways that these seven Gifts might bear fruit in the lives of those who celebrate Confirmation.

Wisdom The gift of wisdom helps those who are confirmed to see and evaluate all things from the viewpoint of God. To see as God sees, that is the heart of wisdom. This gift helps someone who is confirmed to make practical judgments that are wise, because they are in accord with God's will.

Many saints not educated in a formal way were renowned for their wisdom because they were so close to God and thus could more easily discern his path in many complex situations. The Holy Spirit helps those confirmed to possess this sort of "simple wisdom."

Understanding The gift of understanding helps those who are confirmed to grasp more easily the meaning of God's revealed truths, to penetrate to the deeper significance that religious truths hold for their lives of faith. Understanding is a kind of "intuition" guided by the Holy Spirit that allows the confirmed to get beneath the surface of things and see deeper meanings and value.

Counsel (Right Judgment) The gift of counsel helps those who are confirmed to make proper judgments about actions that will lead them closer to or away from God. This gift allows them to listen more easily to the prompting of the Spirit within their consciences. It helps them to recognize the better course of action in difficult and unclear situations. It also guides the confirmed to give better counsel to others who are seeking to discern God's will for their own lives.

Fortitude (Courage) The gift of fortitude gives to those who are confirmed God's special help in being courageous when faced with difficulties or sufferings. By reassuring them that they can, with God's assistance, overcome all evil and win his blessing in heaven, this gift strengthens those who have been confirmed to resist evil and stay on the right path, no matter what obstacles they face.

Knowledge The gift of knowledge helps those who are confirmed to recognize how earthly things can cause them to stray from their path to God. Or, to put it another way, they are helped by this gift to make correct judgments regarding what can harm their spiritual well-being so they will not be led astray by worldly temptations. This gift is the basis for the Church's teachings about the "sense of the faithful," that is, the innate sense that faithful believers have for what "fits" with authentic faith and what does not.

Piety (Reverence) The gift of piety helps those who are confirmed to reverence God the Father, to respect him, and to stand in thankfulness for his loving goodness and for the work of his Son, Jesus. This gift makes it more natural for those who have been confirmed to be prayerful and to call on the Holy Spirit for guidance and strength. Those who respond to this gift in their lives have an increased respect for the things of God. This gift also helps them to see others as God's children, and therefore to respect every human being as one who is made in the image and likeness of God.

Fear of the Lord (Wonder and Awe) The gift of fear of the Lord helps those who are confirmed to deepen their resolve and desire never to offend or be separated from God. The *fear* in question here is not a cowering before a punishing or threatening God. Rather, it is the fear one has of hurting or betraying one who loves us and whom we love above all things. It is an awareness that our God is a loving and just God to whom we are accountable for our actions.

This gift allows those who have been confirmed to deepen their awareness that they are God's children and depend on him for everything, and thus to abhor the thought of losing friendship with him.

FAITH ACTIVITY

Models of Virtue List the seven Gifts of the Holy Spirit and put beside each one the name of a person who embodies that virtue for you. Give a brief explanation of how and why that person is an example of the gift listed. Identify one way you can better live out or respond to each of the Gifts of the Holy Spirit.

✔ Quick Check

1. What are some of the Spirit-led transformations mentioned in the New Testament?
2. What does the phrase *Gifts of the Holy Spirit* mean?
3. What is the character received in Confirmation and its significance?
4. What are the seven Gifts of the Holy Spirit?

Understanding Our Experience of God in Confirmation

We saw in the previous chapter how the Church from the very beginning has sought to deepen her understanding of the faith experience of Jesus' disciples, thus giving rise to a way of reflecting what we call today "theology." The two Greek words (*theos* + *logos*) that are the roots of the word *theology* might be roughly translated as "discourse about God." Theology seeks to understand God and his design for us by means of rational reflection on human experience in light of Scripture and the Church's living Tradition. The nature of God is infinite, and we are finite creatures. We would not be capable of knowing God as Father, Son, and Holy Spirit if God had not chosen to tell us about himself. The word *revelation* is the term we use to describe this process of God telling us something of himself, both in Sacred Scripture and in Sacred Tradition.

While our relationship with God is expressed and strengthened in many ways and places, the experience of the Trinity in the liturgy is unique. The Church teaches that we truly encounter the presence of the divine in the sacred liturgy, in the Person of Jesus Christ (see the *Catechism*, 1084–1090), through the working of the Holy Spirit (see the *Catechism*, 1089–1109). The *Catechism* explains that it is Christ who pours out the Holy Spirit on the members of his Body:

> . . . to nourish, heal, and organize them in their mutual functions, to give them life, send them to bear witness, and associate them to his self-offering to the Father and to his intercession for the whole world. Through the Church's sacraments, Christ communicates his Holy and sanctifying Spirit to the members of his Body.
>
> *Catechism of the Catholic Church,* 739

Some early Church members sometimes referred to the liturgy as "primary theology," while what we today call theology was called "secondary theology." This helps us to appreciate how fundamental our experience of God in the liturgy is to the Church's faith. The bishops at the Second Vatican Council, in the *Constitution on the Sacred Liturgy*, said, "To accomplish so great a work [i.e., our redemption] Christ is always present in his Church, especially in her liturgical celebrations. (7) . . . In the earthly liturgy we take part in a foretaste of that heavenly liturgy which is celebrated in the Holy City . . . where Christ is sitting at the right hand of God." (8)

We encounter God the Father in the liturgy in the Person of his Son, Jesus Christ, through the power of the Holy Spirit. It is that encounter that forms the basis of the Church's reflection, her theology, which leads us to a deeper understanding of the mystery of our salvation.

The Effects of Confirmation

Over many centuries the Church, under the guidance of the Pope and bishops, has reflected on our encounter with God in the liturgy of the Sacrament of Confirmation. Reflecting on the experience of confirmed believers has enabled the Church to identify and teach about what happens to a person who has had this life-transforming encounter, the Gift of the Holy Spirit, bestowed in Confirmation. This teaching is summarized in very concise form in the *Catechism*.

FAITH ACTIVITY

Conduct an Interview Identify three people who have recently been confirmed. Ask them what part of the celebration made the deepest impression on them, and why. Find out what difference being confirmed has made in the way they look at themselves, their faith, and the Church community.

- Confirmation increases and deepens the grace of Baptism.

- Confirmation roots us to God more deeply as sons and daughters, which as Paul says moves us to cry, "Abba! Father!" (*CCC*, 1303).

- Confirmation increases the Gifts of the Holy Spirit in us.

- Confirmation draws us more definitely into Christ.

- Confirmation makes our bond with the Church stronger.

- Confirmation more closely connects us with the mission and work of the Church.

- Confirmation makes us more capable of giving witness to our faith by the things we say and do.

The Very Life of God The first thing we note in terms of the effects of Confirmation is that the sacrament serves as the "completion and perfection" of the graces of Baptism. We learned from our review of the early history of the Sacraments of Initiation that the Church originally celebrated these two sacraments together in a single ritual (as they still are in the Eastern Churches). This was not just an accident of history, nor a casual connection. A deeper reflection on the relationship between Baptism and Confirmation reminds us of the role of the Trinity in our lives and in the sacraments. The *Rite of Christian Initiation of Adults* expresses this truth in the following words:

> The conjunction of the two celebrations [i.e., Baptism and Confirmation] signifies the unity of the paschal mystery, the close link between the mission of the Son and the outpouring of the Holy Spirit, and the connection between the two sacraments through which the Son and the Holy Spirit come with the Father to those who are baptized.
>
> *Rite of Christian Initiation of Adults,* 215

This passage from the RCIA is saying that Confirmation completes Baptism by making known the full mystery of the Blessed Trinity—Father, Son, and Holy Spirit—at work in our salvation. To say that the Trinity is "at work in our salvation" is yet another reminder that we have been "born again" as God's adopted children in Baptism. One of the effects of Confirmation is to deepen our awareness and experience of being children of the Father, drawn into the very life of the Trinity himself. The Father "has given us a new birth into . . . an inheritance that is imperishable," (*1 Peter 1:3–4*) and that "gift" has made us Temples of the Holy Spirit, sharers in the eternal life of God himself. The teaching that Confirmation completes Baptism is more than a statement about the sequence or order of celebrating the sacraments. Rather, it gives us a glimpse into one of the most mysterious truths of our faith; namely, that through the sacraments we are inserted into the very life of God.

GROUP TALK

1. What elements and symbols of the Rite of Baptism are also present in this liturgy? You may want to review the chart on the Sacrament of Confirmation (pages 77-79).

2. Why is it important to make a connection between the two sacraments?

Drawn into Christ and the Church The next two effects of Confirmation—drawing us more definitely into Christ and making our bond with the Church stronger—are two sides of a single coin. One has only to read Saint Paul's letter to the community at Corinth, in which he discusses their membership in the Body of Christ and the unity of the Church, to understand how these two effects of Confirmation go hand in hand. Saint Jerome once said that ignorance of Scripture is ignorance of Christ. We might borrow this kind of expression and say that the more deeply we are plunged into the mystery of Christ, the more robust is our connection to the Body of Christ, the Church.

The Gift of the Holy Spirit that we receive in Confirmation connects us more fully both to Christ and to the Church—our parish, our diocese, and the broader universal Church. In every liturgy, the Father sends the Holy Spirit so that we can be brought into communion with Christ, and in doing so become his Body. We are spiritually transformed into Christ's image, forming with all other believers his Body on earth.

Sent Forth to Evangelize The next two effects of Confirmation—connecting us more closely with the Church's mission and helping us give witness to the Christian faith, both in our words and by our deeds—are also two sides of a single coin. Pope Paul VI, in his Apostolic Exhortation on evangelization, said this:

> We wish to confirm once more that the task of evangelizing all people constitutes the essential mission of the Church. . . . Evangelizing is in fact the grace and vocation proper to the Church, her deepest identity. She exists in order to evangelize[1].

Apostolic Exhortation On Evangelization In The Modern World, 14

The Holy Father's teaching in this regard could not have been clearer. It is a teaching that his successor, Pope John Paul II, often repeated, calling for a "new evangelization" suited for the challenges of today.

▲ Pope Benedict at World Youth Day 2005

From the very first generation of believers, the Church has recognized the connection that exists between the Gift of the Holy Spirit and the disciple's enthusiasm for spreading the Gospel to all nations. The Acts of the Apostles was written by Saint Luke in great part to show how the Spirit is at work in the Church (just as he had been at work in the ministry of Jesus) in order to bring the Good News to all people. The courage and boldness with which the Apostles and first disciples spread the Gospel, even in the face of persecution and death, was for Saint Luke a testimony that the gift of the Spirit had transformed these men and women into the Body of Christ. Thus, one of the effects of Confirmation is that we are helped to give witness to our faith, both by what we say and by what we do. Pope Paul VI's Apostolic Exhortation underlines the significance of this form of evangelization:

> Above all the Gospel must be proclaimed by witness. Take a Christian or a handful of Christians who, in the midst of their own community, show their capacity for understanding and acceptance, their sharing of life and destiny with other people, their solidarity with the efforts of all for whatever is noble and good. Let us suppose that, in addition, they radiate in an altogether simple and unaffected way their faith in values that go beyond current values, and their hope in something that is not seen and that one would not dare to imagine. Through this wordless witness these Christians stir up irresistible questions in the hearts of those who see how they live: Why are they like this? Why do they live in this way? What or who is it that inspires them? Why are they in our midst? Such a witness is already a silent proclamation of the Good News and a very powerful and effective one.

On Evangelization in the Modern World, 21

This simple way of evangelizing by the witness of our lives is essential, but as the Holy Father also taught, "this always remains insufficient, because even the finest witness will prove ineffective in the long run if it is not explained, justified—what Peter called always having 'your answer ready for people who ask you the reason for the hope that you all have' (*1 Peter 3:15*)" (22). A further effect of Confirmation, then, is that the Holy Spirit helps us to find the words—and the courage—to speak out boldly in sharing the Good News with others, explaining and defending the faith we have in God, in Jesus, and in the Holy Spirit.

At the conclusion of the Sacrament of Confirmation, the bishop prays a final blessing or chooses to pray the following "Prayer over the People." This prayer echoes the commitment of all confirmed to give witness to Christ in all they say and do. As a prayer over all gathered, it calls forth an evangelizing spirit among the whole assembly gathered, not only the newly confirmed.

God our Father,
complete the work you have begun
and keep the gifts of your Holy Spirit
active in the hearts of your people.
Make them ready to live his Gospel
and eager to do his will.
May they never be ashamed
to proclaim to all the world Christ crucified
living and reigning for ever and ever.

Rite of Confirmation, 33

Quick Check

1. What does the term *Revelation* mean?
2. What are the effects of Confirmation?
3. How are Baptism and Confirmation connected?
4. What does evangelization have to do with the Gifts of the Holy Spirit and Confirmation?

GROUP TALK

The "new evangelization" described by Pope John Paul II demands that we who have first heard the Good News must be confident and competent in sharing the faith with others through word and action.

1. What are the ways that you stir up the hearts of those around you by the way you live?

2. How prepared are you to share your faith with those who don't know Jesus?

3. What are the wordless ways that you can witness and evangelize?

❯Person of Faith

Saint Cyril of Jerusalem (c. 315–386)

Cyril was born in or near Jerusalem around the year 315. This date is significant because it means Cyril grew up in the years immediately after the Roman Emperor Constantine gave legal status—and eventually imperial support—to the Christian religion. Constantine not only allowed Christians to worship in public, he also began to build many grand structures in which they were able to worship. During his youth, Cyril witnessed the discovery of the Holy Sepulcher (in 326) and other locations associated with the death and Resurrection of Jesus. He was a newly ordained deacon when Constantine's magnificent Church of the Resurrection, built over the Holy Sepulcher, was dedicated in 335.

The First Ecumenical Council at Nicaea had been held in 325, and there the bishops formulated the Nicene Creed as a guide to orthodox faith. However, in the years following the declarations of Nicaea, there was tremendous controversy within the Church over how one ought to understand the two natures of Jesus Christ. The heretical Arian sect denied the divinity of Jesus, while orthodox Christians insisted that Jesus was "one in being with the Father" and therefore divine. The bitter controversy over this issue consumed the better part of the fourth century, pitting bishop against bishop and dividing communities along fiercely held party lines. Cyril was caught up in this struggle for the whole of his tenure as bishop of Jerusalem. He was ordained a priest in the year 345, and made a bishop shortly thereafter, around the year 350. As bishop, he sought ways to reconcile opposing factions during the Arian controversy, seeking language satisfactory to both sides, but he was ultimately unsuccessful. As a result of his efforts to find middle ground, he was deeply involved in the political and theological struggles raging throughout the Christian Church, and three times during his episcopacy—for a total of eleven years—his enemies had him exiled from the See of Jerusalem.

When Constantine ended the era of persecution, there was a flood of converts to Christianity, and Cyril worked diligently overseeing their formation and instructing them in the faith. As bishop he also initiated many changes in the way the liturgy was celebrated, developing rituals that were much more lavish and expressive than had been possible when Christians were not allowed to worship in public. Many of the ceremonies we now observe during Holy Week can be traced back to innovations introduced by Cyril during his ministry as bishop of Jerusalem. Although we do not know much about the details of his personal life, we do have a good feel for the strength of Cyril's faith, thanks to the fact that many of his writings and homilies have been preserved. He is best known for the instructions he gave to the catechumens in Jerusalem. In one of his homilies (called a *mystagogical catechesis*) preached during Easter Week, he explains to those he had baptized at the Easter Vigil something of the meaning of their

Confirmation. This passage from Edward Yarnold's *The Awe-Inspiring Rites of Initiation* gives us a feel for Saint Cyril's passionate preaching and wise pastoral care of his flock:

> But be sure not to regard the chrism merely as ointment. Just as the bread of the Eucharist after the invocation of the Holy Spirit is no longer just bread, but the body of Christ, so the holy chrism after the invocation is no longer ordinary ointment but Christ's grace, which through the presence of the Holy Spirit instills his divinity into us. It is applied to your forehead and organs of sense with a symbolic meaning; the body is anointed with visible ointment, and the soul is sanctified by the holy, hidden Spirit . . . Just as Christ after his baptism and visitation by the Holy Spirit went out and successfully wrestled with the enemy, so you also, after your holy baptism and sacramental anointing, put on the armor of the Holy Spirit, confront the power of the enemy, and reduce it saying, "I can do all things in Christ who strengthens me." (III, 3, 4)

The Awe-Inspiring Rites of Initiation, 80–82

We get a final glimpse of Cyril's character from one of the charges leveled against him on one occasion when he was exiled from Jerusalem. He was charged with selling vestments and furnishings belonging to the Church in order to feed the poor during a time of famine. His actions and demeanor throughout such periods of affliction eventually earned him respect as a holy and ascetical shepherd. His reputation was vindicated as a defender of orthodox faith at the Second Ecumenical Council, that of Constantinople in 381, in which he participated along with 150 other Church fathers. He died five years later in 386 (probably on March 18) at about the age of seventy.

REFLECT

1. Why is Saint Cyril an appropriate person to read about in connection with the Sacrament of Confirmation?

2. Cyril was a very gifted and effective teacher. What teachers have you had in your life who were similarly gifted and effective, and what influence did they have on your life?

3. What elements of Cyril's character would you most like to emulate?

Pentecost Sequence:
Come, O Holy Spirit
(Veni, Sancte Spiritus)

Come, O Holy Spirit, come!
And from your celestial home
Shed a ray of light divine!

Come, O Father of the poor!
Come, O source of all our store!
Come within our bosoms shine!

You, of comforters the best;
You, the soul's most welcome guest;
Sweet refreshment here below;

In our labor, rest most sweet;
Grateful coolness in the heat,
Solace in the midst of woe.

O most blessed Light divine
May that Light within us shine,
And our inmost being fill!

In your absence, we have naught,
Nothing good in deed or thought,
Nothing free from taint of ill.

Heal our wounds, our strength renew;
On our dryness pour your dew;
Wash the stains of guilt away:

Bend the stubborn heart and will;
Melt the frozen, warm the chill;
Guide the steps that go astray.

On the faithful who adore
And confess you evermore
In your sev'nfold gift descend;

Give them virtue's sure reward;
Give them your salvation, Lord;
Give them joys that never end.
Amen. Alleluia.

Study Guide

▶Check Understanding

1. Highlight some of the differences in the way Confirmation was celebrated across the centuries as well as what remained unchanged.

2. Summarize what the New Testament says regarding the role of the Spirit in the ministry of Jesus and in the ministry of the early Church.

3. Describe the significant change made by Pope Paul VI when he promulgated the new Rite of Confirmation after Vatican II.

4. Identify some of the differences in the way Eastern Catholic Churches and the Roman Catholic Church celebrate Confirmation.

5. Summarize the minimum requirements for a person to celebrate the Sacrament of Confirmation.

6. Outline the structure of the Rite of Confirmation as it is customarily celebrated today.

7. Explain the meaning of the symbols of laying on of hands and anointing with chrism.

8. Define *virtue*.

9. Give some examples of the Spirit-led transformation mentioned in the New Testament.

10. Define *Gifts of the Holy Spirit*.

11. Explain the character one receives in Confirmation and its significance.

12. Name the seven Gifts of the Holy Spirit and give a brief explanation or definition of each.

13. Describe the term *Revelation*.

14. List the effects of Confirmation.

15. Explain the connection between Baptism and Confirmation, and what this connection says about the Trinity.

16. Expand upon the relationship between evangelization, the Gifts of the Holy Spirit, and Confirmation.

▶Apply and Develop

17. Write an essay describing the significance of the essential elements of Confirmation remaining unchanged over the centuries.

18. Illustrate in words or images the meaning of the rites and symbols of the Sacrament of Confirmation.

19. Using texts from Isaiah 11:1–3 and Luke 4:14–18, support how God's self-disclosure of himself as a Trinity of Persons was only gradually revealed over the course of time.

20. Distinguish between the terms *primary theology* and *secondary theology* and explain the significance this distinction has for our appreciation of the importance of the liturgy in deepening our understanding of God.

▶Key Words

See pages noted for contextual explanations of these important faith terms.

chrismation (p. 72)

Eastern Churches (p. 73)

Gifts of the Holy Spirit (p. 85)

Revelation (p. 83)

virtues (p. 80)

While they were eating, [Jesus] took a loaf of bread, and after blessing it he broke it, gave it to them, and said, "Take; this is my body." Then he took a cup, and after giving thanks he gave it to them, and all of them drank from it. He said to them, "This is my blood of the covenant, which is poured out for many."

Mark 14:22–24

EUCHARIST

CHAPTER 4

CHAPTER GOALS

In this chapter, you will:

★ learn how the Eucharistic liturgy was celebrated in the early Church and how it has been renewed since Vatican II.

★ consider what it takes for us to participate fully, consciously, and actively in the Mass.

★ explore the connection between our participation in the Eucharist and how we are called to live our lives.

★ learn more about the Church's beliefs regarding Sunday as the Lord's Day, Real Presence, the Mass as a sacrificial banquet, and the fruits of Holy Communion.

★ learn about the life of Oscar Romero.

Julia's Story

Julia had an extraordinary talent for music. She played several instruments to near perfection. Her voice's natural range and quality matched what others might work for years to achieve only with the assistance of a voice coach. Julia had been in several pick-up bands with kids from her neighborhood, but she always quickly lost interest. For some time she had been wondering what to do with her musical talents, when Mr. Wilson, the director of the school's musical program, approached her one day in the hallway. Julia had always admired Mr. Wilson, and in fact had often thought she'd like to make a difference in kids' lives in the way Mr. Wilson did.

"Julia, I need some help with a project I've been asked to undertake, and I wonder if you'd be interested in working with me?" Mr. Wilson then explained to Julia that he had agreed to start a youth choir at St. Mary's (Julia and Mr. Wilson were both parishioners there), and he needed someone with Julia's leadership skills to help him make it happen. Julia was taken aback by the fact that Mr. Wilson saw her as a leader, and she couldn't help wondering whether the timing of this invitation was more than coincidental. Mr. Wilson explained his vision for the choir. It would enrich the celebration of Sunday liturgy and hopefully be a way to help young people have a deeper understanding and love for the Mass. Julia was embarrassed at how shallow her own knowledge of the Mass really was, but she was honest enough to admit that she felt unprepared to be a real leader since she knew so little herself. Mr. Wilson promised to help her; and, he added that he wanted Julia to grow not only her musical talents but in her faith as well. More out of her admiration for Mr. Wilson than for any spiritual motive, Julia agreed to help.

Over the course of the next two years, Julia worked with Mr. Wilson to develop one of the finest youth choirs in the city. Julia's musical skills were called upon frequently, but just as often Mr. Wilson made her part of the spiritual formation efforts that were an integral and regular part of the group's gatherings. Julia found herself studying the history of the Mass so she could explain its development and principal parts to the younger children. She learned about the many other liturgical ministries, besides music, that a parish must develop and that must work in harmony to produce a smoothly run celebration every Sunday. She was introduced to how the Lectionary readings each week guided the choice of music, and she even led simple faith-sharing sessions that opened their weekly rehearsal and that were always built around the Gospel for the coming Sunday.

By the time she graduated from high school and headed off to college, Julia had grown tremendously in more ways than she had imagined possible. She had an impressive knowledge of the liturgy and Sunday Mass. More importantly, she had grown spiritually, learning how to give of herself in service to others and how to participate more fully in the Mass. Countless hours of working with younger children had refined leadership skills she did not know she had. Julia had learned how to connect the meaning of the Mass with the values that she was living through her ministry in the choir. She had discovered how to be part of the celebration of the Eucharistic liturgy, by sharing in Christ's self-offering to the Father, and by participating more deeply in the worship of the parish community. Julia had, indeed, grown not only in her musical talents but in her faith as well.

The Church Celebrates the Paschal Banquet

A careful study of the Scriptures indicates that the origins of our Eucharistic liturgy lie in the Jewish Passover meal, which commemorates God's deliverance of the Jewish people from slavery in Egypt. The New Testament contains several descriptions of Jesus instituting the Eucharist in a Passover context, at the Last Supper. We will consider this in greater detail later in this chapter.

The significant issue to emphasize here is that Jesus clearly instructed his disciples to continue to gather in memory of him, blessing and breaking bread, committing themselves to follow him and honor the new covenant.

> *While they were eating, Jesus took a loaf of bread, and after blessing it he broke it, gave it to the disciples, and said, "Take, eat; this is my body." Then he took a cup, and after giving thanks he gave it to them, saying, "Drink from it, all of you; for this is my blood of the covenant, which is poured out for many for the forgiveness of sins."*
>
>  Matthew 26:26–28

Other key texts are found in Mark 14:22–25, Luke 22:15–20, and 1 Corinthians 11:23–25. The Gospel of John presumes familiarity with these narratives of the institution and reflects instead on the meaning of the Eucharist rather than its institution. (See *John 6,* the Bread of Life discourse, and *John 13–17,* Jesus' washing of the disciples' feet and his discourses at the Last Supper.)

FAITH ACTIVITY

Bread of Life Discourse Read John 6:22–59. Make a list of the different ways Jesus speaks of bread, life, eating, and drinking. Using that list, highlight three main points from Jesus' teaching. Indicate what meaning they have for us as Catholics.

The Lord's Supper (1997) by Laura James ▼

We know that the disciples followed Jesus' command to bless and break bread in his memory. In the Acts of the Apostles we can read about the way the community gathered:

They devoted themselves to the apostles' teaching and fellow-ship, to the breaking of bread and the prayers. Awe came upon everyone, because many wonders and signs were being done by the apostles. All who believed were together and had all things in common; they would sell their possessions and goods and distribute the proceeds to all, as any had need. Day by day, as they spent much time together in the temple, they broke bread at home and ate their food with glad and generous hearts, praising God and having the goodwill of the people.

 Acts 2:42-47

After the New Testament was completed, we have very little by way of written records describing how the Eucharist was celebrated during the next hundred or so years of the Christian era.

Justin Martyr (c. 100–165) was an Apologist. An apologist was someone who explained and defended the Christian faith to his contemporaries. Justin's writings allow us to pick up the story of how the Christian community celebrated the Eucharistic liturgy in the mid-second century. In his *Apologia* (I, 65–67) Justin describes the shape of a Sunday Eucharistic celebration. What we find there is a remarkable similarity to the basic structure of the Mass with which we are familiar today. Justin describes the following elements that appear already to have become the normative way of celebrating the Eucharist:

- Gathering Rites
- Liturgy of the Word (Readings + homily)
- Prayer of the Faithful
- Sign of Peace
- Offertory Procession
- Eucharistic Prayer
- Communion Rite.

GROUP TALK

In small groups compare the liturgy as described here with your present-day experience of Sunday Mass. Discuss the similarities and the differences.

From the time of Justin onward, we have an increasingly detailed written record of how the Eucharist has been celebrated. Another text from Rome, written less than 75 years later, further substantiates that this pattern of Eucharistic worship was fixed very early on in the Church's life. That document from the early third century, called the *Apostolic Tradition of Hippolytus,* reports on customs already considered very ancient by that time. They also clearly follow the same pattern described by Justin. In addition, it contains one of our very earliest Eucharistic Prayers—one that in recent years has been put back into regular use as Eucharistic Prayer II. These ancient sources allow us to recognize that certain elements are always included in the Eucharistic celebration as a single act of worship:

- proclamation of the Word of God

- thanksgiving to God the Father for all his benefits, especially the gift of his Son

- consecration of bread and wine

- participation in the liturgical banquet by receiving Christ's Body and Blood.

A Time of Renewal

When the bishops of the world gathered for the Second Vatican Council, the first task they undertook was a massive project of reform and renewal of the Church's worship. In the *Constitution on the Sacred Liturgy,* they laid out general principles that governed the entire project, as well as directives concerning individual aspects of specific liturgical rites. Central to this effort was the revitalization of the Eucharistic celebration, which they called the "source and summit" of the Church's life (10).

Here are some of the most significant instructions regarding the celebration of the Mass (50–55):

- Make clearer the nature and purpose of the parts of the Mass and their interconnections

- Simplify the rites of the Mass

- Omit parts that had been added "with little advantage" or duplicated over the centuries

- Restore other parts lost over the course of time

- Provide a richer share of readings from the Scriptures

- Restore the prayer of the faithful (General Intercessions)

- Permission was granted for Mass to be said in the language of the people as well as in Latin

- Communion of the faithful under both species was permitted.

In the years immediately following the promulgation of the *Constitution,* the Church revised the rite of the Mass. In many ways the structure and simplicity described by Justin Martyr were recovered. The two principle parts of the Mass—the Liturgy of the Word and the Liturgy of the Eucharist—were given more balanced prominence so that it would be clear that the faithful are fed from two sources—the twin tables of Word and Sacrament.

The Council Fathers also reflected deeply on the wonderful reality of the sacred liturgy. In their teachings they highlighted many traditional doctrines that seemed particularly helpful for the revitalization of the community's celebration of the Eucharist.

Perhaps the single most significant theme that the bishops emphasized was the understanding that in the liturgy we are joined to the Paschal Mystery of Jesus. Each of the sacraments, in its own way, plunges us more deeply into the reality of Christ, dying and rising for the sake of our salvation. But especially in the Eucharistic meal, Christ associates his Church and all her members with his sacrifice of praise and thanksgiving, offered once and for all on the cross to his Father. In fact, it is Christ himself through the ministry of the priest who offers the eucharistic sacrifice. The liturgy of the Eucharist is the living memorial of Christ's Passover sacrifice. It makes present in a sacramental way that timeless self-offering of Christ to his Father. And because Christ is truly present in the ritual actions of the Mass, we are able to enter in a sacramental way into the reality of his sacrifice.

This notion of Christ's *sacramental presence* is crucial, because it is by his Paschal Sacrifice that Christ has poured out the graces of salvation on his Body, the Church. The Mass embodies not only the meaning, but more fully the *reality* of Christ's sacrifice. This is why the Council Fathers call repeatedly for the faithful to participate more fully, consciously, and actively in the liturgy. It is by our fuller participation in the Mass that we are able to reap the fruits of Christ's redemption ever more fully. Because we are joined to Christ and his Paschal Mystery when we participate in the Eucharist, we offer worship to the Father, through him, with him and in him; and, in so doing, "God is perfectly glorified and men are sanctified" (7). In the next section, we will explore what is required to achieve the kind of participation called for in the *Constitution.*

GROUP TALK

Sanctification means, "to be made holy."

1. How does our participation in the celebration of Eucharist Sunday after Sunday make us a holy people?

2. In your parish community, what are signs that the people who gather for worship are being transformed into a holy people?

Changing Forms but an Unchanging Reality

It's important to realize the continuity and consistency in the basic shape and the essential elements of the Eucharist for more than two thousand years. This is quite remarkable. Jesus' command to "Do this in memory of me" has been a cornerstone of Catholic faith from the beginning, and remains so today.

Celebrating the Sacrament		
Part of the Mass		**Toward a Deeper Understanding**
Introductory Rites	Entrance Song and Procession Greeting of the Altar and People Blessing and Sprinkling with Holy Water Penitential Rite (Confiteor and Kyrie Eleison) Gloria Collect (Opening Prayer)	· These rites serve to gather us as an assembly of God's people, joined together as the Body of Christ to give thanks and praise. · As a community, we are prepared to hear and be receptive to God's Word and to properly participate in the celebration of the Eucharist.
Liturgy of the Word	Readings Homily Profession of Faith General Intercessions (Prayer of the Faithful)	· In the proclamation of Scripture, God himself speaks to the assembly his saving work in our lives. · Through the Responsorial Psalm and responses, those gathered make God's Word their own, and through the homily they apply the Word to their lives. · In the Profession of Faith, the assembly shows their commitment to the word they have heard and accepted. · Having been guided by God's Word, the assembly offers prayers for the needs of the Church and the whole world.

Liturgy of the Eucharist	Preparation of the Altar and Gifts
	Prayer over the Gifts
	Eucharistic Prayer
	Communion Rite
	    Lord's Prayer
	    Sign of Peace
	    Fraction (Breaking of the Bread)
	    Communion
	    Communion Song
	    Prayer after Communion
		· The community offers gifts of bread and wine that will be consecrated. They offer themselves as well.
		· The center of the entire celebration is the Eucharistic Prayer, a prayer of thanksgiving and sanctification.
		· During this prayer, the prayers of the entire assembly are joined to that of the priest. Through his words and actions, and by the power of the Holy Spirit, the bread and wine become the Body and Blood of Christ.

Chart continued on next page

Part of the Mass		Toward a Deeper Understanding
Liturgy of the Eucharist		· The entire assembly "joins itself to Christ in acknowledging the great things God has done and in offering the sacrifice" GIRM, 54. · After being united through the praying of the Lord's Prayer and offering of Christ's peace, those properly disposed receive the Body and Blood of Christ. · Those gathered become what they receive: the Body of Christ in the word.
Concluding Rite	Greeting Blessing Dismissal	· Nourished by word and sacrament, the assembly is sent forth to do good works, praising and blessing the Lord.

Connecting the Rite and Symbol to Everyday Life

· Why do we prepare before an important event? How can what happens as we gather for Mass have an impact on our participation?

· In what ways are you open to God speaking to you in your life?

· Listen carefully to what is prayed for in the General Intercessions. Make a list of ways that your parish and school might work to bring about some aspect of what the community is praying for.

· What do you offer of yourself to God during the week? At Sunday Mass?

· How can you be a sign of Christ's peace at home, in school, and with friends?

· What are some ways your family continues the work of Christ after Mass? How do you praise and bless the Lord by the things you say and do?

Quick Check

1. What is the context in which Jesus instituted the Eucharist?
2. What do we know about how Mass was celebrated in the year 150?
3. What were the key directions given in the *Constitution on the Sacred Liturgy* regarding how the order of the Mass was to be revised?
4. What are the parts of the Mass as it is celebrated today?

What Does It Take?

The question, "What does it take . . . ?" to celebrate a particular sacrament can be answered on two levels: the first being the bare minimum requirement of the essential elements needed for validity, and the second being what is needed for a fuller and richer experience of the grace present in the sacramental celebration. The first answer is usually quite clear-cut; the second more elusive.

For a valid celebration of the Sacrament of the Eucharist, a validly ordained priest calls upon the Holy Spirit to transform the wheat bread and grape wine. The priest then uses the words of consecration Jesus spoke at the Last Supper:

> Take this, all of you, and eat it:
> this is my body which will be given up for you. . . .
>
> Take this, all of you, and drink from it:
> this is the cup of my blood,
> the blood of the new and everlasting covenant.
> It will be shed for you and for all
> so that sins may be forgiven.
> Do this in memory of me.

From Eucharistic Prayer II, *The Roman Missal*

FAITH ACTIVITY

Guidelines for Reception In 1996, the National Conference of Catholic Bishops approved a set of guidelines on the reception of Communion. Look up those guidelines at **www.harcourtreligion.com** and write a brief essay about these policies.

The wheat bread and grape wine, the invocation of the Holy Spirit, and the words of consecration are the essential signs or elements of the Eucharistic celebration.

At a bare minimum, these are the requirements for receiving Holy Communion: The person must be a baptized Catholic, approach the sacrament with faith, and be in the state of grace. Anyone who is aware of having sinned mortally must first receive sacramental absolution in the Sacrament of Penance before taking Communion (see *1 Corinthians 11:27–29*). A person must fast for one hour before receiving Communion, unless circumstances related to health or age makes such a practice inadvisable. The Church encourages the faithful to receive Holy Communion whenever they participate in the Mass, but she obliges them to receive once a year, during the Easter season.

These bare minimum requirements are relatively easy to identify and follow. It is more challenging, however, to address the issue of that "something

more" which is required for the celebration to be truly beneficial to the participant. What is it that we need to bring to the celebration of the Eucharist, and how must we participate in it, in order for the Mass to be as grace-filled for us as possible?

From Bare Minimum to Full, Active Participation

The bishops clearly stated the purpose of the liturgical reform and renewal that they mandated.

> In order that the Christian people may more certainly derive an abundance of graces from the sacred liturgy, holy Mother Church desires to undertake with great care a general restoration of the liturgy itself.
>
> *Constitution on the Sacred Liturgy,* 21

The Council Fathers were well aware that the way certain aspects of Mass were being celebrated at the time of the Council did not sufficiently engage people's faith. They knew that while every Mass contains an infinite reservoir of God's grace, *how* a particular celebration of Mass takes place can affect people's openness to the grace that is available. This idea connects to the principles of sacrament and Incarnation discussed in Chapter 1: We are human, and God calls us to salvation in ways that respect how we as humans operate.

Because the bishops had in mind this pastoral aim of enlivening the faith of God's people, they identified an overriding principle that would serve as a guide for any and every change introduced into the liturgy: "In the restoration and promotion of the sacred liturgy, this full and active participation by all the people is the aim to be considered before all else . . . " (*Constitution on the Sacred Liturgy,* 14).

The ongoing work of accomplishing this liturgical renewal in the generations following the Council has now shifted to the local level. Liturgies in our home parishes are celebrated in a way that encourages—more or less, depending on how well they are done—the full, conscious, and active participation of all parishioners. That is why parish liturgy committees exist to collaborate with their pastors in preparing and coordinating celebrations with the goal of making them more meaningful, engaging, and worshipful. That is also the reason why so many lay ministries support and enrich the Eucharistic celebration: lectors, cantors, choirs, extraordinary ministers of Holy Communion, ushers, greeters, sacristans, environmental artists, and many more.

FAITH ACTIVITY

Research Ministries Using your parish bulletin, parish hall postings, or parish Web site, find out what liturgical ministries are open to parishioners in your parish. Find out how people your age can get involved. Look into which of those ministers are also active in your school celebration of the Mass. Write about how you would like to be involved in one of those ministries.

Cooperating with God's Grace While the liturgy is the source and summit of the Church's life, those gathered need to be open to all that is offered them.

> But in order that the liturgy may be able to produce its full effects, it is necessary that the faithful come to it with proper dispositions, that their minds should be attuned to their voices, and that they should cooperate with divine grace lest they receive it in vain.
>
> *Constitution on the Sacred Liturgy*, 11

What are the "proper dispositions" with which we must come to the Eucharist in order for it to bear fruit in our lives to the degree that God wishes for us? How must we approach each celebration of the Mass so that God's grace can be most fruitful in our lives? The following are some elements that answer this question, "What does it take?"

- **Bring the mindset of a participant, not a spectator.** Many of us are so saturated with the spirit of a consumer society that we do not realize how such attitudes can affect our worship and our ability to be open to God's grace. We might tend to critique everything from a spectator's viewpoint: "I didn't like the music," "The homily was boring," "The lector mumbled," and so forth. Nothing will keep us at a distance from encountering God in the celebration as much as this detached attitude of a spectator waiting for someone to entertain or satisfy our personal tastes.

- **Think of the gift you bring to offer, not only on what you will get.** In the Eucharist we are being invited to join our minds and hearts to those of Jesus in an act of *sacrificial self-offering.* The impact of a Eucharistic liturgy for us should be measured more by what we give than what we get. How often have you heard someone say after Mass, "I didn't get anything out of it," when the real question should be, "How much did I give myself to it?" Every celebration of the Mass is a remembering and making present of Jesus' sacrifice for us; every Mass is an act of praise and thanks to the Father, offered first and foremost by Christ himself. Try to come to every Eucharist with the thought that you are entering into the Paschal Mystery of Jesus by offering up to God some specific sacrificial dimension of your life.

- **Approach the Eucharist as the worship of the community in which you participate, rather than as your private prayer.** Our culture is highly individualistic, and our religious attitudes are heavily influenced by a privatism that closes us to many of the values of community worship. We must remember how countercultural the Mass truly is, because there we worship as a community, as the Body of Christ, and not as a collection of individuals. At Mass we become part of something bigger than us.

FAITH ACTIVITY

Spectator or Participant? Reflect on the difference between being a participant and a spectator at a public event. Apply your insights to your own involvement in Sunday worship. Choose two things you could change about your attitude or behavior that help you participate actively in the liturgy. Put your plan into action.

- **Work at developing specific "skills" needed to participate more fully, consciously, and actively.** The *Constitution on the Sacred Liturgy* says, "To promote active participation, the people should be encouraged to take part by means of acclamations, responses, psalmody, antiphons, and songs, as well as by actions, gestures, and bodily attitudes. And at the proper times all should observe a reverent silence" (30). Think about all of the skills that you need to do all of these things more fully. Certain skills may be innate, but in general they are abilities that we cultivate and develop gradually over time by hard work and practice. Skills needed for liturgical participation are no different. We must learn the music and the words, practice singing our parts, and so forth. We must learn how to listen to the Scriptures, the prayers, and the homily more attentively, with deeper understanding, and with a more proactive desire to "make connections" between what we hear and how we act.

GROUP TALK

The liturgical renewal stresses the importance of fuller participation by all of the people.

1. What are the things in your parish that help or hinder people's participation in Sunday Mass?

2. What are some things your parish could do differently to better engage and involve people your age in the celebration?

A Raised Awareness Pope John Paul II was tireless in his efforts to encourage Catholics to deepen their awareness of the Eucharist as what he called a "mystery of presence." He wrote his encyclical letter on the Eucharist, *Church of the Eucharist*, he said, to "rekindle this Eucharistic 'amazement'" (6) among Catholics. In his Apostolic Letter, *Mane Nobiscum Domine (Stay with us, Lord)*, in which he proclaimed a Year of the Eucharist, he wrote,

> There is a particular need to cultivate *a lively awareness of Christ's real presence*, both in the celebration of Mass and in the worship of the Eucharist outside Mass . . . The presence of Jesus in the tabernacle must be a kind of *magnetic pole* attracting an ever greater number of souls enamored of him, ready to wait patiently to hear his voice and, as it were, to sense the beating of his heart. 'O taste and see that the Lord is good!' (*Ps* 34:8).

Apostolic Letter for the Year of the Eucharist, 18

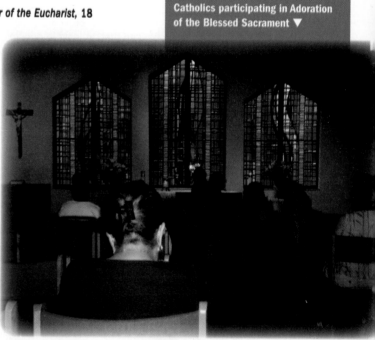

Catholics participating in Adoration of the Blessed Sacrament ▼

The growing number of people spending time in Adoration of the Blessed Sacrament seems to be yet another way that many Catholics have responded to the Holy Father's call for a renewal of awareness—a renewal that leads back again to more active participation in the Eucharistic celebration and in the many ministries associated with a community's liturgical life. It is an interesting historical note that reservation of the Eucharist outside of Mass was originally begun to have it available to take Communion to the homebound. From the fact of its reservation, however, there has arisen a deep piety of prayer before the Blessed Sacrament that has reinforced Catholic faith in Christ's Real Presence in the Eucharist and has drawn believers to participate in Eucharistic celebrations all the more fully and enthusiastically. "The worship of the Eucharist outside of the Mass," the Holy Father has said, "is strictly linked to the celebration of the Eucharistic sacrifice" (*Church of the Eucharist*, 25).

True liturgical renewal, however, is not accomplished simply by a greater participation in the liturgical celebration. The Eucharist, Pope John Paul II wrote, "increases, rather than lessens, *our sense of responsibility for the world* today. I wish to reaffirm this forcefully . . . so that Christians will feel more obligated than ever not to neglect their duties as citizens of the world" (*Church of the Eucharist*, 20). Adoring the Real Presence of Christ in the Eucharist teaches us about his presence in us and in all whom we encounter.

Quick Check

1. What are the essential elements required for a valid celebration of the Eucharist?
2. What are the minimum requirements for a Catholic to receive Holy Communion?
3. What does it mean to have the "proper dispositions" for participating fully in the Eucharist?
4. What is Adoration of the Blessed Sacrament?

Liturgical Inculturation

One very significant innovation introduced in the *Constitution on the Sacred Liturgy* was the possibility of adapting liturgical rituals to specific cultures. This kind of liturgical inculturation had taken place informally and as part of a very natural process throughout the first 1,500 years of the Church's history, as the Gospel was spread in various lands and among new cultural and linguistic groups. However, in light of what Rome considered the excessive and misplaced liturgical changes of the Protestant Reformation, the Council of Trent mandated a nearly absolute uniformity of practice in order to safeguard Catholic traditions. For four hundred years, up to the Second Vatican Council, the liturgy was celebrated in a single format with virtually no adaptation.

The Council Fathers changed that, at least in principle, by acknowledging the appropriateness and on occasion even the need for ongoing adaptation of liturgical forms to specific cultural situations. In 1994, the Congregation for Divine Worship and the Discipline of the Sacraments issued guidelines for the inculturation of liturgy in a document, called *The Roman Liturgy and Inculturation.* One striking example of a successful inculturation has taken place in Africa.

When Pope Paul VI visited Africa in 1969 he specifically encouraged liturgical inculturation on that continent. In that same year the project of the Zairean Mass was begun and eventually presented to Rome for approval in 1973 as the *Zairean Rite of Eucharistic Celebration.* It was approved fifteen years later by the Congregation for Divine Worship on April 30, 1988, as the *Roman Missal for the Dioceses of Zaire.* These are some aspects of that inculturated ritual that have had widespread success since its introduction:

- The presider is dressed in the robes and insignia of a chief.
- The servers carry spears symbolizing the traditional guardians of a chieftain.
- The presider dances in with the servers and encircles the altar, which is reverenced by the priest on all four sides with arms outstretched in a V-form.
- An invocation of the saints and ancestors, who are ever present and guarantee family and community functions, follows next.
- The congregation is sprinkled with holy water and peace is exchanged.
- The people sit while the Gospel is read.
- During the Prayer of the Faithful, incense is burned.
- The Penitential Rite is placed after the homily and Creed, and it calls for the head to be bowed and arms placed on the chest.
- At the offertory members of the assembly dance in with gifts for the needy.
- The congregation echoes and accompanies the priest's prayers with short responses, and all raise hands with him during his prayers.
- The Eucharistic Prayer is punctuated by responses of the congregation.

FAITH ACTIVITY

Ideas for Cultural Adaptation With a partner, create a list of ideas you would want to suggest if you were charged with making cultural adaptations to the Mass that would help people in our country to pray better. Be sure to name some that would specifically help teenagers. Remember, inculturation is not about changing the elements of the Mass or their meaning; it's about the manner in which these are celebrated and making that more meaningful to the participants.

Liturgy and Life

The prophets in ancient Israel often warned the Jewish people that their worship counted for nothing if they were not being faithful to the Lord's Covenant. Though they followed all of the prescribed rituals, God rejected the hypocrisy of their liturgies. The prophets insisted, in particular, that the Jewish people must care for the poor and powerless if they were to be pleasing in God's sight.

> *What to me is the multitude of your sacrifices?*
> *   says the LORD;*
> *I have had enough of burnt offerings of rams*
> *   and the fat of fed beasts;*
> *I do not delight in the blood of bulls,*
> *   or of lambs, or of goats. . . .*
> *Even though you make many prayers,*
> *   I will not listen; . . .*
> *Wash yourselves; make yourselves clean; . . .*
> *seek justice,*
> *   rescue the oppressed,*
> *defend the orphan,*
> *   plead for the widow.*

✝ Isaiah 1:11,15–17

Jesus, too, recognized the importance of love of neighbor if one's worship is to be meaningful and pleasing in God's sight. The judgment scene in Matthew 25:31–46 is startling in how intimately Jesus identifies himself with those in need. In his great teaching in the Sermon on the Mount, Jesus says:

> So when you are offering your gift at the altar, if you remember that your brother or sister has something against you, leave your gift there before the altar and go; first be reconciled to your brother or sister, and then come and offer your gift.
>
> ✝ Matthew 5:23-24

FAITH ACTIVITY

Parable Search Make a list of parables in the Gospels that depict Jesus dining with people. Who are the people Jesus eats with? Why is it important that he does so? What do these parables tell us about the Kingdom of God?

The *Catechism of the Catholic Church* is very succinct in its expression of this linkage between liturgy and life.

> *The Eucharist commits us to the poor.* To receive in truth the Body and Blood of Christ given up for us, we must recognize Christ in the poorest, his brethren. . . .
>
> Catechism of the Catholic Church, 1397

In his Apostolic Letter for the Year of the Eucharist (*Stay with us, Lord*) written not long before his death, Pope John Paul II was even more pointed in saying that the authenticity of our Eucharistic celebrations is directly tied to how we live our lives, particularly with regard to those who are poor and suffering.

> There is one other point which I would like to emphasize, since it significantly affects the authenticity of our communal sharing in the Eucharist. It is the impulse which the Eucharist gives to the community for *a practical commitment to building a more just and fraternal society.* . . . We cannot delude ourselves: by our mutual love and, in particular, by our concern for those in need we will be recognized as true followers of Christ (cf. *Jn* 13:35; *Mt* 25:31–46). This will be the criterion by which the authenticity of our Eucharistic celebrations is judged.
>
> Apostolic Letter for the Year of the Eucharist, 28

Taken together, the texts quoted above show an unbroken thread from the Jewish prophets, through Jesus' teachings in the Gospel, down to the Church's magisterium in our own day. The lesson is inescapable—that what we do in our liturgy must have real consequences in the rest of our lives, or else our worship is empty and in vain.

Participating in the Eucharist

We will now explore three of those consequences of our participation in the Eucharist.

Sharers in the Paschal Mystery Pope John Paul II wrote, "The Church was born of the paschal mystery. For this very reason the Eucharist, which is in an outstanding way the sacrament of the paschal mystery, *stands at the centre of the Church's life . . .*" (*Church of the Eucharist*, 3). All of the other sacraments, our moral lives, our mission to spread the Good News, and our acts of social justice all flow from and lead to the Eucharist. As the very heart of our Church life, the Eucharist defines who we are as a People, what we believe, and how we live out that belief.

It is not by chance that Jesus instituted the Eucharist in the context of the Passover, at the Last Supper, just as his passion was beginning to unfold. For his Jewish contemporaries the Passover celebrated the truth that God's deliverance never fails. The Jews had learned in Egypt that God could and would deliver his people even when their fortunes seemed impossibly low. When the Israelites passed dry-shod over the sea with Pharaoh's army in hot pursuit, and again when they were delivered from exile in Babylon, the deep meaning of Passover as God's continuing deliverance was renewed for them. Thus, it was profoundly significant for his disciples that Jesus instituted the Eucharist at a Passover Supper. His sacrificial death-Resurrection was the great Passover of the New Covenant, and Jesus linked the Eucharist to it.

> He said to them, "I have eagerly desired to eat this Passover with you before I suffer . . ." Then he took a cup, and after giving thanks he said, "Take this and divide it among yourselves; for I tell you that from now on I will not drink of the fruit of the vine until the kingdom of God comes." Then he took a loaf of bread, and when he had given thanks, he broke it and gave it to them, saying, "This is my body, which is given for you. Do this in remembrance of me." And he did the same with the cup after supper, saying, "This cup that is poured out for you is the new covenant in my blood."
>
> ✠ Luke 22:15–20

Immediately after making this linkage, Jesus underlined the consequences for his disciples. He taught that the one who serves others is "greatest" in his Kingdom (*Luke 22:24–30*). In the Gospel according to John, the author tells us that Jesus "got up from the table . . ." and

FAITH ACTIVITY

How Aware Are You? On your way to and from church this week, take two different routes. Notice the poor among you. With your family, brainstorm how the parish community might include those who are poor, outcast, or vulnerable into their practice of the Christian faith. How might your family participate in this important work? Share your ideas with the class.

proceeded to wash the disciples' feet, insisting that they must do the same if they are to share his supper and be part of his Kingdom. (See *John 13:4–8*.) To "serve others" or to "wash feet" are important metaphors for embracing the Paschal Mystery of Jesus in our everyday lives. We embrace this mystery in our own lives by living for others, offering the "sacrifice" of our lives lived in obedience to the Father's will, putting the needs of others before our own, dying to self in order to follow the Great Commandment that links love of God and love of neighbor, and so forth.

In a "me first" culture such as ours, these Gospel values are challenging, to say the least. It is one thing to profess that by Baptism we have been joined to the Paschal Mystery of Jesus Christ. It is quite another thing to learn over a lifetime how to embrace that mystery in our daily lives, by choosing to die to what is selfish and unloving in ourselves so that we can experience a newness of life that leads us to act more like Christ, love more like Christ, and grow closer to the Father. The Eucharist not only celebrates the truth that we are members of Christ's Body; it also nourishes us on his Body and Blood in Communion. In so doing, this sacrament makes it possible for us to live as the Body of Christ in the world, "completing what is lacking in Christ's afflictions," as the audacious expression of Saint Paul puts it, "for the sake of his body, that is, the church" (*Colossians 1:24*).

The early Christian community shaped the narratives of the Last Supper to drive home a point that they knew to be at the core of discipleship: Jesus' followers must share in the Eucharistic meal, but they must also live lives that are consistent with the meaning of the Eucharist, lest hypocrisy cause them to perish. Saint Paul wrote some of his strongest admonitions when he rebuked the Christians at Corinth over behavior that was inconsistent with their participation in the Lord's Supper. (See *1 Corinthians 11*.) When he told them, "as often as you eat this bread and drink the cup, you proclaim the Lord's death until he comes" (*1 Corinthians 1:26*), he was explaining the linkage between sharing in the Eucharist and living the Paschal Mystery.

GROUP TALK

Revisit the story of the Last Supper as retold in John 13:1–17. Then discuss the following.

1. Why do you think "washing feet" is an essential ritual of the Evening Mass of the Lord's Supper on Holy Thursday?

2. How do you feel about letting someone wash your feet?

3. How would you relate "washing feet" to both the Sacrament of Baptism and the Celebration of Eucharist?

Reconcilers and Peacemakers In the Gospel according to Matthew, 5:23–24, Jesus commands us to be reconciled with our brother or sister *before* coming to offer our gift at the altar. Historical studies have established the importance of the exchange of a sign of peace among the early Christian community, especially in a liturgical context. Those first disciples understood that they could not participate in a banquet of peace if they were not at peace with one another. Paul's admonitions to "Greet one another with a holy kiss" (*Romans 16:16; 1 Corinthians 16:20; 2 Corinthians 13:12; 1 Thessalonians 5:26*) were more than mere rhetoric. They were a pointed reminder that those who share in the Eucharist must be reconcilers (see *2 Corinthians 5:18–20*).

At every Eucharist we exchange a sign of peace. In the early Church, that gesture was performed before the community offered their gifts at the altar to more vividly highlight the Gospel command of Jesus. In subsequent centuries, the ritual of being reconciled through exchanging a sign of peace was placed closer to the Communion Rite, where we find it today. This position highlights an important implication of participating in Holy Communion: If we are to share in the Eucharist, then we must be peacemakers and work actively for reconciliation—both in our own personal relationships and in the larger world around us.

GROUP TALK

Jesus was clear that before offering our gift at the altar, we need to be reconciled with our brothers and sisters in Christ. Yet, in practice there are often strained relationships that are not so easily resolved.

1. How does your parish resolve conflicts? Your school? Your family? Your circle of friends?

2. What can these groups do differently to follow Christ's example of being a peacemaker?

3. Who are the peacemakers in the various communities to which you belong?

Christian Stewards Before ending this section, we will consider one further example of the connections between our full, conscious, and active participation in the Eucharistic liturgy and the way we live as Jesus' disciples during the rest of the week. In 1992 the United States bishops wrote a very important letter to Catholics in our country on the topic of stewardship. That document, called *Stewardship: A Disciple's Response,* defines a Christian steward as "One who receives God's gifts gratefully, cherishes and tends them in a responsible and accountable manner, shares them in justice and love with others, and returns them with increase to the Lord." Stewardship is about sharing time, talent, and treasure. The document offers a profound reflection on the biblical notion of stewardship, and it also offers practical teaching on how Catholics can develop stewardship as a way of life.

The bishops' explanation of stewardship points out that stewardship is a spirituality—a way of life—grounded in an attitude of gratitude. But how do we develop gratitude as a fundamental outlook on life, so that we can live up to the definition as one who receives God's gifts gratefully? The answer, of course, is suggested by the English translation of the Greek word *eucharistia*, or Eucharist, which means "thanksgiving." We call the Mass the "Eucharist," and in doing so we are naming the whole rite for its most important part—the Eucharistic Prayer. The heart of every Mass begins when the priest invites the assembly to join him in the Eucharistic Prayer by saying, "Let us give thanks to the Lord our God . . ." The Great Thanksgiving then continues with an opening segment that we call the Preface, a prayer that always includes the phrase, "we do well always and everywhere to give you thanks. . . ." A careful review of the various prefaces used at Mass would show that they invariably go on to name the many reasons we have to be grateful and offer thanks to God: for the gift of creation, for forgiveness and redemption won for us in his Son's death and Resurrection, for the gift of the Holy Spirit, and for a share in the very Body and Blood of Christ.

FAITH ACTIVITY

Attitude of Gratitude Spend some time quietly reflecting on the blessings in your life. For whom and for what are you grateful? How might God be acting in and through those people and events in your life? Write a short prayer of thanks, and pray it every day this week.

Quick Check

1. What are some of the Scriptural foundations for the connection between liturgy and life?
2. What does it mean that authenticity of our Eucharist is tied to building a more just society?
3. How is our participation in the Eucharist a sharing in the Paschal Mystery of Christ?
4. How does our participation in the Eucharist call us to be peacemakers?

Over the course of a lifetime, Catholics who participate regularly in the Eucharistic liturgy are gradually but progressively formed—if they participate fully and consciously—in an outlook on life that is mindful of God's many blessings and that overflows in a spirit of gratitude. The basis of stewardship is a grateful heart, and we become ever more grateful the more we are mindful of the many, many blessings that God has showered upon us. Those who are attentive as they join in the Eucharist every week cannot help but become more aware of those gifts. Likewise, praying with the Church the great Prayer of Thanksgiving over and over again instills deep within us a spirit—a spirituality—that is rooted in gratitude and overflows in a life of stewardship. It is true, as we said above, that we should not come to Mass for what we get, but rather for what we can give, intent on offering ourselves as gifts to God. Nonetheless, we know from experience that the more we give of ourselves, the more conscious we become of being blessed by God—to a measure that far exceeds anything we can offer. Indeed, receiving the Bread of Life and Cup of Salvation as pure gifts cannot help but awaken in us a sense of being blessed, and thus our hearts are moved to gratitude.

The Church Believes

We have seen in previous chapters how, over the centuries, the Church has continually deepened her understanding of the ways that God is present to us in the sacraments. The Church teaches that Divine Revelation was complete with the close of the apostolic era and the composition of the last books of the New Testament. But because God's self-communication is an ongoing process, the Church—under the continuing inspiration and guidance of the Holy Spirit—will never exhaust her ability to grow in a deeper understanding of the mysteries of salvation.

The term *deposit of faith* (see *2 Timothy 1:14*) is sometimes used to describe the treasures of divine truth entrusted to the Church for the salvation of humankind. But that image does not mean or imply that we might someday exhaust all there is to know about God and how he works to save us. Led by the Holy Spirit, we will always search for a deeper appreciation and understanding of Revelation.

Sunday Eucharist

From the very beginning, the Apostles and the first disciples gathered weekly to mark the day that Jesus rose from the dead. That particular day was not a "special" day, either in the Jewish calendar or in the pagan Roman calendar. For Jews, the previous day, the Sabbath, was considered a sacred day for worship. According to Justin Martyr, in secular Roman society the "day named after the sun" was just another workday and held no religious significance. Yet, the Jewish followers of Jesus, and later the Gentile converts as well, steadfastly gathered on the day that was the weekly "anniversary" of the Resurrection; for this reason it was special to them. When they gathered they shared their fellowship meal "in remembrance" of Jesus, just as he had commanded (see *1 Corinthians 11:24*). For them, every Sunday was an Easter celebration, and only later did an annual commemoration of the Resurrection (Easter) take on greater importance in the Church's liturgical life.

Choosing Sunday as the day above all others on which to celebrate the Eucharist was part of the inspired guidance of the Holy Spirit. But it meant that poor laborers had to arise in the darkness—often at the risk of their very lives—to gather in secret with other believers for the breaking of the bread before starting their workday. Everyone knew that by doing so they were being faithful to the Lord's command, "Do this in remembrance of me." It was only centuries later, after Constantine gave imperial support to the Christian religion, that it was possible to make Sunday a weekly holiday, thus permitting Christians to gather openly and to worship in public buildings where the Eucharist was celebrated in more elaborate rituals.

With the passage of time, Sunday became known to all as the day when believers assembled for Eucharist, nourished at the tables of word and sacrament, expressing and achieving the unity they shared in Christ. Sunday became the day of the Church.

The universal obligation to participate in Sunday Eucharist as a matter of Canon Law didn't take written form until the start of the twentieth century. Prior to that, we have records dating back as early as the fourth century—exhortations and expectations that were preached or decreed in local councils and in other ways—always assuming that Sunday is the day when every follower of Jesus must gather with other believers to celebrate Eucharist "in remembrance" of his Resurrection. Today, the obligation to celebrate Eucharist on Sundays and holy days is one of the five precepts of the Church.

GROUP TALK

Sunday is a day of grace and rest from work. We honor the Lord's Day by worshiping, relaxing, and activities of service. Sunday helps people nurture their familial, social, and religious lives.

1. How does your family observe Sunday?

2. What are some of the challenges in today's culture to keeping Sunday as a day of worship and rest?

3. What are some things you would like to do to honor Sunday?

Real Presence

Another theme that manifests the way the Church's understanding of the Eucharist has deepened across the centuries is that of the presence of Christ in the Eucharist. The Gospel according to John, in Chapter 6, reveals how the early Christian community began to meditate in a profound way on the reality of Christ's presence in the Eucharist. As early as the middle of the second century Justin Martyr was able to articulate in clear and precise manner this central truth of our faith: ". . . the food over which the eucharist has been spoken becomes the flesh and blood of the incarnate Jesus. . . ."

Nearly a thousand years later, during a period of renewed theological reflection called Scholasticism, the Church felt the need for a deeper grasp of the mystery of Eucharistic presence in more sophisticated, philosophical categories. Using concepts as old as Aristotle, theologians brought new precision to our understanding of Christ's presence by making a distinction between "substance" (the essence of a thing) and "accident" (its physical appearance). They taught that through the words of consecration, the "substance" of the bread and wine is changed into Christ's Body and Blood, while the "accidents" remain those of ordinary bread and wine. This change is called transubstantiation. It captures in a very precise way the ancient faith of the Church that the whole person of Christ, living and glorious—Body and Blood, his soul and divinity—is *really, truly, substantially* present under the consecrated species of bread and wine.

The concept of transubstantiation captured the Church's faith in Christ's Eucharistic presence. Its specialized vocabulary resonated among theologians. Gradually, many ordinary Catholics learned it as well. The Catholic community also referred to this as Real Presence. The grace-filled flowering of Catholic devotional piety concentrated on the Real Presence of Christ in the Blessed Sacrament. This belief is an eloquent testimony to the way the faith of the Church has been passed on over many centuries. Christ's Real Presence is one of the bedrocks of Catholic faith. It is an inexhaustible source of comfort and inspiration for those who ponder the mystery of Christ's sacramental presence in the Eucharist.

The Church is constantly deepening her grasp of the sacraments, and in the *Constitution on the Sacred Liturgy* the Council Fathers developed yet another dimension of our faith that Christ is present in the Eucharist. In paragraph seven of the *Constitution*, the bishops teach that in addition to Christ's true presence in his Body and Blood, he is also truly present in the following ways:

- in the **priest** who stands in his place to lead the community's prayer

- in his **word** as the one who speaks when the holy Scriptures are proclaimed

- in the **community** of believers, his Body the Church, gathered in song and prayer.

These forms of Christ's Presence are "real" also, but in a different way. The term *Real Presence* is specifically reserved for Christ's unique presence in the Blessed Sacrament.

FAITH ACTIVITY

Communion and Community The U.S. Bishops' *Happy Are Those Who Are Called to His Supper* states, "The reception of Holy Communion is . . . not a private devotion. Rather, the reception of Holy Communion is an integral part of our worship as a community of faith." Make a list of ways receiving Communion is an act of the Church as a whole.

Sacrificial Banquet

Another theme that we shall consider in this section is the balanced way the faith of the Church has joined two distinct but inseparable understandings of the nature of the Mass—sacrificial memorial and sacred banquet. Christ linked them together from the beginning by his words at the Last Supper as he offered his Body and Blood to eat and drink. This revealed to his disciples that the deeper meaning of the meal was his sacrificial offering of himself to the Father.

Pope John Paul II commented on this linkage in his Apostolic Letter *Stay with Us, Lord*.

> There is no doubt that the most evident dimension of the Eucharist is that it is a *meal* . . . As such, it expresses the fellowship which God wishes to establish with us and which we ourselves must build with one another. Yet it must not be forgotten that the Eucharistic meal also has a profoundly and primarily *sacrificial* meaning. (15)

The Eucharist is a sacrifice because it makes present Christ's sacrifice on the cross. It does this because it is the memorial of his Paschal Mystery and makes available the effects of Christ's redemptive sacrifice. We share in this sacrifice by joining in Christ's offering, both for our own sins and for the entire Communion of Saints—all the faithful on earth, in heaven, and in purgatory. Our participation truly is a "holy communion" since our prayers are joined with those of the entire Mystical Body, living and dead, with whom we are united in Christ through Baptism. It is a wondrous mystery that is called a "holy communion" because it unites us with Christ in heaven, perpetually interceding with his Father on our behalf, as well as with the members of the Body of Christ, who join their earthly prayers to our own. To describe in words the scope of this mystery requires the skill of a poet, in addition to that of a theologian. This ancient prayer seems to be the work of both:

> O sacred banquet in which Christ is received as food,
> The memory of his Passion is renewed,
> The soul is filled with grace,
> And a pledge of the life to come is given to us!

The Fruits of Holy Communion

How are we to name the fruits of our sharing in Holy Communion? What are the effects of this sacrament for those who receive it worthily? They are manifold, of course, but the Catechism provides a helpful summary that can focus our appreciation for the gifts that are ours in this wondrous sacrament.

- **Holy Communion deepens our union with Christ.** It does this by increasing and renewing the life of grace that we receive in Baptism. The Eucharist is the third of the Sacraments of Christian Initiation. It completes our Christian initiation. We become what we receive in this mysterious exchange, so that with Saint Paul we can say that we have "put on the Lord Jesus Christ" (*Romans 13:14*). (See *CCC*, 1391–1392.)

- **Holy Communion separates us from sin.** It does this by cleansing us from venial sin and defending us against mortal sin. As we grow in virtue, constantly being cleansed from our lesser faults, the terrible possibility of mortal sin becomes more remote. (See *CCC*, 1393.)

- **Holy Communion strengthens our bond with the Church.** It does this by deepening our incorporation into the Body of Christ. It is a happy coincidence of our language that reminds us that in Holy Communion we are joined to the holy "communion of saints," the full Body of Christ that embraces both the living and the dead. (See *CCC*, 1396.)

- **Holy Communion commits us to the poor.** It does this by helping us to recognize Christ in the poorest, who are his brothers and sisters. Recognizing him there, our hearts are filled with the grace of love and charity, and we cannot help but put into action the compassion of Christ whose Body we are. (See *CCC*, 1397.)

- **Holy Communion deepens our longing for the unity of all Christians.** It does this by making us pray all the more urgently that the full unity of Christ's Body might one day be restored. Because it is both a sign and a cause of the unity of Christ's Body, Holy Communion cannot help but make us long ever more urgently to be able to share at the table of the Lord with everyone who carries the name Christian. (See *CCC*, 1398.)

FAITH ACTIVITY

First Communion Recall your own preparation for First Communion. What do you most remember about the preparation? How has your understanding of the Eucharist developed since you first received your First Communion? List those new understandings. What new faith practices have you developed since that time?

Quick Check

1. How did Sunday develop as the primary day for the Church to gather and celebrate the Eucharist?
2. What do transubstantiation and Real Presence mean?
3. What are fruits of Holy Communion?
4. How is the Mass a meal and a sacrifice?

›Person of Faith

Archbishop Oscar Romero (1917–1980)

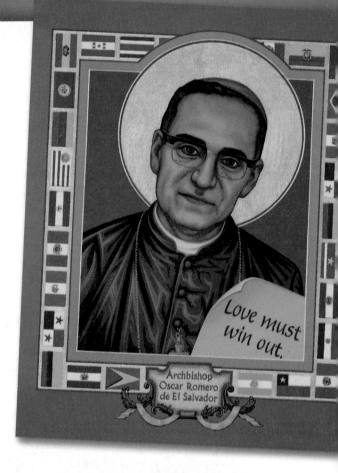

Archbishop Oscar Romero de El Salvador

"The Eucharist commits us to the poor" (*CCC*, 1397).

"I must tell you, as a Christian, I do not believe in death without Resurrection. If I am killed, I shall arise in the Salvadoran people" (Oscar Romero).

Oscar Arnulfo Romero y Galdámez was born on August 15, 1917, in Cindad Barrios, a town in the mountainous east of El Salvador near the border with Honduras, the second of seven children. He left school at the age of 12 to begin learning the trade of carpentry, but soon thereafter expressed a desire to study for the priesthood. His early seminary training was in El Salvador, but his final years of preparation were in Rome, where he studied at the Gregorian University and was ordained in 1942. Two years later, his bishop recalled him from Rome and gave him an assignment first in a country parish and later as a seminary teacher. His talents were recognized by his ecclesiastical superiors, and he undertook a series of administrative responsibilities that earned him a reputation as an organized, hard worker. During this period, he began to give talks on local radio stations, a practice that he was to continue throughout the remainder of his priestly ministry. He had often expressed doubts about his "people skills," and radio broadcasts seemed well suited to his shy nature.

In 1970, he became auxiliary bishop of San Salvador. Two years later he was made bishop of a rural diocese, Santiago de Maria, and in February 1977, Oscar Romero became archbishop of San Salvador. At the time of his appointment, many considered Archbishop Romero a conservative, a "safe" choice who would not involve the Church in the growing political and social unrest of the country. He had, however, a pastor's heart, and he stayed close to his people, especially the poor. It was not long

before he was drawn into their sufferings and began to defend them against the powerful forces that exploited them.

An important turning point in the archbishop's life came in March 1977, with the murder of Father Rutilio Grande, S.J., a social crusader and activist who denounced the injustices being perpetrated against the poor. After the priest's murder, government officials brought Archbishop Romero to view his body as a warning and a threat. Instead, the archbishop pushed for an official government inquiry. When it was clear that there would be no effort to bring his killers to justice, the archbishop held a service for him in the cathedral that was attended by thousands. In his homily, the archbishop called Father Grande and the two who were killed with him "co-workers in Christian liberation." He then went on to say, "The government should not consider a priest who takes a stand for social justice, as a politician, or a subversive element, when he is fulfilling his mission in the politics of the common good." The following week, he made a bold public move, prohibiting the celebration of Mass anywhere in the diocese on the following Sunday, except at his own Cathedral. He invited the faithful to gather with him at the Cathedral, and 100,000 came. The event galvanized the poor and cast the archbishop decisively on their side in the struggle against their powerful oppressors.

From that point onward, it was only a matter of time before Archbishop Romero would have to confront the full fury of the right-wing forces arrayed against him. He became increasingly outspoken on behalf of the poor, and he appealed even beyond the borders of his own country for help in bringing an end to the violence in his homeland. During a visit to the Pope in May of 1979, Archbishop Romero presented him with seven dossiers filled with reports documenting institutionalized torture, murder, and other human rights violations in El Salvador. The scope of the escalating violence that was to consume El Salvador is suggested by the following figures: In a nation of 5.5 million inhabitants, the bloody civil war that eventually broke out and lasted more than a decade resulted in 300,000 "disappearances" and more than 75,000 confirmed deaths. One million fled their homeland, and another million became fugitives within their own country, pursued by the military and police.

In an article published just two weeks before his death, Archbishop Romero wrote, "I am bound, as a pastor, by divine command to give my life for those whom I love, and that is all Salvadorans, even those who are going to kill me." On March 24, 1980, he was celebrating a funeral Mass in the chapel of the hospital where he lived, and in his homily he spoke about the parable of the wheat. He said, "Those who surrender to the service of the poor through love of Christ will live like the grain of wheat that dies. It only apparently dies. If it were not to die, it would remain a solitary grain. The harvest comes because

of the grain that dies. . . . We know that every effort to improve society, above all when society is so full of injustice and sin, is an effort that God blesses; that God wants; that God demands of us." Minutes later, a paid assassin burst through the doors of the little chapel and shot him while he was standing at the altar, about to begin the Eucharistic Prayer.

REFLECT

1. How does Archbishop Romero's life connect with the Sacrament of Eucharist?

2. Who do you know personally, from current events, or from history who demonstrates solidarity with the poor as Archbishop Romero did?

3. What virtue of the life of Archbishop Romero would you most like to model?

Prayer

If we truly believe that Christ, in the Eucharist of our church, is the living bread that feeds the world, and that, as a believing Christian who receives this host, I am the instrument, then I should bring it to the world. I have the responsibility of being the leavening of society, of transforming such an ugly world. This, yes, would change the face of the country, to truly inject the life of Christ in our society, in our laws, in our politics, in all relationships. Who is going to do this? You are! If all of you, the Salvadoran Christians, don't do this, then don't expect El Salvador to be fixed. El Salvador will only be leavened with divine life if the Christians of El Salvador truly propose not to live a lazy faith, a fearful faith, rather truly as the saint—I think it was Saint John Chrysostom—said, "When you take communion, you receive fire." You ought to leave breathing joy, with the strength to transform the world.[1]

Archbishop Oscar Romero, May 28, 1978

Study Guide
▶Check Understanding

1. Describe the context in which Jesus instituted the Eucharist, as recorded in the New Testament.

2. Summarize what we know about how Mass was celebrated in the year 150 using Justin's *Apology.*

3. List the key directions given in the *Constitution on the Sacred Liturgy* regarding how the order of the Mass was to be revised.

4. Outline the parts of the Mass as it is celebrated today.

5. Identify the essential elements required for a valid celebration of the Eucharist.

6. Name the minimum requirements for a Catholic to receive Holy Communion.

7. Describe some of the "dispositions" a person must bring to the Eucharist in order to participate as fully as possible.

8. Explain the development of the Adoration of the Blessed Sacrament.

9. Summarize how we can trace the teachings in the Judeo-Christian tradition regarding the connection between liturgy and life.

10. Explain what Pope John Paul II meant when he said the authenticity of our Eucharist is tied to our practical commitment to building a more just society.

11. Describe how our participation in the Eucharist is a sharing in the Paschal Mystery of Christ.

12. Highlight how our participation in the Eucharist calls us to be peacemakers.

13. Describe how Sunday came to be acknowledged as the primary day for the Church to gather and celebrate the Eucharist.

14. Define the term *transubstantiation* and explain its connection to Real Presence.

15. Name and explain the fruits of Holy Communion.

16. Explain how the Mass is a meal and a sacrifice.

▶Apply and Develop

17. Choose two restorations in the liturgy that took place after Vatican II and illustrate how these reflect the significance of the concepts of the Paschal Mystery and sacramental presence.

18. One of the key aspects of entering into the celebration of Mass more fully is the idea of joining ourselves to the self-offering of Jesus. Write an essay explaining what needs to take place within a person in order to achieve this goal of making the Mass a time of sacrificial self-offering with Jesus.

19. Observers of our culture have noted a rise in narcissistic ("me first") attitudes and behaviors in our society. Evaluate some of the challenges of this trend for communities that are trying to form disciples of Jesus Christ, and what the impact might be on the Church's worship.

20. Prepare a presentation on Christ's presence in the liturgy; be sure to point out the various ways Christ is with us and why this is significant to the whole of the Mass and how we grow from it.

▶Key Words

See pages noted for contextual explanations of these important faith terms.

Communion of Saints (p. 122)

deposit of faith (p. 119)

inculturation (p. 112)

Mystical Body (p. 122)

Real Presence (p. 111)

transubstantiation (p. 121)

Receive the Holy Spirit. If you forgive the sins of any, they are forgiven them; if you retain the sins of any, they are retained.

John 20:22-23

PENANCE AND RECONCILIATION

CHAPTER 5

CHAPTER GOALS

In this chapter, you will:

★ learn how the Sacrament of Penance and Reconciliation was celebrated in the past and how it is celebrated today.

★ consider contrition and confession as essential parts of the sacrament.

★ explore what Penance or satisfaction—the third essential part of the sacrament—was in the past and how it is still meaningful today.

★ understand how the faith of the Church is expressed in the fourth essential part of the sacrament, absolution.

★ learn about the life of Saint John-Baptiste-Marie Vianney, the Patron of Confessors.

Mark's Story

Mark had been growing more and more miserable for months. In fact, as he looked back on it, the last couple of years had been a downward spiral involving turmoil and fights at home, neglect of his school work, partying that involved drugs and drink, and lately even some shoplifting with his buddies. He was ashamed of who he'd become. A close call with what could have been a fatal car accident had finally made him take a hard look at the mess his life was in.

It was a Thursday late afternoon and he had planned on just stopping by church to spend some quiet time thinking, but he discovered there was a "First Confession" celebration just getting started for the parish second grade class and their families. Father Carson was telling the children about how much Jesus loved people who had strayed from the right path, and how the story of the Prodigal Son was really an invitation to each of us to "come home" and receive God's forgiveness. Something about the whole experience moved Mark deeply, stirring memories of how happy he used to be years ago, and making him want to recapture something of the innocence he saw in the smiling faces of those second graders.

When Father Carson invited family members and anyone else present to join the children as they approached one of the visiting priests for individual confession, Mark felt it was Jesus speaking to him, to his troubled heart, inviting him to a fresh start. He was surprised at how easily he was able to open up to the priest and admit the mess of his life. The priest helped him, in just a few minutes time, to name the ways he'd sinned, and even gave him a penance that made sense as a way to show (God and himself) that he was really serious about beginning over again. When the priest put his hands on Mark's head and said the words of absolution, a very deep peace filled his heart, and in that moment he understood in a new way what the word "grace" really means. Returning to his pew, he even found himself singing with gusto the Song of Thanksgiving along with the families and First Penitents.

Mark's story can help us understand a great deal about how the Church celebrates God's love today, two thousand years after Jesus told his disciples to share with others the forgiveness that his Heavenly Father had sent him to bring to our sinful human condition. Mark experienced the Sacrament of Penance and Reconciliation in its communal form, with individual confession of sins and absolution. The communal form of the sacrament that Mark experienced is quite similar to what happens when one person receives the sacrament: God's Word of forgiveness is proclaimed, a sharing of one's sin's is followed by the priest giving counsel and assigning a penance, the prayer of absolution is pronounced and a concluding expression of praise and thanksgiving is offered to God for the gift of forgiveness just received.

GROUP TALK

How does Mark's story compare to your own story of finding forgiveness in the Church and receiving the Sacrament of Reconciliation?

The Church Celebrates God's Forgiveness

I n this very simple ritual format, the Church continues to make available the healing mercies of God, announced by Jesus at the very beginning of his ministry—Repent, and believe in the good news" *(Mark 1:15)*. These have continued to be celebrated by the Church in various ways across the centuries. All of the essential elements of this ancient ritual unfold naturally in a process of conversion that "brings us home" to the Church where we experience the healing touch of Jesus today, just as surely as did the sinners of his own time and place.

In addition to making repentance and forgiveness a central theme of his preaching, Jesus showed by his actions that sharing the Father's forgiving love was at the heart of his ministry. When he told the paralytic man that his sins were forgiven, the bystanders were shocked and some even infuriated at his claim of such power. But his subsequent cure of the paralyzed man was done specifically "so that you may know that the Son of Man has authority on earth to forgive sins" *(Luke 5:24)*.

It was that same authority that Jesus passed on to the Church in the person of the Apostles when he appeared to them after the Resurrection, breathing on them the power of his Holy Spirit and saying,

> 'Peace be with you. As the Father has sent me, so I send you...If you forgive the sins of any, they are forgiven them; if you retain the sins of any, they are retained.'
>
> ✝ John 20:22-23

Mark, a person of faith, knew that in the Church that same forgiveness continues to be available.

Changing Forms, but a Single Message

The *Catechism* reminds us that, "Over the centuries the concrete form in which the Church has exercised this power received from the Lord has varied considerably." (1447) In the early centuries of the Church's history, the sacrament was reserved for extremely grave sins—for example, murder, apostasy, adultery, or idolatry. There developed what was called the Order of Penitents, a process of public penance meant to foster conversion and heal the sinner's wounded state of soul.

Enrollment in the Order of Penitents was reserved to those guilty of such a grave sin, and often was allowed only once in a lifetime. Then, as today, lesser sins were forgiven by acts of charity, prayer, participation in the Eucharist, and so forth. To verify that the sinner's repentance was genuine, and as a sign of that repentance, public penances were given, often lasting years before the penitent was reconciled and allowed to participate fully in the Church's life. Sin offended the community, and public penance was a way to reconcile the penitent to the community. It was a punishment for sin and a means for healing. In a positive light, it was part of the healing process, helping the sinner to turn away from sin, and reminding the members of the Church to pray for the person who was thus excluded from the grace of the sacraments.

The rigors of such a severe penitential discipline began to be relaxed in the seventh century when Irish missionaries brought to the rest of Europe a practice that had its origins in the Fathers of the Desert, among (Eastern) monastic communities. The practice of celebrating the sacrament, as we know it today, developed in Ireland. Penances assigned were made less harsh and could be accomplished more quickly without public notice. Besides permitting immediate reconciliation at the time when one's sins were confessed, this discipline allowed penitents to celebrate the sacrament more frequently than once in a lifetime. This form of celebrating the sacrament quickly spread and developed into the practice that is commonplace today. For more than a thousand years, this form of celebrating Penance and Reconciliation remained virtually unchanged.

▲ Augustinian Abbey Church in Limerick, Ireland

Vatican II Renews the Sacrament

It was only in the last century, as part of the liturgical reform of the Second Vatican Council, that further changes were made in the liturgy of the sacrament. These consisted in the creation of three distinct ritual forms according to which the sacrament may be celebrated:

- **Form One,** individual confession with individual absolution, is basically the familiar way of celebrating introduced by the Irish missionaries.

- **Form Two,** a communal celebration with individual confession and absolution, is an entirely new ritual form. Although its basic elements are familiar, this way of celebrating the sacrament had never before been part of the Church's official liturgical repertoire.

- **Form Three,** a communal celebration but with no individual confession and with general absolution, was formerly permitted only in times of serious emergency, when a priest was not available to hear individual confessions (such as soldiers about to go into battle). If a mortal sin (grave sin) is confessed through Form Three, this sin must be confessed according to its kind and number the next time a person receives the sacrament under Form One or Two. The use of this form today is *restricted to very limited circumstances* and is rarely celebrated in this country.

Compassionate Listening Today the ordinary way that a person is reconciled with God and with the Church is by celebrating either Form One or Form Two of the sacrament. Both forms show the ecclesial or communal nature of the Sacrament of Penance. In either of these forms, a person is expected to make a careful and sincere examination of conscience in order to identify whether there are any grave (mortal) sins to be confessed. If so, they must be fully disclosed to the priest. If a person forgets about a sin and so fails to confess it, the sin is nonetheless forgiven. However, if it is remembered at a subsequent confession, it should be confessed at that time.

If someone is aware of a grave sin and deliberately conceals it from the priest in confession, there is no forgiveness that takes place since a deliberate deception has been introduced into the sacramental ritual. This is a very serious matter, and if it should ever occur the person needs to return to the sacrament as soon as possible to seek the priest's help in making an honest and full confession. It is very easy to mislead a priest in confession, but God looks into our hearts and is never misled. It goes without saying, of course, that one must have the intention and the desire not to sin in the future in order for sins to be forgiven.

▲ The Prodigal Son by Marc Chagall

FAITH ACTIVITY

The Forgiving Father Read Luke 15:11–32, The Parable of the Prodigal and His Brother. What are similarities between the son's return home to reconcile with his family and Mark's experience of the Sacrament of Reconciliation? Correlate the steps of the Rite of Penance to the process of reconciliation for the Prodigal Son and Mark.

Most often, concealing one's sin from a priest in confession happens out of a sense of embarrassment or shame. Sometimes there is also fear that the priest will scold or reprimand. In such a case, the person needs to focus on the loving, compassionate Christ who is present in the sacrament and who is really the one to whom our sins are being disclosed. Jesus already knows the secrets of our hearts, and he loves us unconditionally. He has already died on the cross to win forgiveness for our sins, and his only desire is our happiness and that we be freed from our sins, no matter how serious or ugly they may be. Priests receive years of training and are very mindful of the fact that they represent Christ in the sacrament. Their sole concern is that the person celebrating the sacrament encounter—through them—the compassionate and forgiving face of Jesus.

GROUP TALK

1. Who are some people in your life who have shown you compassion?

2. What difference did their sensitivity, love, and possible forgiveness make in your life?

3. How can you be a more compassionate person to family and friends? To people you do not know well?

How to Participate in the Sacrament · Form One

The Rite of Penance	Toward a Deeper Understanding
Reception of the Penitent · Welcoming the penitent · Sign of the Cross · Invitation to trust in God	· The priest warmly and kindly welcomes the penitent. An informal dialogue may take place before the formal opening of the liturgy. · There is no mention in this rite of the traditional formula "Bless me Father for I have sinned, it's been _____ since my last confession." However, that custom may still be maintained. · After the Sign of the Cross, the priest invites the penitent to trust in God.
Reading of the Word of God (optional)	· Unlike communal celebrations, in the individual form of the sacrament a Liturgy of the Word is optional. However, a number of passages are suggested, and permission is given for either the priest or penitent to select any text that seems appropriate. · This is a wonderful way to begin one's confession and places all that follows in a context of faith.
Confession of Sins & Acceptance of Satisfaction	· This part of the rite is meant to be a kind of dialogue between the priest and the penitent. First, the penitent discloses to the priest the sins for which healing and forgiveness are being sought. It is a time to express sorrow, to admit honestly one's guilt, and to seek forgiveness. · At a minimum, the priest responds by assigning a penance, but ideally he will accompany that with wise counsel, words of reassurance and encouragement, and so forth. The words of the priest are meant to be healing, overflowing with the compassion of Jesus, and spoken in the power of the Holy Spirit.

Chart continued on next page

The Rite of Penance	Toward a Deeper Understanding
Prayer of the Penitent Penitent uses one of the formulas or prays spontaneously	The penitent says an "Act of Contrition." The rite gives a number of sample texts that may be used (45, 85–92), but it also allows the penitent to formulate this prayer in his or her own words.
Prayer of Absolution · Priest extends his hands over the penitent · Priest makes the Sign of the Cross · Penitent answers "Amen"	· It is as important for the priest to listen to the prayer of the penitent as it is for the penitent to listen to the prayer of the priest. · The text that the priest uses is called the prayer of absolution, and it is the Church's official pronouncement of God's forgiveness for the penitent's sins.
Proclamation of Praise · Priest says, "Give thanks to the Lord, for he is good." · Penitent answers, "His mercy endures for ever." (*Rite of Penance*, 47)	· This exchange between the priest and penitent is one of the new elements in the revised liturgy of the sacrament. It highlights the celebration of the sacrament as a shared prayer between both priest and penitent. · When we celebrate this sacrament we are called to full and active participation in the Church's liturgy, just as we are at Mass each Sunday.
Dismissal by the Priest Priest says, "The Lord has freed you from your sins. Go in peace," or uses one of the other dismissals. (*Rite of Penance*, 47)	The rite provides a number of texts that the priest may use in sending forth the penitent. All of them aim to impart a final sense of peace as the penitent returns to the world renewed, cleansed and healed of sin, ready to complete the penance and once again to live the faithful life of the baptized.

Connecting the Rite and Symbol to Everyday Life

Reflect on the following questions.

· Why is it important to be able to trust in God? Has someone you know modeled that trust for you? What might keep people from trusting God or those close to them?

· What are some areas of your life that might need reconciliation and healing? Have you been able to discuss them with anyone? Have you considered bringing them to the Sacrament of Penance?

· Think of a time you asked for and received forgiveness. How did the experience affect you?

· How might the peace of this sacrament help people your age respond to the challenges you face? How can the newness of life help you faithfully follow Christ?

Quick Check

1. What role did the Irish missionaries have in the celebration of the sacrament in the seventh through eighth centuries?
2. What was the Order of Penitents?
3. What are the three Forms under which the sacrament may be celebrated today?
4. What takes place during the celebration of the Rite of Penance for an individual?

Timeless Elements

FAITH ACTIVITY

Names of the Sacrament Look up the meanings of *conversion, Penance, confession, forgiveness,* and *Reconciliation* in the Glossary of the *Catechism of the Catholic Church.* Why do you think these different names are sometimes extended to the Sacrament of Penance and Reconciliation as a whole? Then read *CCC 1423–1424* to check your answers.

The *Constitution on the Sacred Liturgy* reminds us that, "the liturgy is made up of immutable elements divinely instituted, and of elements subject to change" (21). So the Church has sought to adapt the outward form of this sacrament to the changing needs of God's people. Corresponding to the different ways that the sacrament has been celebrated, there are a number of different names that have been used to refer to this sacrament: the Sacrament of conversion, confession, Penance, and Reconciliation. However, a core reality has always been present, a timeless essence that has never changed. Saint Paul captures this in his Second Letter to the Corinthians, as he describes his own ministry in terms of reconciliation.

All this is from God, who reconciled us to himself through Christ, and has given us the ministry of reconciliation; that is, in Christ God was reconciling the world to himself, not counting their trespasses against them, and entrusting the message of reconciliation to us.

✝ **2 Corinthians 5:18–19**

Always in the Church's ministry of Reconciliation, Christ has been present in the ritual signs and symbols, especially in the person of the priest confessor who acts on his behalf. Always, the Holy Spirit has been at work, moving sinners' hearts so that they might encounter Christ more deeply in the ritual. He reveals Christ to the believers who receive the sacrament, making the power of Christ's grace present, transforming sinful lives with forgiveness and healing.

In every age, in order for the Sacrament of Penance and Reconciliation to bear fruit in the lives of sinners who celebrate it, the same fundamental structure has been followed, made up of two equally essential parts.

- **On the one hand,** there is the human experience of conversion, led by the power of the Holy Spirit. This inner reality of conversion is expressed externally by three acts of the penitent, which are called **contrition, confession,** and **penance** (or **satisfaction**).

- **On the other hand,** there is God's action, which is accomplished through the Church and finds expression in the priest's prayer of **absolution**.

GROUP TALK

1. In what ways does sin harm or even rupture our relationship with God and with others?

2. How could you help someone understand the impact of sinful behaviors on themselves and others?

3. How can true sorrow for sin be an impetus to avoid turning away from God in the same way in the future?

Contrition

As we noted in the chapter on Baptism, personal sin is a thought, word, or action that we freely and knowingly commit, or in the case of omission, fail to do. Sin is disobedience of God's law, and offense against God . . . an act contrary to reason (CCC, 1871–1872). Sin simply does not make sense; it counters all that we know to be good and right and weakens the unity and communion among all people.

Venial sin refers to sin that weakens our relationship with God and others and diminishes God's grace within us. Mortal, or grave, sin is a very serious offense against the law of God. Mortal sin destroys God's grace within the soul of the sinner and requires repentance in order to share in God's Kingdom and experience eternal life with him. For a sin to be mortal, it must have three conditions (1) The matter involved is seriously wrong (contrary to God's law). (2) The person acting knows that it is seriously wrong but (3) freely chooses to commit the wrong anyway.

While human nature is inclined to sin, the Holy Spirit leads us to turn away from sin and toward God. Contrition is the term used to describe sorrow for our sins that includes a genuine desire to change our sinful ways and resolution to avoid sin in the future. But sorrow comes in many forms, and it is helpful to know that the Church recognizes two different degrees or kinds of contrition.

- **Perfect contrition** is sorrow that springs from a pure love of God, whereby we love God above all else. The power of such love is so great that it frees us not only from venial sin, but even our mortal sins, as long as we intend to confess them in the sacrament as soon as possible.

- **Imperfect contrition,** which is also a gift of the Holy Spirit stirring in our hearts, springs more from fear of sin's consequences and a loathing for the ugliness of sin than from a pure love of God. Such sorrow requires sacramental confession to free us from our mortal sins, but it is often a motive that leads us to the sacrament.

Prepare an Examination To most fully participate in the sacrament, one needs to do a good examination of their conscience—how they have loved as God has loved them and how they have failed to love as God does. With a partner, create a list of phrases or questions that can help someone your age reflect on how they have and have not lived a life of love of God and neighbor. Be sure to address all the different aspects of life: home, school, parish, friends, family, and so on. Use the Ten Commandments, the Beatitudes, etc. (see pages 253–257) as your model for discerning what it means to live a moral life.

Often we are led by imperfect contrition. The action of the Holy Spirit fills us with disappointment and even disgust at how empty our life has become. We feel shame and regret for sins we have been committing. However, in the course of the celebration of the Sacrament of Penance, we can be touched by an awareness of how much God loves us. When our hearts are moved and stirred with a deep and selfless love for God, imperfect contrition can become perfect contrition. Disgust over sinful ways does not cease at that point— on the contrary, it most likely becomes even deeper. But if our focus is on God and his love, we approach the sacrament out of a spirit of perfect contrition. This is what happened to Mark in the opening story.

This helps us to see what an important part the liturgical celebration of the sacraments plays in our spiritual life. It would be ideal if we always approached every sacramental celebration with a pure and perfect frame of mind. But that is simply not the case. We come to the liturgy often with very mixed motives and with a jumble of distractions and attitudes that can easily keep us from entering deeply into the mysteries being celebrated. But one aspect of the mission of the Holy Spirit in the liturgy is to prepare us to encounter Christ there. In addition to his hidden workings deep within us, the Spirit uses the human dimensions of our liturgy (signs and symbols, music, the words spoken, and so forth) to open up our hearts and to awaken our faith. For Mark, it may have been the words of the Scripture, or something the priest said in his homily, or a song that was sung, or simply the faith he saw on the faces of those second graders. Whatever human elements of the liturgy it may have been, the Holy Spirit used them to draw Mark from imperfect to perfect contrition.

Mark's move from imperfect to perfect contrition testifies to how we can encounter Christ in the liturgy of the Church and be transformed by that encounter and the grace it provides—just as the paralyzed man who was forgiven and cured in the house at Capernaum was transformed by his encounter with Jesus.

Confession

Confession is the second essential element of the Sacrament of Reconciliation. As humans we are made up of both body and spirit, and our spiritual conversion must be expressed in both words and actions for it to be fully realized. Furthermore, because sin wounds our relationship with God and the Church, our relationship with both must be healed. We must be reconciled with God *and* the Church, and this can only happen through our confession to and absolution from the Church's minister.

Confession of Venial Sins We are obliged to confess all our mortal sins according to their kind, number, and any circumstances that change their nature. We have already mentioned that in confessing our sins, we must tell the priest all of the mortal sins we remember that we have committed since our last confession. The "seal of confession" assures us our sins will not be repeated to anyone. **Venial** (less serious) **sins** may be confessed as well—even though this is not required. The Church recommends the regular confession of our venial sins as an important way of becoming a more faithful disciple of Jesus. The *Catechism* encourages the practice of regular confession, even with only venial sins, and it points out the benefits of doing so. (See *CCC*, 1458.)

Frequent confession helps us to form our conscience, to develop a keener sense of right and wrong, and to recognize when we have strayed, even a little, from the path of discipleship. The Introduction to the Rite of Penance reminds us that confession helps us to develop "true knowledge of self before God" (6b). It is so easy for us to ignore our little faults and to live in denial of how they are impacting our lives in negative ways.

The habit of examining our conscience regularly before confession and confronting even our slightest faults can help us. The Church teaches that our conscience is a judgment of reason we make about whether a specific act is good or bad, right or wrong. But a properly formed judgment (conscience) does not simply happen automatically. Our conscience is formed gradually as we read the Scriptures, learn more about the Church's teachings, pray more fervently, listen to the stirrings of the Holy Spirit in our heart, and so forth.

Frequent confession strengthens us in the fight against sin and evil in our lives. The repetition of sins, even venial sins, can lead to vices and more serious sin. But, just as weight training gradually builds our body's strength, a regular practice of confession adds to our spiritual strength by opening us more and more deeply to the grace of the Holy Spirit in our lives. We gradually replace vices—habits of sin—with virtue—good habits, and our lives are progressively transformed to become more like Christ. This is what Saint Paul was encouraging in the many places in his letters where he urged his followers to put aside the ways of sin and to put on the strength of Christ Jesus. (See *Romans 13:12–14*; *Ephesians 6:11–15*; *Colossians 3:5–10, 12–17*.)

Frequent confession opens us up to allow Christ to heal us.
There is a very subtle temptation that we can fall prey to
when we live generally good lives and manage to avoid serious sin. It is this: We can begin to think that we are doing
well and avoiding sin on the basis of our own strength. Such
an attitude is really a sinful pride that ignores the truth of
how we grow in holiness. Every gain we make is in reality a
gift of God's grace. And every gain we make in virtue is the
result of God's abundant grace flowing into our lives and
making us capable of being better, more loving persons.
Regular confession reminds us that we need constant healing
and that Jesus' forgiveness is what makes us whole.

***Frequent confession stimulates growth in our spiritual
lives.*** Conversion is an ongoing process, not a "once-and-for-
all" event. The *Constitution on the Church* (*Lumen Gentium*)
acknowledged that we are a Church of sinners and always "in
need of cleansing, and so . . . unceasingly intent on repentance
and reform" (8). The Introduction to the Rite of Penance
recalls this teaching of the Council and adds:

> the people of God accomplish and perfect this continual repentance
> in many different ways. . . . Thus the people of God become in the
> world a sign of conversion to God. All this the Church expresses in its
> life and celebrates in its liturgy when the faithful confess that they
> are sinners and ask pardon of God and of their brothers and sisters.
>
> *Introduction to the Rite of Penance,* 4

This same passage also reminds us that every confession of
our sins is made "in light of God's mercy." This is, perhaps, a
key to understanding the importance of frequent participation
in the Sacrament of Reconciliation. At the deepest level of our
being, holiness resides in our capacity to allow ourselves to be
loved by God and to return that love, both to God and neighbor. The more we confess our sinfulness "in light of God's
mercy," the more will our hearts learn of the depth of God's
love for us. And as we gradually learn to open ourselves to
that love, the more we will find ourselves *responding* to love
by *returning* love.

Why Confess to a Priest? People often ask why they "have
to" confess their sins to a priest when God already knows
their heart and sees their sorrow. We need to be prepared with
an answer and able to help someone understand not only why
we must, but also, why we are enriched by doing so. Jesus
established the Sacrament of Reconciliation as the ordinary
means for the forgiveness of sins, so that we could experience God's mercy and receive his forgiveness. Jesus gave the
Apostles, and their successors, the authority to forgive sins in
his name. The bishops share this authority with priests.

We are not spirits, beings without bodies. And because we are flesh-and-blood creatures, something deep within our nature cries out for the interior (spiritual) realities of who we are to be given external expression, to be "embodied" in ways that are tangible and concrete. If a young man courts a young lady whom he loves deeply, but never bothers to put into words his feelings for her, thinking *"She already knows what's in my heart,"* the two of them will not last very long as a couple.

From our own experience, we know that we need to apologize to one another, to say we're sorry in real, human words in order for healing after hurts. That same necessity is present in our religious lives. To be true to our "embodied" nature, we must approach the Church to be reconciled for our sins. That means engaging in a human dialogue with the Church's minister, from whom we seek God's forgiveness and healing. The Church makes this very easy to do. Any priest who has received from proper Church authorities the faculty to hear confessions may celebrate the sacrament with any person, and in doing so he always forgives sins in the name of Christ and by the power of the Holy Spirit.

Our nature needs not only for us to say, "I'm sorry" when we have sinned. It also needs to hear, "You're forgiven." The dialogue with the priest accomplishes exactly that and helps us re-establish "habits befitting a disciple of Christ" (*CCC,* 1494). By reconciling us to the Church at the hands of her official minister, we hear and experience the truth of our Reconciliation with God. Mark knew that he needed to express his sorrow out loud to the priest, who represents Jesus Christ, and his experience of confessing those sins and being absolved was one of relief and an unburdening that brought him immediate peace. Nothing could have been more rewarding for Mark than this powerful experience of the sacrament.

Quick Check

1. What are the four essential parts of the Sacrament of Reconciliation?
2. How are perfect and imperfect contrition different?
3. What is required for a person's confession of sins to be "complete" and "sincere"?
4. How does regular confession of venial sins benefit Catholics?

GROUP TALK

Our Catholic faith challenges us to be a people who can forgive others.

1. Why is it sometimes hard to ask for forgiveness?
2. Why is it often hard to say, "I forgive you" in our society?
3. What can you do to change that mentality in your everyday life?
4. What are some reasons why people resist participating in the Sacrament of Penance?
5. What would you say to them to help them see the benefit of doing so?

Led to a Life of Conversion

FAITH ACTIVITY

Demonstrating the Sacrament
Read and study *CCC* 1480. Work in groups to create a skit that would explain what the Sacrament of Penance and Reconciliation is ordinarily like to a person about to receive this sacrament for the first time.

In the previous section, we considered two of the timeless elements of the Sacrament of Penance, contrition and confession. In this section, we will take a closer look at the element that is called *penance* or *satisfaction*. For those who think of going to confession and getting a penance from the priest is something like, "Say three Hail Marys," this section may come as something of a surprise. You will discover in the pages that follow a considerable richness is associated with the practice of penance that far exceeds saying a few brief prayers.

The Lessons of History

In order to recover this deeper understanding of the sacrament, we must hearken back to the ancient practice of the sacrament when the penitent was required to complete the doing of a penance *before* celebrating the sacrament and being reconciled with the Church. We mentioned above that in the middle of the first millennium the Church developed what was known as the Order of Penitents, a formally recognized group of individuals who had committed serious, usually public, sins and had therefore been excluded from participating in the community's Eucharist. Their doing of public penance did not involve a public confession of their sins—a popular misconception—although in many cases those sins were already well-known within the community.

Once the penitents admitted their guilt and sought reconciliation with the Church, they were admitted—usually with prayer and ritual—into the group of those who were committed to undergo a lengthy process of penitential discipline—the Order of Penitents. Often they wore distinctive dress (sackcloth and ashes in some cases), and sat begging in front of a church as the faithful gathered on Sunday morning, beseeching their prayers. The specifics of the penitential disciplines that each one had to undergo varied considerably and were decided upon by the bishop or local priest. Usually these disciplines aimed at correcting whatever root faults drove the penitents into sin in the first place. Eventually, after a lengthy period of doing penance, they were reconciled to the Church with prayer and ritual and readmitted to the Eucharist.

A Community Concern It is helpful to remember that the practice of penance varied widely from place to place in the early centuries. In some instances, sinners were reconciled with less fanfare and more quickly; in other situations, readmission to the Eucharist was delayed until one was at the point of death. Despite this diversity of practice, one thing that was common everywhere—and is difficult for us to appreciate fully from our modern viewpoint—was a keen sense that the sin of any individual, no matter how secret or private, truly harmed the entire Church community. Healing that sin's effects was a matter of concern not only for the sake of the individual's soul, but also for the well-being of the community at large. To use modern terminology, early Christians had a more highly developed sense of the *social nature of sin*.

In every aspect of their lives, early Christians experienced how interconnected they were, and there was no exception to this in matters of sin and grace. They lived in what anthropologists today call a *collectivist culture*, as opposed to the *individualist culture* prevalent in our country. From within our highly individualistic culture, with its emphasis on the distinct identity of each person, it is extremely challenging for us to appreciate the depth of this experience of interconnectedness. But the following passage from Saint Paul's First Letter to the Corinthians gives us a glimpse into the realism with which the members of the early Church experienced the profound unity they shared in Christ.

*As it is, there are many members, yet one body. The eye cannot say to the hand, 'I have no need of you,' nor again the head to the feet, 'I have no need of you.'… But God has so arranged the body, giving the greater honor to the inferior member, that there may be no dissension within the body, but the members may have the same care for one another. **If one member suffers, all suffer together with it; if one member is honored, all rejoice together with it.** [emphasis added] Now you are the body of Christ and individually members of it.*

 1 Corinthians 12:20–21, 24–27

GROUP TALK

In some aspects of their lives, people may struggle with accepting the fact that they need other people to accomplish something, to share something, or to simply "be" to their fullest potential.

1. What aspects of our culture undermine the positive side of needing others?

2. How can we get caught up in our own lives and lose sight of the impact our actions have on others and other cultures?

3. Who are some people that remind you that you are important and needed?

The Practice of Penance The purpose of doing penance as part of sacramental Reconciliation, then, has always been twofold. In the first place, it is about healing the hurt caused by sin to the Christian community. The *Catechism* says that one must repair the harm done to the neighbor by one's sin. "Simple justice requires as much" (*CCC*, 1459). In the second place, penance is aimed at strengthening the weakened sinner, helping the sinner to recover full spiritual health. The *Catechism* suggests that the penance assigned by the confessor should take into consideration one's personal situation and seek the spiritual good of the penitent. It should also correspond in some way to the seriousness and nature of the sins committed.

The following kinds of penance are suggested by way of example, but are certainly not meant to be an exhaustive list:

- saying prayers
- almsgiving
- doing corporal or spiritual works of mercy
- performing some service to one's neighbor,
- engaging in some kind of voluntary self-denial
- making a specific sacrifice of some sort
- patient acceptance of whatever cross we must bear

In the matter of doing penance or making satisfaction for our sins, a very subtle danger must be avoided. The language of "making amends for our sins" can be misleading and give the impression that by our own efforts we can somehow "make up for" the evil of sin. Nothing could be further from the truth, of course. The *Catechism* reminds us that it is "Christ, who alone expiated our sins, once for all . . . The satisfaction that we make for our sins . . . is not so much ours as . . . done through Jesus Christ. We . . . can do nothing ourselves . . . man has nothing of which to boast..." But the *Catechism* also points out the following.

" all our boasting is in Christ . . . in whom we make satisfaction by bringing forth 'fruits that befit repentance.' These fruits have their efficacy from him, by him they are offered to the Father, and through him they are accepted by the Father.[1] "

Catechism of the Catholic Church, 1460

As long as we keep these truths in mind, we will not fall prey to the temptation to think it is the penance we do that "makes up for" our sins. Rather, the penance that we do helps us to be more closely one with Christ, to be, as Saint Paul says, "conformed to the image of [God's] Son" (*Romans 8:29*).

A Vehicle for God's Action

We don't know what anyone confesses to their priest, but imagine for a moment the following example. One of the sins that Mark confessed to the priest was that recently he and some buddies had gone out after a night of drinking and spray-painted graffiti on the homes of several minority families. The priest was deciding on a penance, and asked Mark what sin he was most ashamed of. Mark indicated that it was the vandalism. The priest asked Mark what he thought might be the dollar value of the damage he had done. Mark could only guess—maybe a couple hundred dollars.

After the discussion Father Carson concluded that Mark could not directly return money for the damage to the family involved without facing serious consequences. At that point, Father Carson asked Mark if he would be willing to "work off" his debt by volunteering to help the local Habitat for Humanity on one of their homebuilding projects. "Sure, Father," replied Mark, happy that he could really do something to make amends and as a sign of his gratitude for God's forgiveness. "Okay then," Father Carson said. "Let's say your labor is worth ten bucks an hour. See to it that you volunteer with Habitat until you've 'donated' a couple hundred dollars' worth of labor. Don't worry how long it takes you—just do it."

It took Mark over one month to do his penance. But in the course of his working side by side with volunteers of every age, ethnic background, and socio-economic class, he soon forgot that his labors were a penance. He got to know the family of Haitians for whom the home was being built, and he learned from their plight more about discrimination than he ever suspected existed. They became real people to him, not just an ethnic minority. He saw their struggle to survive in a foreign land, their determination to give their children a better life, their faith in God that had sustained them through perils that Mark found nearly unbelievable.

Mark also started to feel better about himself that summer, and he began to break away from the drinking buddies with whom he usually got into trouble. He began to think about what he wanted to do in college, and he got excited about a career as an architect who would work in underdeveloped countries building affordable housing.

In the above example Mark's penance worked, which is to say that it became a vehicle for God's action in his life. Without any high drama, a very natural unfolding of grace happened for Mark. His penance served as a catalyst for a genuine conversion experience. He probably would never recognize or name it that way, but a conversion it was—a turning away from sin and a turning toward a life of more faithful discipleship. This is one instance of what our religious language refers to as our participation in the Paschal Mystery, a dying to sin and a rising to new life in Christ. Sacraments work that

FAITH ACTIVITY

Moving Toward Christ Find an article or news story that obviously depicts someone in need of reconciliation and God's mercy. If you were a priest, what types of penance would you assign this person in an effort to move him or her "to be more closely one with Christ?" What would you hope this person's life would look like after doing penance?

way—they connect us more deeply to Christ. In so doing we are immersed more fully into the mystery of Christ's Death and Resurrection. Mark certainly did not become a saint overnight, and his struggle with sinful ways continued in the years ahead. But the satisfaction suggested by Father Carson on that Thursday afternoon was a real turning point. It helped to set him on a new course at a crucial stage of his young adult development. Often, that is how God's grace works.

Social Sin

One of the consequences of our living in such an individualistic society is that we tend to think of sin almost exclusively in very personal terms. Pope John Paul II recognized this tendency in modern societies, and so he addressed the issue of social sin in a very important document called his *Apostolic Exhortation on Reconciliation and Penance* (December 2, 1984). The association of penance or satisfaction with our tradition of sacramental Reconciliation is one way that this notion of social sin has been kept alive across the centuries. Doing penance reminds us that the consequences of even our most hidden, personal sins are social. As the Holy Father says, "every sin is *social* insofar as and because it also has social repercussions" (15). The *Catechism* teaches, "'Structures of sin' are the expression and effect of personal sins. They lead their victims to do evil in their turn. In an analogous sense, they constitute a 'social sin'2" (*CCC*, 1869).

The Pope goes on in paragraph 16 of his *Apostolic Exhortation* to explain some very important understandings of social sin. He acknowledges that an individual commits only individual sins, since sin "is always a *personal act* . . . an act of freedom on the part of an individual person and not properly of a group or community." However, the Pope insists that we can and do participate in social sin, and to that extent we must take responsibility for both the individual and social sins in which we are involved. He says, in fact that we must not

> underestimate the responsibility of the individuals involved . . . [each of whom must] shoulder his or her responsibility seriously and courageously in order to change those disastrous conditions and intolerable situations [of social sin].
>
> *Apostolic Exhortation on Reconciliation and Penance*, 16

The Holy Father is referring to massive situations of evil such as wars between nations, racism, and economic structures that are radically unjust and exploitative, systematic violations of human rights, and so forth.

FAITH ACTIVITY

Think Globally, Act Locally Sin is a reality of life. It wounds human nature and injures human solidarity. It even impacts the planet we call home. Based on what you have learned in this section, make a list of the five most serious "social sins" that you believe are present in our world today. Name one concrete thing your class or family can do to counter them.

In his analysis of social sin the Holy Father points out that social sins "are the result of the accumulation and concentration of many personal sins." His enumeration of the kind of personal sins that give rise to social sin includes the following:

- actions or omissions that cause or support an evil condition

- actions or omissions that exploit an evil condition

- failure to avoid, eliminate or at least limit the evil condition out of laziness, fear, indifference, or a conspiracy of silence

- taking refuge in the impossibility of changing the evil condition

- sidestepping the effort and sacrifice required to address the evil condition

- rationalizing why one cannot engage in actions to address evil conditions.

This list is an uncomfortable one for us to ponder. In today's world of globalization and instantaneous communication, we are keenly aware of situations that easily qualify as social sin. We know about sweatshops in underdeveloped countries that produce cheap consumer goods for our enjoyment. We see graphic images of ethnic cleansing and genocidal hatred. We are all too familiar with racism and consumerism in our everyday lives, our schools, and neighborhoods. The causes for and the solutions to these massive structures of sin are complex and beyond our ability to fully grasp. But the Holy Father's teaching will not let us off so easily. It will not let us claim immunity from any involvement or responsibility in the face of social sin. Conversion from social sin may not require us to address *every* situation of evil in the world. But it surely requires that we address *something, somewhere.* The bumper sticker often seen says it succinctly: "Think globally. Act locally."

Quick Check

1. What is the purpose of the penance given by the priest in the sacrament?
2. What are some of the types of penances that may be given?
3. What is social sin and in what sense can an individual person be said to be responsible for it?
4. What are some kinds of personal sins that give rise to social sin?

GROUP TALK

Omissions (things that we fail to do to show love of God or neighbor) are personal sins that can give rise to social sins. Working in small groups, give three or four examples of this in your school or community. How could these situations be changed? Discuss why you think John Paul II wrote extensively about this and not just personal sins.

Understanding the Reconciliation Offered

A great deal of what the Church believes about a particular sacrament can be uncovered by an attentive consideration of the way that sacrament is celebrated. This is no less true of the Sacrament of Reconciliation. In previous sections, we looked at three essential elements of the sacrament that have to do with the participation of the penitent, i.e., contrition, confession, and penance or satisfaction. In this final section, we will reflect on the fourth essential element of the sacrament, absolution, which concerns what God does through the action of the Church. In fact, the prayer of absolution summarizes the key elements of the sacrament.

Here is the text of what the priest prays as he extends his hands over the penitent and pronounces the words of God's forgiveness on behalf of the Church:

God, the Father of mercies,
through the death and resurrection of his Son
has reconciled the world to himself
and sent the Holy Spirit among us
for the forgiveness of sins;
through the ministry of the Church
may God give you pardon and peace,
and I absolve you from your sins
in the name of the Father, and of the Son,
and of the Holy Spirit.

Rite of Penance, 46

Before we consider the words themselves, we should take note of a very important gesture that the priest makes while speaking the words of absolution. In the Introduction to the Rite of Penance and Reconciliation (6d), we are reminded that "...God uses visible signs to give salvation and to renew the broken covenant." The way nature can communicate and symbolize deeper spiritual realities is what theologians often call the *sacramental principle.* Simply put, it means that God's saving grace comes to us in tangible, human ways—by means of our senses—rather than by some disembodied divine intervention that happens unseen in the depth of our souls. God could have saved the human race simply with a decree of his will, instantaneously removing all sin from the human heart. But instead he chose to take flesh in human form, in the birth of Jesus who has "visibly appeared to us," so that we might experience and know salvation in our humanness. The mystery of the Incarnation—Jesus being true God and true man—is the foundation of this sacramental principle: it helps to explain why God the Father makes his saving grace available to us through the signs and symbols of the liturgy of each of the sacraments through the power of the Holy Spirit.

The visible, tangible signs used in the liturgy (e.g., bread and wine, oil, water, candles, etc.) are important like the words that accompany them. We note that the rite directs that "the priest extends his hands over the penitent's head" as he pronounces the words of absolution (46). The ritual envisions a full gesture here, with both hands over the head—perhaps even resting upon the penitent's head if it seems appropriate. Only by default, as might be the case when the penitent is separated from the priest by a screen, does the rite say that the priest "at least extends his right hand" over and toward the penitent.

This gesture is very significant because of its long history in our sacramental Tradition. Scripture is filled with examples of Jesus, first, and later the Apostles using this gesture as a sign of healing and in conjunction with the gift of the Holy Spirit. For the priest to extend hands over, or lay hands on, one of the faithful is a symbolic gesture used in nearly all of our sacramental rituals. It is one of our most ancient sacramental signs by which the Church expresses the invocation of the Holy Spirit. The technical name for the invocation of the Holy Spirit is *epiclesis*, and it is always one of the most solemn moments in any ritual. The fact that the priest is directed to make this epicletic gesture while saying the words of absolution serves as a reminder that the power of the Holy Spirit is at work in the sacrament, not mere human, wishful thinking. Catholics are sometimes challenged and accused of acting as if human beings had the power to forgive sins on their own. But for one who knows the history of a prayer of *epiclesis*, there is no mistaking whose power is at work as the priest extends his hands and prays for forgiveness in the name of the Church.

Words of Faith

The words of absolution begin by naming the source of all forgiveness: God, who is called the "Father of mercies." Entire volumes can be (and indeed have been) written about how we have come to know our God as one who is all-merciful, "slow to anger and abounding in steadfast love." (See, for examples,

FAITH ACTIVITY

Mercy Collage One definition of mercy is "compassion or forbearance shown especially to an offender or to one subject to one's power" (Webster's). Collect images of people showing compassion to others. Create a poster or presentation and discuss how we might learn about God's limitless compassion from the examples.

Psalms 86:15; 103:8; 145:8.) Immediately after naming God the Father as the source of all forgiveness, the prayer proclaims the core truth of our faith—that forgiveness of sin has been accomplished through the death and Resurrection of his Son. Every celebration of a sacrament is in some way making Christ's Paschal Mystery present again in our midst. We are saved by being joined to the dying and rising of Christ, as Saint Paul says in Romans 6. Here, we are reminded that it is through the Paschal Mystery that God has "reconciled the world to himself." Saint Paul sums up this truth in his Second Letter to the Corinthians, where he links the work of Christ to his own—and the Church's—share in that work.

> *All this is from God, who reconciled us to himself through Christ, and has given us the ministry of Reconciliation; that is, in Christ God was reconciling the world to himself, not counting their trespasses against them, and entrusting the message of Reconciliation to us.*
>
> ✝ 2 Corinthians 5:18–19

The prayer of absolution expresses wonderfully that it is the entire Trinity at work in our salvation. After naming the "Father of mercies" and the Paschal Mystery of Jesus, the prayer proclaims that the Holy Spirit has been sent among us "for the forgiveness of sins." Each Person of the Blessed Trinity is named in turn, and only then does the prayer turn to the role of the Church.

The *Catechism* teaches that among the spiritual effects of the sacrament there is a two-fold Reconciliation: with God and with the Church. This is a significant teaching, because the two are linked together. In the words of absolution, the priest proclaims that it is "through the ministry of the Church" that this double reconciliation takes place. Christ entrusted to Peter the keys of the Kingdom of Heaven, and to all the Apostles, the power to bind and loose. (See *Matthew 16:19*.) Even today, it is a very solemn teaching that only priests who have received from the Church the faculty of absolving can forgive sins in the name of Christ.

FAITH ACTIVITY

Reflect on Renewal Spend some time quietly considering experiences of renewal you have had. What role did the sacraments have in that experience? How did that sense of rebirth change the way you thought and acted? Write about the difference it made in your life.

Indulgences

In pronouncing the words of absolution the priest indicates that God grants to the sinner "pardon and peace." These brief words are very suggestive and point to much larger truths. Of what does this "pardon" consist? Most obviously, for one in a state of mortal sin, the consequence of unforgiven mortal sin is the loss of eternal life with God. That punishment is lifted in the sacrament, but another consequence of sin is what the Church calls **temporal punishment** due because of sin.

In the *Catechism* treatment of temporal punishment is alluded to as "an unhealthy attachment to creatures" from which we must be purified, even after being forgiven for our mortal or venial sins. The purification can take place here on earth or after death in purgatory. (See *CCC*, 1472). One of the spiritual effects of the sacrament is a lessening of this temporal punishment, but often this is not complete with the words of absolution. The wound of sin resulting from the attachment to creatures over the Creator is not healed instantaneously, yet the Church never ceases in her efforts to help sinners recover their spiritual health. The temporal punishment can be lessened through prayer, penance, fervent charity, suffering, and works of mercy.

The doctrine and practice of indulgences are closely linked to the spiritual effects of this sacrament. The redeeming power of Christ's Paschal Mystery is infinite, but as finite creatures we often gradually open ourselves to that grace, over time.

The Church continues throughout human history to pour out the merits of the redeemer from her treasury of grace. This treasury refers to the spiritual goods that flow among all members of Christ's Body in heaven, purgatory, and on earth. As members of this Communion of Saints, we are linked through charity and through the Church's treasury of grace, which can never be exhausted. Because of the profound union shared in Christ, all members of the Church, living and dead, are immersed in this mystery of grace. We stand in solidarity with one another and can pray for one another, whether living or dead. The communion we share in Christ's love allows us to assist one another with our prayers, to help lessen the temporal punishment due to our sins that may remain after our sins are forgiven.

An **indulgence** is the remission before God (partial or plenary) of the temporal punishment that remains after our sins are forgiven. In granting an indulgence, the Church, with the authority from Christ to bind or loosen us from sins, dispenses and applies with authority the treasury of Christ's merit, those of Mary, his mother, and the saints joined to him in holiness. Indulgences remove the temporal punishment due our sins. They help us to lessen our attachment to creatures and more fully set our hearts on God alone. In a wondrous mystery of solidarity, the members of the communion of saints are able to help one another in this process of spiritual transformation.

Hopi Virgin & Child,
by Father John Giuliani ▼

GROUP TALK

We ask Mary and the saints to intercede on our behalf with Christ, for they are close with him in heaven. They help the Church grow in holiness by their example and prayers.

1. How comfortable are you asking others to pray for you? How often do you offer to pray for someone or something?

2. How would you describe the role of prayer in your family and/or in the lives of those you know?

3. Which saints do you feel closest to and why?

Shalom

The words of absolution ask God to grant "pardon and peace." Among the spiritual effects of the sacrament are the gifts of peace and serenity of conscience. This is sometimes called *spiritual consolation.* It is "the peace of God, which surpasses all understanding," a peace for which Saint Paul prayed in his Letter to the Philippians (4:7).

In our example from earlier, when Mark finished his confession to Father Carson, he surely felt a sense of relief. He was unburdened from his guilt and shame, and his emotional state was more calm and untroubled than it had been prior to his confession.

But the spiritual benefit described in the *Catechism* as peace and serenity of conscience are deeper than any psychological state that may be temporary or even in some cases fleeting. Rather, the *shalom* offered in this sacrament touches the very core of our spiritual self. Because we truly have been reconciled with God, neighbor, and ourselves, we experience an interior harmony that includes but is deeper than feelings of well-being. It is a spiritual state of soul that flows from the fact that we are loved unconditionally by God, that our sins no matter how serious have been washed away in the blood of Jesus, that the promise of eternal life first given at Baptism has been renewed, and that we have been given a "second birth."

The *shalom* we experience as one of the effects of this sacrament wells up from the new life into which we are reborn. The Penitent who receives God's forgiveness at the hands of the priest is restored to God's grace and brought back to intimate friendship with him. Listen to how Saint Peter in his First Epistle describes the birth of a Christian to new life as the source of the *shalom* we born-again children of the Father experience.

By his great mercy [God] has given us a new birth into a living hope through the resurrection of Jesus Christ from the dead, and into an inheritance that is imperishable, undefiled, and unfading, kept in heaven for you, who are being protected by the power of God through faith for a salvation ready to be revealed in the last time.

 1 Peter 1:3–5

Quick Check

1. What is the sacramental principle?
2. What is an indulgence?
3. What are the spiritual effects of the sacrament?
4. With whom are we reconciled in the sacrament?

Penance and Reconciliation in the East

In this chapter, our focus is on understanding the history and practice of the Sacrament of Reconciliation in the Roman Catholic Church. As indicated in our brief historical overview, Irish missionaries in the seventh century introduced into the Christian churches of the West—those we today call "Roman" Catholic churches—a new way of celebrating the sacrament.

It is helpful to remember that our Western way of celebrating the sacraments is not the only possible expression of Christian faith. The churches of the East—both those in union with Rome and those of the Orthodox tradition who still remain separated from Rome—trace their liturgical traditions back to apostolic times.

Eastern Christians have distinctive ways of understanding and living their faith that are every bit as ancient and authentic as are those of our Roman tradition. Today's Western Christians can always be enriched by learning more about the traditions of our Eastern sisters and brothers and how they celebrate the healing mercies of Christ.

As early as the third century, we can trace in the Eastern Fathers many of the emphases that still characterize how Eastern Christians approach Penance. A third-century document from north Syria, called the *Didaskalia,* describes a well-developed penitential discipline. In the writings of the Eastern fathers Clement of Alexandria (*c.* 150–215) and Origen (*c.* 185–284), we see a strong emphasis on spiritual direction and the healing function of the Church's minister, in contrast to a more legalistic approach in the West.

The role of the Holy Spirit in the process of healing is more pronounced in the liturgical traditions of the East than in the West. The Catechism gives us a flavor of the spirituality of the East by quoting one of the formulas of absolution presently in use in the Byzantine Liturgy:

▲ Cathedral of St. Basil the Blessed, Moscow, Russia

> May the same God, who through the Prophet Nathan forgave David when he confessed his sins, who forgave Peter when he wept bitterly, the prostitute when she washed his feet with her tears, the publican, and the prodigal son, through me, a sinner, forgive you both in this life and in the next and enable you to appear before his awe-inspiring tribunal without condemnation, he who is blessed for ever and ever. Amen.

Catechism of the Catholic Church, 1481

❯Person of Faith

An Unlikely Saint: John-Baptiste-Marie Vianney (1786–1859)

It has been said that the ministry of Reconciliation is the most difficult, delicate, taxing, and demanding of all ministries that a priest must do. Even the saint who has been named the Patron of Parish Priests and of Confessors was someone who found it so hard to learn that he first was dismissed from his seminary training, readmitted, and then failed the academic requirements once again, before being eventually ordained a priest.

John-Baptiste-Marie Vianney was born on May 8, 1786, in France, near Lyon, and worked on a farm, as a shepherd, until the age of 18. He was drafted into Napoleon's army and inadvertently became a deserter, further compounding the hurdles he faced in his desire to become a priest. His persistence, however, eventually prevailed, and he was ordained at the age of 29 in Grenoble. Three years later, he was sent to a tiny parish in a non-descript village called Ars; hence, the title he is known by today, the Curé of Ars.

When his bishop sent him as pastor to Ars, he warned John that the people there were quite weak in their faith. What he found was, in fact, a distressing situation of lax faith and sinful practices, about which few seemed concerned. John Vianney immediately began to pray for, as well as do penance for, the sins of his people—asking God's forgiveness and healing mercy on their souls. The zeal the young pastor showed, for his priestly ministry soon began to awaken the people's fervor. He was tireless in caring for the sick, spent hours preparing his sermons, and practiced personal sacrifices and mortifications that were extraordinarily difficult.

His holiness eventually began to attract interest beyond his tiny parish. Word spread, especially about the special gifts he had as a confessor. He used an intuitive ability to read the hearts of those who came for confession in a way that led them more deeply into the mystery of God's grace. Many reported a profound conversion as a result of their encounter with him in the Sacrament of Penance. He was able to say the right word, to challenge or comfort as needed, and even sometimes to reveal that he knew a person's sins before they confessed them. During the forty years that he served as Pastor, his fame grew steadily, and eventually tens of thousands of pilgrims made their way each year to the little village. The influx was so great that a railway line was constructed to Ars to handle the crowds!

This flood of pilgrims took its toll on the frail and ascetic priest. The demands on his time and energy were overwhelming. His health suffered, and cramped hours in the confessional box, sweltering in summer and freezing in winter, only added to his physical misery. He also had dramatic encounters and struggles with evil spirits who tormented him and were outraged at the way he was delivering sinners from their grasp. The number of those who wished to confess to him was so great that he often spent 10–15 hours a day in the confessional. There were so many pilgrims' requests for his priestly ministry that he sometimes slept as little as two or three hours a night.

Many of his sermons and instructions are preserved. In the passage that follows, we can glimpse the simplicity with which he taught the people, and the love of God and neighbor that so permeated his entire life:

> My children, we cannot comprehend the goodness of God towards us in instituting this great Sacrament of Penance. If we had had a favour to ask of Our Lord, we should never have thought of asking Him that. But He foresaw our frailty and our inconstancy in well-doing, and His love induced Him to do what we should not have dared to ask. If one said to those poor lost souls that have been so long in Hell, 'We are going to place a priest at the gate of Hell: all those who wish to confess have only to go out,' do you think, my children, that a single one would remain? The most guilty would not be afraid of telling their sins, nor even of telling them before all the world. Oh, how soon Hell would be a desert, and how Heaven would be peopled! Well, we have the time and the means, which those poor lost souls have not. And I am quite sure that those wretched ones say in Hell, 'O accursed priest! if I had never known you, I should not be so guilty!' It is a beautiful thought, my children, that we have a Sacrament which heals the wounds of our soul!

REFLECT

1. How is Saint John Vianney associated with the Sacrament of Penance?

2. Name some servants of God who had massive followings.

3. What area of your spiritual life would you like to focus on right now? How could you give more importance to your faith growth? Who in your family, circle of friends, or local community are reconcilers? How do they show forgiveness and act to bring people back together?

 **Prayer**

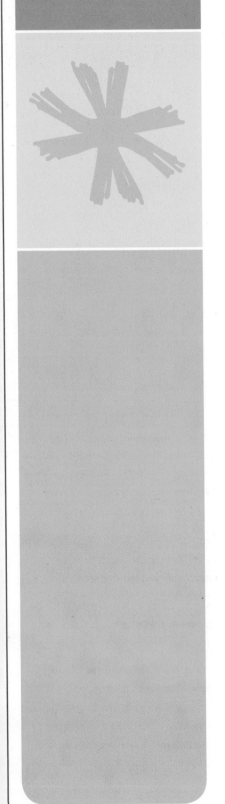

An Act of Love composed by Saint John Marie Vianney

I love You, O my God, and my sole desire is to love You until the last breath of my life.

I love You, O infinitely lovable God, and I prefer to die loving You than live one instant without loving You.

I love You, O my God, and I do not desire anything but heaven so as to have the joy of loving You perfectly.

I love You, O my God, and I fear hell, because there will not be the sweet consolation of loving You.

O my God, if my tongue cannot say in every moment that I love You, I want my heart to say it in every beat.

Allow me the grace to suffer loving You, to love you suffering and one day to die loving You and feeling that I love You.

And as I approach my end, I beg you to increase and perfect my love of You.

Study Guide
▶Check Understanding

1. State the contribution to the development of this sacrament made by Irish missionaries in the seventh through eighth centuries.

2. Describe the Order of Penitents.

3. Explain the three Forms under which the sacrament may be celebrated today.

4. Outline what takes place during the celebration of the Rite of Penance with an individual.

5. Identify the four essential parts of the Sacrament of Reconciliation.

6. Distinguish between perfect and imperfect contrition.

7. Recall what is required for a person's confession of sins to be "complete" and "sincere."

8. Summarize the benefits of regular confession of venial sins.

9. Explain the purpose/benefit of the penance or satisfaction given by the priest in the sacrament.

10. Identify some of the types of penances that may be given.

11. Describe social sin and in what sense can an individual person be said to be responsible for it.

12. Recall the kinds of personal sins that give rise to social sin.

13. Define the *sacramental principle.*

14. Explain what an indulgence is.

15. Tell about the spiritual effects of the sacrament.

16. Name with whom we are reconciled in the sacrament.

▶Apply and Develop

17. The Sacrament of Penance has been experienced in many ways since the time of the Apostles. Compare and contrast how its various ritual forms were appropriate for each of the eras in which it was used.

18. Catholic teaching insists that a full experience of forgiveness requires contriteness of heart and confession of our sins to a priest in the Sacrament of Penance. Write an essay developing the need for us to put our heartfelt sorrow into words in a sacramental ritual.

19. The problem of how a single individual can address the enormous complexity of social sin is very real. In a group discussion, develop strategies that are realistic ways for someone your age to be part of meaningful efforts to get rid of social sin.

20. Analyze the priest's prayer of absolution to show how it sums up what we believe about the Sacrament of Penance.

▶Key Words

See pages noted for contextual explanations of these important faith terms.

absolution (p. 136)

confession (p. 136)

conscience (p. 133)

contrition (p. 136)

epiclesis (p. 149)

Incarnation (p. 149)

indulgence (p. 151)

mortal sin (p. 133)

penance (satisfaction) (p. 136)

social sin (p. 146)

temporal punishment (p. 150)

venial sin (p. 139)

Are any among you sick? They should call for the elders of the church and have them pray over them, anointing them with oil in the name of the Lord. The prayer of faith will save the sick, and the Lord will raise them up; and anyone who has committed sins will be forgiven.

James 5:14–15

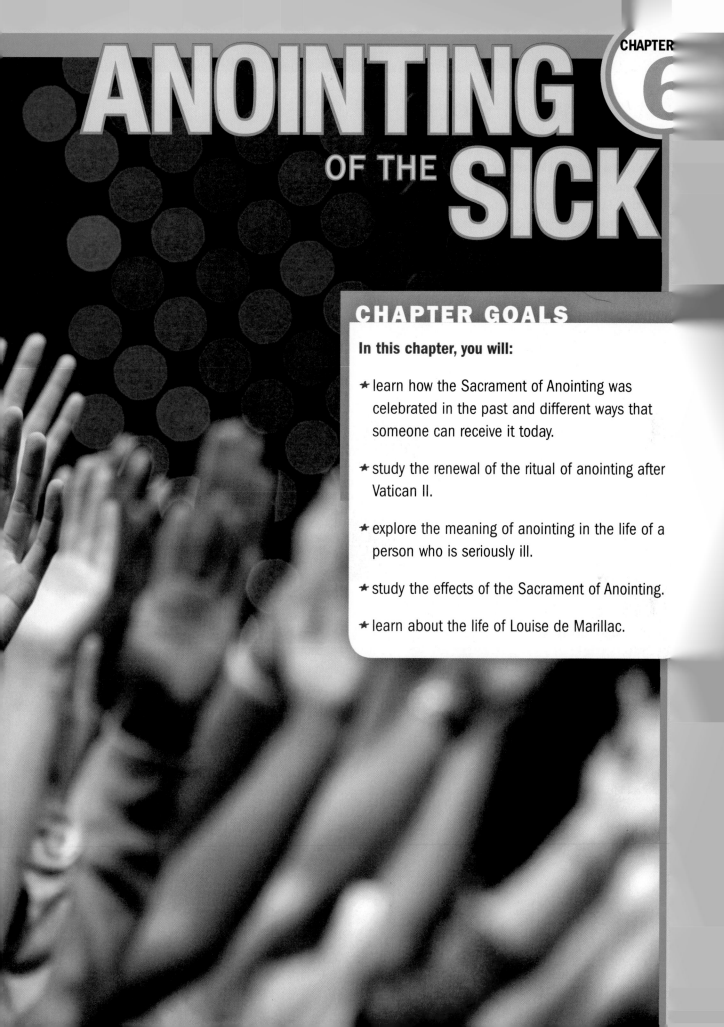

ANOINTING OF THE SICK

CHAPTER 6

CHAPTER GOALS

In this chapter, you will:

★ learn how the Sacrament of Anointing was celebrated in the past and different ways that someone can receive it today.

★ study the renewal of the ritual of anointing after Vatican II.

★ explore the meaning of anointing in the life of a person who is seriously ill.

★ study the effects of the Sacrament of Anointing.

★ learn about the life of Louise de Marillac.

Catherine's Story

Catherine was one of those people who always seemed to live a charmed life—she had it all. But, then, three days short of her fortieth birthday, her doctor told her she had a Stage Four cancer. Her pastor, Father Richards, was compassionate and supportive as Catherine poured out her heart to him several weeks after her diagnosis. He suggested—and she accepted—celebrating the Sacrament of Anointing at Sunday Mass the following weekend. As she said, "I need all the prayers I can get!"

Nothing could have prepared Catherine for what happened that Sunday morning.

After his homily, Father Richards called Catherine forward and then invited the community to offer prayers of heartfelt faith for Catherine's healing. The cantor sang prayers of a litany of intercession, and the community responded with the familiar refrain "Lord have mercy." Then, as the singing stopped, the church fell silent and Father Richards placed his hands gently on Catherine's head. For what seemed like forever, he silently prayed over her, gazing softly into her eyes that were gradually filling with tears. The silence in the church was deafening. As she felt the slight pressure of Father Richards' hands on her head, Catherine thought to herself, "I wonder if that's how it felt when Jesus touched the sick people."

Tears suddenly flowed from her eyes as she released the tension that had gripped her body, and she felt a deep, calming peace that was almost beyond belief. Father Richards then stepped back and picked up a cruet of golden oil from a nearby table, held it high for the people to see, and said a prayer of thanksgiving and blessing over the oil. Next, he put generous amounts of the Oil of the Sick on her forehead and her hands, while saying a prayer whose words she only briefly caught and barely remembered: ". . . love and mercy . . . Holy Spirit . . . frees you . . . raise you up." Then he said another prayer and told her to return to her pew, as the Mass continued. Catherine didn't know she had that many tears in her, as they poured out of

her for most of the remainder of the liturgy. But they were not tears of sadness or fear. They were welling up from somewhere deeper, and they brought peace and a powerful sense of being held in God's loving care.

Experimental treatments gave Catherine a reprieve, but no final cure. After six months of chemotherapy, her cancer went into remission for just over two years. It came back then with a vengeance. Within a month's time, she was so weakened that she was homebound. The doctors had nothing more to offer her, and so the family arranged for hospice to care for her at home. Father Richards anointed her again, this time at home with just her family and her parents at her bedside. The liturgy of anointing seemed more familiar to her this time, not as dramatic, but still very comforting.

Catherine and her family deeply wanted her to be able to die at home. But the reality of her condition was eventually such that after three months at home she had to be moved to a residential hospice. She lingered there for two more weeks before dying very peacefully in her sleep. Just three days before her death, Father Richards slipped into her room one afternoon and found her alone and quite alert. She asked to be anointed again, which he did, using a shortened rite. He also heard her confession and gave her a special blessing called the Apostolic Pardon for the Dying, had her renew her baptismal promises, and then gave her Holy Communion as Viaticum. He asked Catherine to put in a good word for him when she saw the Lord. She smiled weakly and whispered, "I will."

GROUP TALK

1. Explain the difference between physical healing and spiritual healing.

2. Share a time when you or a loved one suffered. How has this suffering strengthened your faith?

The Church Celebrates God's Healing

During her illness, Catherine celebrated the Sacrament of Anointing three times, each time in a very different setting. In many ways, her experience embodied the long history of the sacrament, from its origins in the healing ministry of Jesus to the renewed ritual forms made available as a result of the Second Vatican Council.

Jewish Roots We find the roots of the Sacrament of the Anointing of the Sick in the religious traditions of our Jewish ancestors in faith. The Old Testament is filled with passages that acknowledge the healing power of Yahweh. In Chapter 38 of the Book of Isaiah, for example, King Hezekiah falls ill and pleads with the Lord to be spared. Witnessing his heartfelt prayer, God says, "I will heal you." The Psalms, too, frequently capture the faith-filled prayers of those who are afflicted and turn to the Lord for healing, forgiveness and strength. (See especially *Psalms 6* and *38*.)

In the culture of the Jewish people, oil was an important product with many uses (cosmetic, medicinal, ritual, and so forth) and meanings. Although the Book of Leviticus, Chapter 14, includes one reference to its use as part of a healing ritual, this seems not to have been a major association in Old Testament times. People used oil to consecrate sacred objects and persons, and, generally, oil was seen as a sign and source of strength, vitality, and life. However, we find no evidence that the Jewish people regularly used it in any rituals for healing.

A final element of the Old Testament roots of the sacrament is the association that was made between illness and sinfulness. Sometimes the connection was seen as directly causal: A person sinned and was therefore punished by God with the scourge of illness. In other cases, the association was less directly causal, but nonetheless still present. Illness was an evil, and sin was the source of all evils. Hence, a widespread perception existed that illnesses were, in some mysterious way, punishment for sins.

Changing Forms but a Timeless Healing

Jesus rejected this connection between illness and sinfulness when he was asked about the source of a man's blindness (see *John 9:2–3*). Nonetheless, we see clearly from the New Testament that Jesus lived in a culture that could not easily separate illness from the idea of evil—even evil in the form of demonic possession. The Gospels do not show Jesus making neat theological distinctions between illness and its relationship to evil. They do show that his ministry was centered on his compassion for them and their redemption—freeing those he met from each and every form of bondage, including sin or sickness.

Jesus was a healer and a miracle worker, his healings were signs of the coming Kingdom of God and he sent out his disciples to share in his ministry.

As you go, proclaim the good news, 'The kingdom of heaven has come near.' Cure the sick, raise the dead, cleanse the lepers, cast out demons. You received without payment; give without payment.

✝ Matthew 10:7-8

The Gospels describe how the disciples of Jesus were sent to:

- proclaim the Kingdom of God
- preach repentance
- cast out demons
- heal the sick.

Christ Healing the Blind Man, by Eustache Le Sueur
▶

The New Testament includes no specific mention of Jesus using oil to anoint, but the Gospel according to Mark reports that when Jesus sent his disciples out on mission, "They cast out many demons, and anointed with oil many who were sick and cured them" (*Matthew 6:13*). In his Parable of the Good Samaritan, Jesus describes how the Samaritan cared for the wounded man in a way that would have been familiar in that culture: "He went to him and bandaged his wounds, having poured oil and wine on them" (*Luke 10:34*). The Acts of the Apostles shows clearly that the early Christian community understood that they should continue to offer Spirit-filled healings to the sick as a sign of the power of the Risen Christ at work in the Church (see Peter's cure of the disabled beggar in *Acts 3*).

Although the Gospels do not report any explicit words of Jesus instituting this sacrament, it is clear that he intended his Apostles to continue to heal in the manner that he did, offering both physical and spiritual relief. The earliest historical record of how the first generation of Christians used oil in a ritual context for healing is found in the Letter of James.

Are any among you suffering? They should pray. Are any cheerful? They should sing songs of praise. Are any among you sick? They should call for the elders of the church and have them pray over them, anointing them with oil in the name of the Lord. The prayer of faith will save the sick, and the Lord will raise them up; and anyone who has committed sins will be forgiven.

 James 5:13–15

FAITH ACTIVITY

Jesus' Healings Read the following passages: Mark 9:14–29, Luke 5:17–26, and Luke 18:35–43. In small groups make a list of the similarities and differences in these stories. Indicate what you think each of these stories teaches us.

GROUP TALK

The Letter of James encourages the suffering to pray; the cheerful, to sing praises; the sick, to bring themselves to be prayed over and anointed.

1. In what ways do you see people suffering, especially those your age?

2. Do you think people pray in times of suffering? Have you prayed in times of suffering, either your own or that of those you care about?

3. Why do you think it's important to sing songs of praise when you are cheerful?

4. Have you ever asked someone to pray for you or someone you know who is sick? What did it feel like asking, and how did the person respond? Have you ever offered to pray for someone, or has someone ever offered to pray for you? Did you pray together in that moment? Why do you think this is important?

FAITH ACTIVITY

Parish Outreach Find out how your parish organizes its care for home-bound parishioners. This would include things like bringing Holy Communion to them, visiting them, transportation to doctors, and so on. Who participates in these ministries? How can your class get involved?

✓ Quick Check

1. How was oil significant during biblical times?
2. What was Jesus' ministry among the sick and how were his disciples involved in continuing his healing work?
3. What is the earliest record of the Church celebrating the Sacrament of Anointing after the Resurrection?
4. How did the emphasis of anointing shift historically?

Developing Forms After the New Testament era, there is a gap of many centuries in our knowledge of specifically how the Church celebrated the Sacrament of Anointing. We do have some ancient Christian prayers for the blessing of oil to be used for the sick, and these may be as old as the second or third centuries. It is very likely that just as the consecrated Eucharist was taken home by the faithful for those unable to be at Mass, so the blessed oil was likely taken home in the early centuries to be used by those who were sick.

Manuscripts and other sources from the eighth and ninth centuries give us a much fuller picture of how the Church was celebrating anointing for the sick at that time. By then the emphasis in anointing had already shifted from a sacrament of healing and recovery for those who were ill to a final anointing for those on their deathbed. We find evidence of this from the Council of Chalon, in 813, and from the Synod at Aachen, in 836. The influence of the emperor Charlemagne played a strong role in these councils.

Blessing of the oil was reserved for the bishop, and the actual anointing was reserved for the ordained. The notion of recovery of physical health had not disappeared entirely from the prayers and rites. However, they primarily emphasized the forgiveness of sins and a spiritual healing that would prepare the dying for their final journey to God. This practice continued right up into modern times. The teaching of the Council of Trent (1545–1563) set the stage for our practices before Vatican II. In the next section we will learn about how Vatican II restored some of the earlier emphasis of healing the sick.

Reform and Renewal

The ritual for anointing used on the eve of the Second Vatican Council was an amalgamation of prayers and rites that had been used in varying circumstances over more than a thousand years of the Church's history. Traces of an earlier practice focused on healing and recovery were still evident in some of the prayer texts, but the primary focus of the rite was on preparing someone to die. The name Extreme Unction, meaning "Last Anointing," was an apt description of the sacrament, since in practice the faithful were generally anointed only on their deathbed.

The bishops at the Second Vatican Council mandated a reform and renewal of this sacrament, directing that its name should be changed to the "Anointing of the Sick." They specified several other aspects of its revision. They also said that the proper time to celebrate the sacrament was "as soon as anyone of the faithful begins to be in danger of death from sickness or old age" (73–75). In 1972 the Vatican published a revised ritual of the sacrament in Latin. Approximately a decade later, the U. S. bishops published a version of the ritual entitled *Pastoral Care of the Sick: Rites of Anointing and Viaticum* with pastoral adaptations for use in this country.

A careful look at the new ritual book reveals that both the theology and the pastoral practice of this sacrament have been made more consistent, respecting the liturgical and sacramental traditions of its past, but adapting its use to contemporary sensibilities. The ritual book contains:

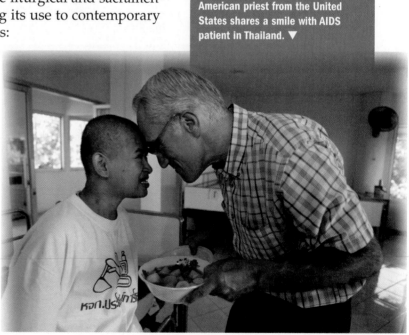

American priest from the United States shares a smile with AIDS patient in Thailand. ▼

- prayers and rites for visiting and bringing communion to the sick, both adults and children, as well as anointing

- abbreviated rites for use in hospitals and emergency situations

- rites for Viaticum, commendation of the dying, and prayers for the dead

- readings, verses, and responses from Sacred Scripture.

FAITH ACTIVITY

Make a Visit Visit someone who is elderly, homebound, or hospitalized. If they wish, talk with them about their life and their suffering, what meaning it has for them. Notice how the person who is suffering teaches and inspires us. Write two to three paragraphs about your experience.

This renewed ritual for anointing covers a variety of pastoral situations. The following chart allows a quick comparison of the three forms of the sacrament received by Catherine in the story opening this chapter. It shows how similar the ritual is within and outside of Mass, and how a very abbreviated form is used with extremely ill persons. The words in brackets [ ] indicate optional elements.

Celebrating the Sacrament		
1. Anointing Within Mass	**2. Anointing Outside of Mass**	**3. Rite for Emergencies**
INTRODUCTORY RITES	**INTRODUCTORY RITES**	
Greeting	Greeting	
Reception of the Sick	Sprinkling with Holy Water	
	Instruction	
Penitential Rite	Penitential Rite	
		[Sacrament of Penance]
		[Apostolic Pardon]
Opening Prayer		
LITURGY OF THE WORD	**LITURGY OF THE WORD**	
Readings	Reading	
Homily	Response	
LITURGY OF ANOINTING	**LITURGY OF ANOINTING**	
Litany	Litany	
Laying on of Hands	Laying on of Hands	
Prayer over the Oil	Prayer over the Oil	
Anointing	Anointing	
Prayer after Anointing	[Prayer after Anointing]	
	The Lord's Prayer	

Chart·continued on next page

1. Anointing Within Mass	2. Anointing Outside of Mass	3. Rite for Emergencies
LITURGY OF THE EUCHARIST	**LITURGY OF HOLY COMMUNION**	
Including Lord's Prayer and Communion	Communion	The Lord's Prayer
	Silent Prayer	Communion as Viaticum
		[Prayer before Anointing]
		Anointing
CONCLUDING RITES	**CONCLUDING RITE**	**CONCLUDING PRAYER**
Blessing	Blessing	Blessing
Dismissal		Sign of Peace

Connecting the Rite and Symbol to Everyday Life

· The revised Rite of Anointing makes a distinction between the sacramental care of the sick and the sacramental care of the dying. Describe the difference. Why do you think the difference is important?

· What does this say about the attitude we should have toward illness and suffering, and those who are sick and those who are dying?

· The Sacrament of Anointing of the Sick and the Sacrament of Reconciliation are both considered Sacraments of Healing. How do these two sacraments provide healing? How are they different?

· Have you, or someone you know, experienced the grace of both of these sacraments? How did you, or they, see the connections?

From Catherine's story in the previous section, we can see how she received the sacrament in three very different contexts. In the first rite (in the chart), within a Mass, the focus was very much on prayer for physical healing, if it were to be God's will, as well as spiritual strengthening to deal with the hardships of her sickness. This way of celebrating was reminiscent of how the early Church must have celebrated the sacrament, often in a communal context—perhaps as part of a Eucharistic gathering—with a focus on physical recovery as well as spiritual healing.

The celebration that took place in Catherine's home with her family (#2 in the chart) was done because her illness had worsened. The revised ritual indicates that the sacrament,

may be repeated if the sick person recovers after being anointed and then again falls ill or if during the same illness the person's condition becomes more serious.

Rite of Anointing, 9

The final way that Catherine received the sacrament, at the hospice with only Father Richards present (#3 in the chart), was quite similar to the medieval tradition that endured until Vatican II. This was a deathbed anointing, with a ritual emphasizing forgiveness for sin and sin's punishments—the Apostolic Pardon, which grants a plenary indulgence—and Holy Communion under the form of Viaticum.

Who Should Be Anointed?

The pastoral introduction to the revised rite goes to some length to address the mindset that one could only be anointed *"in extremis,"* or, "at the point of death," and only once during a given illness. The following excerpts from the rite indicate how eager the Church is for the faithful to celebrate the sacrament rather than put it off or deny themselves its benefits entirely. These quotes from the introduction give an idea of the encouragement contained in the rite to celebrate its healing graces as soon as appropriate.

- "Great care and concern should be taken to see that those of the faithful whose health is seriously impaired by sickness or old age receive this sacrament."

- "A sick person may be anointed before surgery whenever a serious illness is the reason for the surgery."

- "Elderly people may be anointed if they have become notably weakened even though no serious illness is present."

- "Sick children may be anointed if they have sufficient use of reason to be strengthened by this sacrament."

- "[T]he faithful . . . should not follow the wrongful practice of delaying the reception of the sacrament."

- "The Sacrament of Anointing may be conferred on sick people who, although they have lost consciousness or the use of reason, would, as Christian believers, probably have asked for it when they were in control of their faculties."[1]

1. Who are the people in your community most in need of the ministry of healing? What are ways that healing could take place?

2. Identify some of the many different ways the Catholic Church continues the healing ministry of Jesus in today's world through specific institutions, organizations, programs, and practices.

Oil of the Sick

In addition to these ways of encouraging a broader spectrum of the faithful to celebrate the sacrament, the liturgical reform of Vatican II introduced a number of other changes in the revised ritual. Three fairly significant changes had to do with the oil for use in the sacrament. First, depending upon the circumstance, permission was given to use any blessed plant oil, not only blessed olive oil.

The second involved who could bless the oil. From the early centuries of the Church, the blessing of the oil was reserved for the bishop. This was a very symbolic way of expressing the connection of the sick and this sacrament with the larger community of the faithful. The bishop, as the sign of unity, linked all believers to the sick who used the oil that he blessed. The new ritual acknowledges this tradition, but it also gives priests authority to bless oil for the sick themselves when they do not have available any that has been blessed by the bishop. This is to be done within the celebration of the Sacrament of Anointing.

The final change is that the rite now provides three different prayers that may be used for the blessing of the oil. The first of these is the same as the prayer used by the bishop when he blesses the oil of the sick at the Chrism Mass on Holy Thursday. It is one of our most ancient liturgical prayers, found in some of our earliest manuscripts. Its roots can be traced back as far as the blessing of oil in the *Apostolic Tradition* of Hippolytus, from the early third century A.D. It is not only a beautiful prayer, but it captures the rich understanding of the Church about how God works in this sacrament to bring about healing for his people.

Bishop Thomas Wenski blesses oils during Holy Week. ▼

FAITH ACTIVITY

Participate Find a local parish or health care facility where a communal celebration for the Anointing of the Sick is going to take place. Attend the celebration. When appropriate, talk with people before and after. Then share your experience and thoughts with the class.

God of all consolation,
you chose and sent your Son to heal the world.
Graciously listen to our prayer of faith:
send the power of the Holy Spirit, the Consoler,
into this precious oil, this soothing ointment,
this rich gift, this fruit of the earth.
Bless this oil and sanctify it for our use.
Make this oil a remedy for all who are anointed with it;
heal them in body, in soul, and in spirit,
and deliver them from every affliction.

Pastoral Care of the Sick: Rites of Anointing and Viaticum, 123

Toward a Deeper Understanding We can note in this prayer the following points:

- It is Trinitarian, naming all three Persons of the Blessed Trinity.

- It connects our use of this oil as part of the healing ministry of Jesus.

- In an allusion to the "prayer of faith" in James 5:15, it underlines that faith is required for those who use the oil, meaning it is not a magic potion.

- It contains an explicit *epiclesis,* an invocation of the Holy Spirit, thus highlighting the important role that he plays in every sacramental celebration.

- The lush imagery used to describe the oil reminds us of how our sacraments are earthy, rooted in human sensory experience. Theologians would call this aspect of the prayer *incarnational* because it flows from the fact that by becoming man, the Son of God saves us *in* and *through* our human nature.

- The prayer reminds us that the effect of a blessing is that something is sanctified—made holy and becomes a source of holiness for us.

- It includes the dimension of physical healing ("remedy").

- It is holistic in its mention of every dimension of the human person for which we seek healing ("body . . . soul . . . spirit").

- It alludes to the sacrament's penitential effect of removing sin ("deliver them").

From this careful consideration of the prayer of blessing over oil, we get a better sense of its richness and why it has been such an important part of the tradition and history of this sacrament.

Anointing

First, it's important to remember that only priests and bishops can administer the Sacrament of Anointing of the Sick. The directions for how to celebrate the actual ritual of anointing are also worth noting. The laying on of hands in silence is a very significant and very ancient element in the rite. We have seen before how this gesture appears in nearly all of our sacramental rites and is associated with the Church's prayer invoking the Holy Spirit. In this context it is also reminiscent of the way that Jesus touched those whom he healed. As Catherine's story indicates, it can be a very powerful moment in the rite.

The actual anointing is to be done on the forehead and the hands. The rite no longer specifies that the anointing should be done by tracing the Sign of the Cross with the oil, although that is usually still done in actual practice. Neither does it specify whether the hands are to be anointed on the palms or, as was previously required, the back of the hands. The new rite also allows the anointing of other parts of the body as appropriate. The previous rite before Vatican II directed the anointing of eyes, ears, nostrils, mouth, hands, and feet.

The actual words of the anointing have also changed in the new rite. Previously there was an emphasis on anointing as a prayer for forgiveness of sins. In the revised ritual the formula that is part of the essential element of the sacrament is as follows.

Anointing the forehead, the priest says . . .

Through this holy anointing
May the Lord in his love and mercy help you
With the grace of the Holy Spirit.
Amen.

Anointing the hands, the priest says . . .

May the Lord who frees you from sin
save you and raise you up.
Amen.

Pastoral Care of the Sick: Rites of Anointing and Viaticum, 124

Now that we have looked at the ritual used to celebrate the Sacrament of Anointing, we will explore, in the next section, its meaning for the one who is ill and for the larger community that cares for and celebrates with the sick person.

Quick Check

1. What is the most significant change in the practice of the Sacrament of Anointing mandated by Vatican II?
2. What are the settings in which anointing may be celebrated and the circumstances that would dictate each?
3. Who are the various groups of people encouraged to receive the sacrament?
4. What is the significance of the Church's custom of reserving the blessing of oil to the bishop?

What Does It All Mean?

In each of the previous chapters, we have explored the connection that exists between what happens in the ritual of a sacramental celebration and the rest of a person's life outside of the liturgical context. Our assumption, of course, is that there is a connection, that what happens in our sacred rituals is very much about the rest of our lives. The symbols that are used and the ritual actions we perform point to larger meanings beyond the specifics of a particular liturgical celebration.

Catherine's Spiritual Journey

What impact, then, did the Sacrament of Anointing have on Catherine's life after she left Mass on that Sunday morning following her first anointing? The *Catechism* lists as the first effect of the sacrament "*A particular gift of the Holy Spirit*" (CCC, 1520). It then goes on to describe this "first grace" of the sacrament as "one of strengthening, peace and courage to overcome the difficulties that go with the condition of serious illness or the frailty of old age." The *Catechism* is even more specific, explaining that this grace of the Holy Spirit "renews trust and faith in God . . . strengthens against . . . the temptation to discouragement and anguish in the face of death [Cf. *Heb 2:15*]" (CCC, 1520).

The Difficulties Catherine came to know firsthand what the *Catechism* was referring to by the phrase "the difficulties that go with the condition of serious illness" (CCC, 1520). Overnight, the wonderful life she had known was suddenly at risk. Long-range plans of seeing her children grow, get married, and produce grandchildren were suddenly cast in doubt. Dreams of retirement with her husband, when they could reap the rewards of a lifetime, suddenly seemed elusive, evaporating as quickly as the morning mist.

Most unexpectedly, Catherine's very identity was suddenly called into question. She had known who she was—a confident and talented woman, Steve's wife, the children's mother, daughter to her aging parents, friend and neighbor, productive volunteer, and so forth. Now, all of that seemed to take a back seat to her being a cancer patient. Relationships changed with a speed that made her head spin. She was talked *about* by those she formerly talked *with*. She caught the knowing glances, the suddenly hushed conversations when she entered the room, the strained attempts of people to seem normal or upbeat when she was around.

FAITH ACTIVITY

Catholic Hospitals Research how Catholic hospitals began and developed. How is their mission connected to the mission of the Gospel's understanding of healing?

#2

Many people reflect on why tragedy and serious illness come to some people. Some theologians and philosophers refer to this as the "problem of evil." They may probe questions like:

- Why do good people suffer, apparently without reason?

- How can a loving God permit suffering that has no apparent purpose or positive benefit?

Catherine knew nothing of philosophers' or theologians' explanations. What she knew was an immediate panic when she first received the diagnosis, and then a sinking feeling of sadness that settled in as she realized that she was facing the likelihood of an early death. Her mind reeled from the swirl of emotions that competed for her attention, as she tried to focus on complicated medical explanations, reassuring her children, comforting her parents, staying connected with Steve. She felt no stirring of anger toward God; rather, there was just an emptiness that seemed to whisper that God was nowhere to be found in all this mess. She lost her bearings, no longer sure of who she was or what meaning was to be found in the chaos that her life had become.

GROUP TALK

Sickness has a way of isolating people from their friends, family, and faith community. This pain and suffering can lead to a feeling of abandonment and despair.

1. Why do you think sickness isolates people?

2. What can people do to lessen this sense of isolation?

3. Who are some people in your family, school, or parish who embrace those who are ill? How do they do this?

The Healing Her long conversation with Father Richards before her first anointing had begun to help her climb out of the dark pit that she felt she was in. He had not preached to her. Mostly he just listened as she raised her questions, shared her fear and pain, and shed tears of desperation. The few words he did say were hugely important. He told her that she was not alone in what was happening, that he and countless others in the parish community would be with her and her family throughout the coming ordeal, whatever its outcome. He said that others like her had found a new relationship with God in the midst of darkness, a presence more intimate than anything they dreamed possible in days of sunshine. Mostly, she remembered, he told her that "God loves you, no matter what." Without really telling her much about what was going to happen in the liturgy of anointing, he prepared her to receive that *"particular gift of the Holy Spirit"* that the *Catechism* speaks of (*CCC*, 1520).

The celebration of her anointing was, as we described above, surprisingly powerful for Catherine and left her with a sense of peace that she had not expected. Somehow or other, it helped her turn a corner. The faith of the community that surrounded her as she stood before the assembly lifted her up and carried her to a new place. She began to understand—though she still could not put words to it—that we are in this together, that there is solidarity in suffering which is very real and very profound. Some of the extraordinary ministers of Holy Communion who brought the Eucharist to her at home during her months of chemotherapy were themselves cancer survivors. They spoke to her of the power of prayer and hope that had sustained them. When her cancer went into remission, Catherine was convinced that the spiritual strength that she had drawn from the sacraments—Anointing, Penance, and the Eucharist— played a very important part in allowing her body to respond positively to the treatments. She did not naively claim a "miracle cure" when she went into remission. Rather, she saw the return of her health as a gift, a grace that allowed her time to live at a deeper, more aware level, regardless of the number of her days remaining.

- She was able to fight against the temptations to despair and self-absorption that are common reactions to serious illness.

- She worked through issues that allowed her to avoid thinking of herself as "victim," no matter the outcome of her disease.

- When fatigue and irritability overcame her and she found herself being too harsh with the children or Steve, she learned to seek forgiveness and even to forgive herself.

- Gradually, imperceptibly, but very surely, she grew and matured spiritually as a result of her struggle with the cancer.

Someone had told her about the passage in the Book of Genesis, chapter 32, when Jacob wrestled throughout a dark night with a mysterious stranger and emerged wounded, but a survivor. The story captured for her the spiritual struggle she was undergoing, and she had it in mind when she spoke of "my angel" with an ironic smile. In Catherine's mind, the "angel" she was wrestling with was Jesus, who—she knew—

must have felt many of the same emotions as she felt when he was faced with an untimely and unjustified death. Whenever the physical pain or the spiritual darkness threatened to overwhelm her, she thought of Jesus praying in the garden of Gethsemane, wrestling with his own feelings of doubt and despair, yet emerging victorious even as death seemed in the eyes of many to triumph.

New Meaning

The bottom line of her long spiritual struggle was that Catherine came to understand in an entirely new way the depth of meaning contained in so many familiar phrases she had learned growing up Catholic. She learned what it means to share in the Paschal Mystery of Jesus, and how we can offer up our sufferings with his, as a pleasing gift to the Father. Her prayers were often dry and seemingly lacked a depth of emotion, but she learned that intensity of feeling could never be equated with depth when it comes to prayer. Rather, it was her will, her choice to take a particular stand regarding her suffering, that made her prayer a privileged time when her relationship with Jesus deepened beyond words or feelings. She just *knew* that he was present to her through it all.

When Father Richards came to anoint her at home, and then a few months later at the hospice, she understood that she was experiencing a healing grace that was more profound than any physical cure. She knew, again in ways she could not put into words, that the Sacrament of Anointing had brought her *"a particular gift of the Holy Spirit"* by preparing her to make her final journey to God in peace. She still longed for the good life that she had known and lamented the loss of a future that had seemed so promising. But in the end, she was able to let go of all of that and give herself over to God without hesitation. She received what Catholic Tradition has called the "grace of a happy death."

GROUP TALK

Think about the three different times that Catherine was anointed, and how her situation was different each time. Discuss what you think the *"particular gift of the Holy Spirit"* was on each occasion.

The three anointings she had received at the hands of Father Richards over the course of several years punctuated a process of spiritual maturing and growth that steadily prepared Catherine for her final destiny with the Lord in heaven. At their last meeting in the hospice, when he gave her Communion as Viaticum, Father Richards said these words just after she took the tiny piece of the Consecrated Host and swallowed it: "May the Lord Jesus protect you and lead you to eternal life." She whispered her response: "Amen." And then Father added a final prayer from the ritual, just before giving her a last blessing. It was a prayer that seemed to both of them to sum up much of Catherine's spiritual journey.

> Lord God, merciful Father, comforter of the afflicted, look kindly on your servant Catherine, who trusts in you. Though now weighed down with grievous distress, may she find relief through this holy anointing; and may the body and blood of your Son, Jesus Christ, refresh and strengthen her for her journey to life.
>
> *Pastoral Care of the Sick: Rites of Anointing and Viaticum*, 270

In this section, we have looked at the connections between Catherine's experience of the Sacrament of Anointing and her search for the meaning of her illness in her everyday life. In the next section, we will explore how these kinds of experiences have helped the Church to formulate her teachings found in the *Catechism* about the effects of the Sacrament of Anointing.

Quick Check

1. What is meant by the phrase "the difficulties that go with the condition of serious illness"?
2. How does the "problem of evil" relate to the Sacrament of Anointing?
3. How did Catherine experience healing as a result of being anointed?
4. How did Catherine through her experiences participate in the Paschal Mystery?

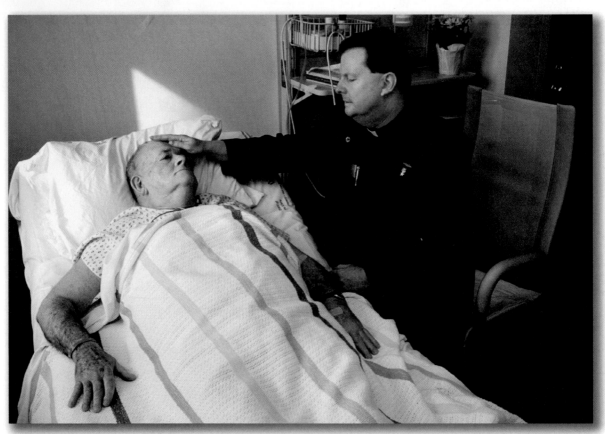

Anointing in the East

Because the Church's use of oil to pray for the healing of the sick stems from apostolic times, it is not surprising to find a well-developed tradition of this sacrament in the churches of the East, just as in the West. As is the case with other sacramental rituals, there are both similar and distinctive elements in the way the Orthodox communities and Eastern Catholic churches celebrate anointing.

In both traditions there has been an association between anointing and forgiveness of sin from the very beginning. More in the East, perhaps, than in the West, the reconciliation of sinners developed in ways that often involved the use of oil. This association has tended to reinforce the notion that the Anointing of the Sick is a primarily penitential liturgy. One cannot always distinguish in the prayers that survive from the early centuries whether the healing associated with a particular use of oil is directed at physical recovery or forgiveness of sins.

One similarity between East and West is the distinction between the blessing of oil and its application. In both traditions, there is a solemn blessing of oil by the bishop or Patriarch generally associated with Holy Week. However, in the East from ancient times, and in the West since Vatican II, the tradition has allowed priests also to bless the oil whenever there was a need. Regardless of who blesses or when the blessing takes place, in both East and West there is a fairly sharp distinction between the act of blessing oil and its use in anointing for healing.

Perhaps the most striking difference between East and West is the very elaborate manner in which the ritual of anointing has developed over the centuries in the East. Whereas the West seems to have developed ritual forms that were more practical and aimed at use in the homes of the sick, the East has maintained a ritual structure more suited to lengthy, grand celebrations in cathedral and monastic churches. There was always provision for a more simplified rite when necessity permitted it, but the primary focus of the ritual evolution was toward an elaborate ceremony in large churches. Some Eastern rituals generally call for seven priests to be involved, each one responsible for one of seven anointings.

In some traditions, the rite opens with prayers of some length for consolation and healing. Then the oil is blessed, again with extensive readings and prayers. Finally, each of the seven anointings is done in the context of its own Liturgy of the Word and with its own distinctive prayers. The rite concludes with the imposition of the Book of the Gospels on the head of the sick and numerous prayers to the saints for their intercession on behalf of the sick.

The Effects of Anointing

We have seen in previous chapters that our understanding of God deepens as we reflect on our experience—both our experience of God at worship and our experience of him in the midst of everyday life. Theology draws upon both of these sources as faith seeks understanding. In this section we will explore the Church's teaching about the effects of the sacrament in light of the story of Catherine and her experience of illness and anointing.

The *Catechism* summarizes the doctrine of the Church regarding the effects of the Sacrament of Anointing in the following way.

> "The special grace of the sacrament of the Anointing of the Sick has as its effects:
> - the uniting of the sick person to the passion of Christ, for his own good and that of the whole Church;
> - the strengthening, peace, and courage to endure in a Christian manner the sufferings of illness or old age;
> - the forgiveness of sins, if the sick person was not able to obtain it through the sacrament of Penance;
> - the restoration of health, if it is conducive to the salvation of his soul;
> - the preparation for passing over to eternal life."
>
> *Catechism of the Catholic Church,* 1532

Looking again at the story of Catherine can help us to deepen our understanding and strengthen our faith in the power of God at work in this sacrament.

United to Christ's Passion Sacraments always involve some sort of change—forgiveness of sins committed since Baptism, transforming the substance of bread and wine into the substance of Christ's Body and Blood, and so forth. The power of the Holy Spirit at work in the Sacrament of the Anointing of the Sick changed Catherine's sufferings, transforming them from meaningless pain into a share in the redeeming work of Christ's passion. The change was primarily in the *meaning* of her disease, not merely in the physical chemistry of illness. This change came about because she approached the anointing as one who believed in the power of the Holy Spirit, present and working in the sacraments. Just as the Apostles were able to cast out demons in his name, bishops and priests today are channels of Christ's healing mercy, empowered as ministers of God's grace to influence the spiritual being of the

one who is anointed. From one-who-is-suffering, Catherine was transformed into one-who-is-suffering-with-Christ. In the sacrament she was united to the passion of Christ in a new and deeper way.

For the Good of the Whole Church Saint Augustine taught that we become what we eat in the Eucharist, the Body of Christ. In a similar way, by becoming one-who-is-suffering-with-Christ, Catherine was transformed into a living sign of God's redeeming love. Her willingness to undergo the trials of her illness as part of a larger mystery of redemptive suffering made her a source of inspiration and hope for the entire community of believers with whom she was connected.

The General Introduction to the Rite of Anointing reads, "By their witness the sick show that our mortal life must be redeemed through the mystery of Christ's death and Resurrection (3).... Moreover, the Church exhorts them to associate themselves willingly with the passion and death of Christ (see *Romans 8:17*),[2] and thus contribute to the welfare of the people of God"[3] (5). Catherine did not think much about it, but in truth, the witness of her faith strengthened countless others with whom she was connected. No longer merely a passive victim of her cancer, Catherine's "full, conscious, and active participation" in the liturgy of anointing had rendered her an active part in the drama of redemption.

The ritual of anointing also contains sections that encourage pastoral care of the sick by the community of which they are a part. At Catherine's parish there was a Caregivers Ministry that provided meals, rides to doctors, and other support to her and her family throughout her illness, in addition to the extraordinary ministers of Holy Communion who brought her Communion while she was homebound. Just as Catherine's faith witnessed to other members of her parish community, so their pastoral concern was a source of strength for Catherine and her family. Sacraments build up the whole Church, not just the individuals who receive them.

FAITH ACTIVITY

Visualize It Discuss in groups how the following statement is true for the Sacraments of Healing: "Sacraments build up the whole Church, not just the individuals who receive them." On poster board create a montage of images, drawn or cut out, that depicts how the sacraments build up the Church, as seen in people's daily lives.

Among Catherine's three children, her fifteen-year-old daughter, Celeste, struggled the most with her mother's illness. Celeste's initial reaction had been one of anger toward God for allowing her mother to contract this dreaded disease, followed by withdrawal and depression. She found going to Mass more and more painful, convinced that people were looking at her and her family with pity, singling them out for negative attention, and only intensifying her sense of isolation in the midst of suffering.

However, Catherine shared openly with her family the struggles she was facing: how her faith was being tested, and eventually how she understood God's grace had worked a genuine spiritual healing within her. Celeste also came gradually to lower her defenses and to open up with other family members about her own sadness, the doubts and confusions that her mother's illness had caused, and her struggle with faith in God. Celeste's father in particular was instrumental in encouraging the children to talk about their feelings, and he modeled for them that believers can have many negative emotions without it meaning their faith is weak. Celeste eventually joined a Rainbows support group for children who have suffered loss, and she found that the parish's youth minister was someone with whom she could also share her questions about faith.

As she reflected on her experience several years later, Celeste was able to acknowledge that her faith had ultimately been strengthened, not weakened, by her mother's illness, and that she had found a spiritual healing not unlike that which had brought comfort to her mother. She recognized and was able to acknowledge that her healing had come in large measure as a result of being part of the graced community of her parish, where pastoral care and faith-filled living had been witnessed so strongly to her and her family.

GROUP TALK

While sickness has a way of isolating people, it also can be a source of conversion for many.

1. Describe the conversion that is evident in the life of Catherine and her family.

2. Do you know anyone who has experienced a turn to God and spiritual renewal because of sickness, either his or her own, or that of someone they love? Share how that person changed.

Courage to Endure in a Christian Manner

The sufferings of illness, like those of old age, are indeed real. We may know those who are embittered at their lot in life, turned in on themselves, and filled with rage over the suffering they are enduring due to illness or old age. We also may know those who exhibit grace under fire, whose attitude towards the suffering they endure is such that the burden seems lighter and their days seem brighter. They inspire those around them with a sense that God walks with them in a very special way.

One of the effects of the Sacrament of Anointing was to help Catherine bear her burden more lightly, in a Christian manner, according to the example of Jesus who carried his cross on the road to Calvary without complaint. Catherine often had long talks with Jesus, asking him to show her how to endure suffering as he had, in a spirit of love rather than bitterness. Her prayers were answered, in a real measure, as a result of the *"particular gift of the Holy Spirit"* of which the *Catechism* speaks and which she received in the Sacrament of Anointing (*CCC*, 1520).

Forgiveness of Sins

Our study of the history of this sacrament has revealed its association over the centuries with the forgiveness of sins. Ideally, anointing is celebrated in conjunction with the Sacrament of Penance, but that is not always the case. Regardless, the Church has discerned that the healing graces of God, spiritual as well as physical, are available in this sacrament. God's merciful forgiveness is obtained by the one whose sufferings are joined to those of Christ through sacramental anointing, just as surely as would be the case through sacramental confession and reconciliation. The scriptural witness is clear: ". . . and anyone who has committed sins will be forgiven" (*James 5:15*). On her deathbed, Catherine asked for sacramental absolution once again, and Father Richards bestowed on her the Apostolic Pardon, the special grant of a plenary indulgence which the Church offers under such circumstances.

Restoration of Health, If It Is Conducive

From her very beginning, the Church has witnessed Christ's healing power revealed in physical cures as a result of faith-filled prayer. The Church has never taught, nor do we know, just how physical healing associated with anointing actually happens. Some consider such cures to be true miracles—the suspension of natural laws through a direct divine intervention. In other words, this would be a sign or wonder that can only take place through God's power. Others believe that more often healing from anointing is part of a more complex natural process in which our body-spirit integrity is restored. An opening on the spiritual level has physical consequences.

FAITH ACTIVITY

Defining Health Research the understanding of health. Write a definition of health based upon your research and understanding of this sacrament. Describe the blessings of good health that might flow from this definition.

While knowing *how* healing takes place may be of interest, it is not relevant to one like Catherine who approached the experience from the perspective of faith. As she saw it, God restored her health for several years after her initial chemotherapy to give her time to put her spiritual house in order. That having been done, she knew that it was time for her to return to God, despite the fact that on a human level she would have wanted to remain with her family for a much longer life. She did not use the exact words of the *Catechism,* but her understanding of God's healing was that it had been "conducive to the salvation of [her] soul" (*CCC,* 1532).

Preparation for Passing Over During the many centuries that anointing was reserved for the final moments of life, theologians explained its effects primarily in terms of it being an "anointing for glory." In the Catholic piety of many generations of believers, the blessing of a final anointing (*Extreme Unction*) just before death was a sign that one had been forgiven for sins committed and rewarded with swift entry into paradise. Despite Vatican II's re-focusing of this sacrament on healing and recovery, this dimension of the sacramental grace of anointing remains a legitimate part of our liturgical tradition. Even though the sick are urged to celebrate the sacrament long before reaching the point of death, its graces still serve to prepare us for that eventual outcome of our life's journey. When the sacrament is celebrated with the elderly, in particular, the shadow of death—even for those not yet critically ill—still looms large. One of the spiritual fruits that anointing has for many people is a greater peace at the approach of death, knowing in an intimate way that the Holy Spirit within is strengthening them for life's "final" journey.

Finding Meaning in Suffering

For many of our contemporaries, sickness is utterly without value. In such a world, it is easy to see why those who suffer are regarded as a burden and expendable. Many in our culture, who see no meaning in suffering and see death as the end of existence, try to justify euthanasia—so-called "mercy killing." The Gospel reveals that every life is a gift from God, precious and sacred and that God does not see or judge by human standards. The Church teaches us to see the meaning of human sickness as part of the mystery of salvation, which includes life beyond death.

We conclude our consideration of the Sacrament of Anointing with several paragraphs from the General Introduction to the Rite. There we find a moving meditation on suffering and illness in light of God the Father's plan, Christ's suffering and death, and the role of the sick in the Church.

Suffering and illness have always been among the greatest problems that trouble the human spirit. Christians feel and experience pain as do all other people; yet their faith helps them to grasp more deeply the mystery of suffering and to bear their pain with greater courage. From Christ's words they know that sickness has meaning and value for their own salvation and for the salvation of the world. They also know that Christ, who during his life often visited and healed the sick, loves them in their illness.

Moreover, the role of the sick in the Church is to be a reminder to others of the essential or higher things. By their witness the sick show that our mortal life must be redeemed through the mystery of Christ's death and Resurrection.

General Introduction, Pastoral Care of the Sick: Rites of Anointing and Viaticum, 1, 3

GROUP TALK

1. Were you ever present when somebody you knew received the Anointing of the Sick? What were the circumstances? What happened? How did you and the others present react?

2. Have you ever received the Anointing of the Sick? What were the circumstances? How did it feel? What are your thoughts about the experience now?

Quick Check

1. What are the effects of the Sacrament of Anointing?
2. How can parishes provide pastoral care of the sick?
3. What does it mean to endure illness "in a Christian manner"?
4. How do those who are sick build up the Body of Christ?

Person of Faith

Louise de Marillac (1591–1660)

The images sometimes presented of saints who lived many centuries ago can make them seem quaint and out of touch with modern-day realities. Often times the stories that are passed down about the holiness of a saint portray an image of piety that we find difficult to relate to. In reality, many saints were strong individuals who lived in a very real world that demanded much more than soft piety. We live today in an age when many question the role of women in the Church. The example of a saint such as Louise de Marillac can help us to appreciate the gritty determination and powerful leadership qualities that distinguished this woman who was so completely dedicated to serving the poor, the sick, and any of Christ's sisters and brothers in need.

Louise was born on August 12, 1591, the child of an unmarried mother she never knew. Her father—a widower at the time, and a member of the French aristocracy—acknowledged his paternity and accepted Louise into his household. However, when he remarried in 1595, Louise's stepmother never accepted her husband's daughter as a full member of the family. The young girl was sent to live in a boarding house where she learned many domestic skills that were later to serve her well in her various ministries to the sick and suffering.

In 1613, at the age of 22, she married Antoine Le Gras, who was a secretary to the French queen, Marie de Medici, and nine months later gave birth to a son, Michel Antoine Le Gras. Louise knew from personal experience about the suffering that comes from illness. She herself struggled with poor health from childhood and with depression as an adult, and her husband also fell ill in 1622, dying three years later after only 12 years of marriage. Following his death, Louise devoted herself to the education of their son, who eventually married in 1650 and had a daughter the following year.

During the years of her marriage, Louise's husband had supported her in her leadership role in the Ladies of Charity, an organization of rich women dedicated to caring for the poor. He defended her against the criticisms of those in aristocratic circles who found her involvements inappropriate, and encouraged her deepening interest in developing her own spiritual life. In 1619 she met Saint Francis De Sales, and around 1623 Saint Vincent de Paul became her spiritual director.

Saint Vincent had been organizing devout, wealthy women to help him care for the poor and the sick, but it soon became clear to him that those of aristocratic background were often ill-equipped for the rough conditions they encountered among the poor. Such was not the case with Louise, however. Despite her own frail health, she undertook a number of missions that Vincent assigned her, and without exception proved her resiliency and competency. Seeing her considerable talents, her spiritual maturity, and her leadership abilities, Vincent chose Louise to train and organize women of lower economic status who would work among the poor. Beginning in 1633 with four country girls in a home that she rented in Paris, she trained groups of women to care for the sick. Eventually the partnership resulted in the opening of an orphanage where the sisters taught the children. Louise established other orphanages and hospitals, nursed plague victims herself in Paris, reformed a neglected hospital in Angers, and worked with galley slaves and prisoners. She traveled extensively throughout France and established more than 40 daughter houses and charities.

Louise had from the earliest days wanted to form a religious order, but Vincent initially resisted. Instead of another religious congregation living a cloistered life, he wanted Louise and her followers to be devoted to the poor. He wrote, "Your convent will be the house of the sick; your cell, a hired room; your chapel, the parish church; your cloister, the streets of the city or the wards of the hospital . . ." Finally, in 1634, he permitted her to draft a rule of life for the growing number of women who were attracted to her company. Unlike other religious women of the day, the Daughters of Charity were non-cloistered so they could move more freely among the poor of the city. They took simple vows, renewable each year, rather than solemn, perpetual vows. In 1655 the Company of the Daughters of Charity was formally approved and established by the Archbishop of Paris. Today, the Daughters of Charity number more than 20,000 members who serve in various charitable ministries among the poor and the sick in nearly 100 countries around the globe. Louise de Marillac died on March 15, 1660, just a few months before Vincent de Paul. She was canonized in 1934.

REFLECT

1. How does the life and ministry of Louise de Marillac relate to the Sacrament of Anointing?

2. Name some people who care for the sick. Are any of these people sick or afflicted themselves? Do you think it is easier to be compassionate to people with whom you can identify?

3. What does the life of Louise de Marillac encourage us to do?

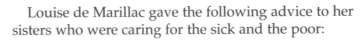

Louise de Marillac gave the following advice to her sisters who were caring for the sick and the poor:

"In serving the sick, you should have God alone in view. You should not be too lenient and condescending when the sick refuse to take remedies or become too insolent, yet you must beware of showing either resentment or contempt in your demeanor toward them. On the contrary, treat the sick with respect and humility, remembering that all harshness and disdain, as well as the services and the honor you render them, are directed to our Lord himself . . . As for your conduct toward the poor, may you never take the attitude of merely getting the task done. You must show them affection; serving them from the heart—inquiring of them what they need; speaking to them gently and compassionately; procuring necessary help for them without being too bothersome or too eager."

This prayer captures in many ways the heart of her spirituality:

"Grant me the grace to spend this day without offending You and without failing my neighbor."

Study Guide

▶Check Understanding

1. Summarize the significance of oil in biblical times.

2. Describe Jesus' ministry among the sick and how he wanted his followers to continue his healing work.

3. Identify the earliest historical evidence we have of the Church celebrating the Sacrament of Anointing after the Resurrection.

4. Explain the way the emphasis of anointing—who was anointed and under what circumstances—shifted historically.

5. Identify the most significant change in the practice of the Sacrament of Anointing mandated by Vatican II.

6. Outline the settings in which anointing may be celebrated and the circumstances that would dictate each.

7. Name the various groups of people encouraged to receive the sacrament.

8. Review the significance of the Church's custom of reserving the blessing of oil to the bishop.

9. Explain what the *Catechism* is referring to by the phrase "the difficulties that go with the condition of serious illness."

10. Describe what is meant by the "problem of evil" and how it relates to the Sacrament of Anointing.

11. Give examples of how Catherine experienced healing as a result of being anointed.

12. Express how Catherine participated in the Paschal Mystery through her experiences.

13. List the effects of the Sacrament of Anointing.

14. Give examples of some of the ways a parish undertakes its pastoral care of the sick.

15. Describe what it means to endure illness "in a Christian manner."

16. Explain the role those who are sick have in building up the Body of Christ.

▶Apply and Develop

17. Propose why you think many people are still reluctant to celebrate the Sacrament of Anointing when they are seriously ill. Include historical or cultural reasons, and be sure to discuss how you could help them to be more open to receiving the sacrament.

18. Write an essay explaining the key beliefs expressed in the "Prayer over the Oil."

19. Develop a presentation on the Sacrament of the Anointing of the Sick highlighted in the *Catechism's* teachings about "*a particular gift of the Holy Spirit.*"

20. Compare and contrast the notions of "physical" and "spiritual" healing, giving attention to how the Sacrament of Anointing relates to both.

▶Key Words

See pages noted for contextual explanations of these important faith terms.

Apostolic Pardon (p. 168)

in extremis (p. 168)

Extreme Unction (p. 165)

Viaticum (p. 160)

Do not neglect the gift that is in you, which was given to you through prophecy with the laying on of hands by the council of elders.

1 Timothy 4:14

HOLY ORDERS

CHAPTER GOALS

In this chapter, you will:

★ learn how the Sacrament of Holy Orders was celebrated in the past and how it is celebrated today.

★ discover the gifts and responsibilities that come with ordained ministry and what the Church requires of those to be ordained.

★ learn about the ministry of bishops, priests, and deacons.

★ study how Vatican II used the theme of priest-prophet-king in considering Holy Orders.

★ learn about the martyrdom of Saint Lawrence.

Daniel's Story

The long line of ministers—altar servers, readers, deacons, and priests—stretched out ahead of him the full length of the cathedral's center aisle. With smiles and nods from well-wishers who filled the pews on either side, Father Daniel walked slowly forward, feeling humble and a bit overwhelmed as the liturgy for the ordination of a bishop began to unfold.

The celebration began with the familiar Introductory Rites and then the Liturgy of the Word, that is, until the Gospel proclamation ended. Instead of everyone taking their seats, the choir and people began chanting the ancient tune of the *Veni, Creator Spiritus*—Come, Creator Spirit—as Father Daniel was led before the principal ordaining bishop. When the music ended, one of the assisting priests asked, on behalf of the local Church, the ordaining bishop "to ordain this priest, Daniel, to the responsibility of the Episcopate." The bishop replied, asking if there was "a mandate from the Apostolic See" for the ordination to take place. The priest answered by reading aloud a very formal document indicating that the Holy Father had chosen Father Daniel to be the new bishop of the diocese. At the end of the letter, the entire assembly rose to their feet and gave their assent by filling the building with a thunderous applause that lasted for what seemed to Father Daniel to be a lifetime.

When the applause subsided, and the principal ordaining bishop had finished his homily, Father Daniel rose and was questioned about his commitment to carry out the duties of the office of bishop. To each of the questions, he answered, "I do," and then he prostrated himself on the floor as a litany of supplication was sung. The assembly first invoked a long list of saints, and then asked the Lord to help Father Daniel with blessings that would allow him to serve worthily as bishop of the flock.

As Father Daniel rose from the floor, he knew that the moment had finally arrived when the essential elements of the sacrament—the laying on of hands and the Prayer of Ordination—would confer on his soul an indeli-ble character, ordaining him forever as one of the successors of the Apostles, a member of the order of bishops. A hush descended on the entire cathedral as the ordaining bishop placed his hands firmly on Father Daniel's head and prayed intently in silence over him. The bishop then stepped aside as all of the other bishops in attendance came forward in turn to lay hands on Daniel. Two deacons carrying the Book of the Gospels then placed it upon Daniel's head as the long Prayer of Consecration was chanted by the principal ordaining bishop.

The final segment of the ordination consisted of what is called the Explanatory Rites, symbolic expressions of the nature of the newly ordained bishop's ministry. First, his head was anointed with the sacred chrism—the sign of the Bishop's distinctive share in the priesthood of Christ. Then, several objects were presented to him: the Book of the Gospels, illustrating that the faithful preaching of the word of God is the pre-eminent obligation of the office of the Bishop; next, his episcopal ring—symbolizing his fidelity to the Bride of God, the Church, a miter—the headdress that signifies his resolve to pursue holiness, a crosier—the pastoral staff that signifies the duty of guiding and governing the Church entrusted to him. Then, after being led to his chair, called the *cathedra*, Bishop Daniel received from all of his brother bishops a kiss of peace that sealed, so to speak, his admittance into the College of Bishops.

GROUP TALK

Based on the story of the ordination of Bishop Daniel, discuss what you think would be for you the most moving part of the celebration and why. If you have ever been to the ordination of a deacon, priest, or bishop, share your experience with the group.

The Church Celebrates Ministries of Service

The Gospels describe in many places how Jesus carefully chose particular men to be his Apostles and entrusted to them the leadership of his Church.

As he walked by the Sea of Galilee, he saw two brothers, Simon, who is called Peter, and Andrew his brother, casting a net into the sea—for they were fishermen. And he said to them, "Follow me, and I will make you fish for people." Immediately they left their nets and followed him. As he went from there, he saw two other brothers, James son of Zebedee and his brother John, in the boat with their father Zebedee, mending their nets, and he called them. Immediately they left the boat and their father, and followed him.

 Matthew 4:18–22

We also read about Jesus' calling his first disciples in Mark 1:16–20.

Then Jesus called the twelve together and gave them power and authority over all demons and to cure diseases, and he sent them out to proclaim the kingdom of God and to heal. He said to them, "Take nothing for your journey, no staff, nor bag, nor bread, nor money—not even an extra tunic. Whatever house you enter, stay there, and leave from there. Wherever they do not welcome you, as you are leaving that town shake the dust off your feet as a testimony against them." They departed and went through the villages, bringing the good news and curing diseases everywhere.

 Luke 9:1-6

We also read about Jesus calling the Twelve (12 apostles) to their mission in Matthew 10:1–16, Mark 3:13–19, and Luke 6:12–16.

In addition to the passages cited and referenced above, we can find more examples of Jesus calling people to be his disciples: Luke 5:1–11; John 1:35–51; Matthew 16:13–20; Mark 8:27–30; and Luke 9:18–21.

FAITH ACTIVITY

Gospel Comparison In small groups, make a list of everything you know about Jesus' call of the Apostles and their ministry. Then read the passages referenced on this page. Note which passages parallel your list, and add to your list as necessary. Discuss what the passages can tell us about Jesus' attitude toward leadership and the reaction of those chosen to be Apostles. How do these apply to the Church today?

Changing Forms but an Unchanging Tradition

The Apostles continued Jesus' tradition of calling leaders. They carefully chose from among worthy men those who would share leadership with them in the Christian community. (See *Acts 1:15–26*.) We lack detailed descriptions of exactly how the early Christian Church ritualized this choice, although it is clear that prayer and laying on of hands were included from earliest apostolic times. The ritual forms, into which these two essential elements have been incorporated, are part of a long and varied liturgical history.

Aside from brief allusions in the New Testament, our earliest documentary evidence of the rites involved in the Sacrament of Orders comes from the *Apostolic Tradition* of Hippolytus at the beginning of the third century A.D. That document describes the ordination of a bishop (2–4) as well as of presbyters (7) and deacons (8). Earlier documents are sketchy about the historical details, but we know that from the beginning that ordained ministry has been conferred and exercised in three degrees: that of bishops, presbyters, and deacons. Although the expression of their respective ministries has evolved over time, these three degrees belong to the very structure of the Church.

GROUP TALK

1. How would you describe Jesus' ministry among the people? What were some of the different aspects of his mission and his work?

2. What are some of the ways the Church has continued Jesus' ministry though the ages? Give some specific examples of how this happens in your parish.

3. What qualities do you think Jesus looked for in those he called to follow him? In those he asked to lead his followers?

4. Who do you know that possesses some of these qualities?

Distinctive Rituals As one might imagine, the rituals associated with the conferral of orders on each of the three degrees took on very distinctive features associated with the practice of each particular ministry in different eras. Very often there were symbolic elements added to the rites to express the meaning of the specific ordination. Many of these symbolic rituals took on an importance over time that seemed disproportionate and threatened to obscure the centrality of the laying on of hands and prayer of consecration. For example, in the medieval rite for the ordination of deacons, a ritual handing over of the Book of the Gospels became so prominent that some might think it was the central moment of the rite. Similarly, in the ordination of priests, the handing over of the paten and chalice seemed in the mind of some to be the most important element in the rite.

In the Western Church "minor orders" arose, stepping-stones to the priesthood, each of which had its own distinctive liturgy. Tonsure, although not a minor order in itself, was the first ritual celebrated as a man entered the clerical state. The minor orders included then porter (doorkeeper), lector, exorcist, and acolyte. The "major orders" that followed them included the subdiaconate in addition to the scriptural orders of deacon and presbyter (priest).

Only the diaconate and priesthood were considered part of the Sacrament of Holy Orders. However, the other offices came to be required as steps toward the sacrament. In 1972 Pope Paul VI dropped tonsure, porter, exorcist, and the subdiaconate. Changing also the language of "minor orders," he retained what are now called the "ministries" of lector and acolyte as steps toward priesthood. The liturgical duties associated with those ministries, however, generally are performed by lay people who have no intention of entering Holy Orders.

Reform and Renewal

On the eve of the Second Vatican Council, the rituals associated with ordination in the Catholic Church were somewhat overgrown with secondary traditions and did not meet many of the standards set forth in the *Constitution on the Sacred Liturgy* for the renewal of each of the sacraments. The *Constitution* directed that the Rites of Ordination were to be revised (76), but it gave little by way of specifics. One of the first of the new liturgical rites issued after the Council, the Sacrament of Holy Orders, was published in 1969, and a revised second edition in 1989. In his Apostolic Constitution promulgating the new ordination ritual, Pope Paul VI pointed especially to two of the major principles of the *Constitution* that had guided the reform: that the rites should express more clearly the holy things they signify, and that the rites should be more easily understood by the people so as to allow for their full and active participation.

Because a bishop receives the fullness of the Sacrament of Holy Orders, the Ordination Rite to the episcopacy serves as a kind of model for ordination to the priesthood and diaconate as well. The chart on the next page allows for an easy comparison of the overall similarities of the three rites and the ritual flow of their individual segments.

Celebrating the Sacrament

Ordination of a Bishop	Ordination of a Priest	Ordination of a Deacon
PREPARATORY RITES	**PREPARATORY RITES**	**PREPARATORY RITES**
Hymn		
	Election —Calling of Candidates	Election —Calling of Candidates
Presentation of the Bishop-Elect	—Presentation of Candidates	—Presentation of Candidates
Apostolic Letter		
Assent of the People	—Election by Bishop and 　Assent of People	—Election by Bishop and 　Assent of People
Homily	Homily	Homily
Examination of the Candidate (Promise of the Elect)	Examination of the Candidate (Promise of Obedience)	Examination of the Candidate (Promise of Obedience)
Litany of the Saints [bishop-elect prostrates himself and everyone else kneels]	Litany of the Saints	Litany of the Saints
ORDINATION	**ORDINATION**	**ORDINATION**
Laying on of Hands	Laying on of Hands	Laying on of Hands
Book of Gospels held above the head		
Prayer of Consecration	Prayer of Consecration	Prayer of Consecration
EXPLANATORY RITES	**EXPLANATORY RITES**	**EXPLANATORY RITES**
	Investiture with Stole and Chasuble	Investiture with Stole and Dalmatic
Anointing of Head	Anointing of Hands	
Presentation of the Book of the Gospels	Presentation of Bread and Wine	Presentation of the Book of the Gospels
Investiture: Ring, Miter, and Pastoral Staff		
Seating of the Bishop		
Kiss of Peace	Kiss of Peace	Kiss of Peace

Connecting the Rite and Symbol to Everyday Life

Discuss the following.

· The peoples' assent is sought in the rituals for ordination *before* the candidate is actually ordained. What do you see as the significance of this placement in the rite? What are some ways your parish community supports your ordained ministers? How can you show your support for the work your priests and deacons do?

· Bishops, priests, and deacons are presented with different items in the Explanatory Rites. What do you think each symbolizes? With what symbols of the faith have you been presented by family or friends? What do those symbols say about who you are?

Toward a Deeper Understanding As we look very carefully at the structure of the Rite of Ordination, we can see that it embodies the *Constitution on the Sacred Liturgy's* goal of a renewed ritual. Worth noting in particular are the following aspects of the ritual:

• The ordination takes place between the Liturgy of the Word and the Liturgy of the Eucharist. This placement characterizes most of the revised rites. It reflects a conviction that full and conscious participation in the ritual happens best after the Scriptures have awakened faith and instructed the faithful in the mysteries to be celebrated.

• The people's assent after the candidate is presented reflects the important role that the faithful play as collaborators with the ordained in their ministry. Both the lay faithful and the ordained share in the one Priesthood of Christ, each in their respective way. Although the ministerial priesthood of the ordained differs in essence and not just in degree from that of the common priesthood of the baptized, both are part of the "royal priesthood" consecrated by the Holy Spirit and both share in Christ's priestly ministry for the salvation of the world.

• The Litany of the Saints is an acknowledgement of the active role that the entire people of God play in prayerful intercession. It is not just the ordaining bishop who prays for the one to be ordained; the entire Church intercedes on his behalf before God.

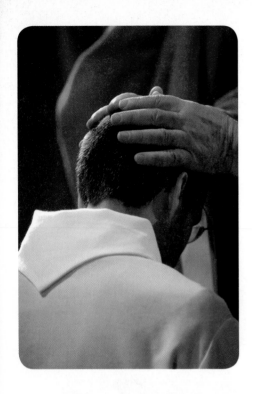

- The placement and the centrality of the laying on of hands and prayer of consecration make their importance stand out in a much clearer way than was the case in the previous ritual in use prior to Vatican II. The consecratory prayer is the most solemn moment in each of the rites.

- All present are directed to answer "Amen" at the end of the ordaining bishop's proclamation of this most important prayer. It is one of many subtle ways that the rite underlines the participation of the faithful in the liturgical action.

- Both bishops (on the head) and priests (on the hands) are anointed with chrism as part of the ritual's Explanatory Rites. We have seen earlier when we studied Baptism and Confirmation that the chrism is used with non-repeatable sacraments (Baptism, Confirmation, Holy Orders) that give a character. Although they do receive the sacramental character, the fact that deacons are not anointed with chrism is a way that the rite distinguishes their ordination to service from the priestly ordination of bishops and priests.

✓ Quick Check

1. How did Jesus' actions establish the tradition of calling and sending forth leaders for the Church?
2. What are the essential parts of the Sacrament of Holy Orders that have remained throughout the centuries?
3. What are some elements of the ritual of ordination that have changed over time?
4. What elements do all three Ordination Rites (bishop, priest, deacon) have in common?

GROUP TALK

Discuss ways that the ministry of your school and parish are connected to the ministry of the bishop.

The Gifts and Responsibilities of Ministry

The ordination of a bishop, priest, or deacon is not merely a selection, a designation, or delegation by the community. Rather, the conferral of Holy Orders in the Church bestows the grace of the Holy Spirit on the recipient.

Jesus chose the Apostles—and their successors, the bishops, and those called to assist the bishops, namely presbyters (priests) and deacons—to act in his person and with his power. The ordination of a bishop makes that person part of an unbroken succession of men since the first Apostles who have received the call to lead God's people. This is what is known as **apostolic succession**.

With every gift comes a corresponding responsibility. In the Sacrament of Holy Orders, a man is given a divine mandate to preach the Gospel and to take leadership in spreading the reign of God. This is the same mandate that Christ gave to the Church when he commissioned the Apostles to go to the ends of the earth on his behalf. (See *Matthew 28:16–20*.) Similarly, when Jesus made Peter the visible foundation of the Church and entrusted to him the "keys" (authority) of the kingdom, he appointed Peter and his successors, the popes, with special responsibilities as the leader of the Apostles and their successors, the bishops. As the *Code of Canon Law* puts it, the pope is the "head of the College of Bishops, Vicar of Christ, and Pastor of the universal Church on earth" (*Canon*, 331).

Catholic youth greeting Pope Benedict at World Youth Day 2005. ▼

The Ministry of Bishops Bishops, who receive the fullness of the Sacrament of Holy Orders, serve as "the visible source and foundation of unity" within their local churches (*Dogmatic Constitution on the Church*, 23). Their unity with the College of Bishops links together all local churches throughout the world in that wonderful communion we call the Catholic Church. In turn, the bishops' unity with their coworkers in their local Church—priests and deacons—is a further expression of the unity all ordained share in Christ through the Holy Spirit.

In the Rite of Ordination of a Bishop, the Church celebrates both the gift of the Spirit and the responsibilities that go with the episcopal office. Part of the ordination ceremony involves the bishop-elect being questioned about his readiness and willingness to undertake those responsibilities. Those questions tell us about his ministry of service in teaching, governing, and sanctifying the faithful in his diocese. The ordaining bishop asks the bishop-elect if he is resolved:

- to preach the Gospel with constancy and fidelity.

- to guard the deposit of faith handed down from the Apostles.

- to build up the Body of Christ.

- to remain in communion with the order of bishops under the authority of Saint Peter's successor, to whom he would render faithful obedience.

- to guide the people of God as a devoted father, together with his fellow priests and deacons.

- to be welcoming and merciful to the poor, to strangers, and to all who are in need.

- to seek out the sheep who stray from the Lord's fold.

- to pray for God's people and carry out this priestly office without reproach.

These points offer an excellent summary of what the bishop of your diocese focuses on, day-in and day-out, as he strives to live out the gift of the Holy Spirit given to him on the day of his episcopal ordination.

Pour out upon this chosen one
that power which is from you,
the Spirit of governance
whom you gave to your beloved Son, Jesus Christ,
the Spirit whom he bestowed upon the holy Apostles,
who established the Church in each place as your
sanctuary for the glory and unceasing praise of
your name.

From the Prayer of Consecration, Rite of Ordination of a Bishop, 26

▲ The Principle Ordaining Bishop performs the Laying on of Hands of the Bishop-elect with two retired bishops looking on.

GROUP TALK

Discuss ways that the work of your school and parish are connected to the ministry of the bishop.

The Ministry of Priests Collectively, the priests of a diocese form a **presbyterium** that shares responsibility with the bishop for the local Church of which they are a part; individually, they receive from him a particular charge to care for a portion of that church's welfare, often a parish.

> Grant, we pray, Almighty Father,
> to this, your servant, the dignity of the priesthood;
> renew deep within him the Spirit of holiness;
> may he henceforth possess this office
> which comes from you, O God,
> and is next in rank to the office of Bishop;
> and by the example of his manner of life,
> may he instill right conduct.
>
> *From the Prayer of Consecration, Rite of Ordination of a Priest, 22*

As the bishop's coworkers, priests share in his responsibilities. Although there are many priests who serve in specialized forms of ministry, most are assigned to work in parishes. The ministry of parish priest includes the following.

- **Teaching** Preaching is the "primary duty" of priests (*Ministry and Life of Priests*, 4). In addition to his homilies at Mass and in other liturgies, a parish priest has frequent occasion to teach as he works with those preparing for various sacraments, speaks at religious education events for parishioners of all ages, writes articles and other pieces in parish bulletins, newsletters, and so forth.

- **Shepherding** A pastor has many leadership responsibilities that include caring for the physical and financial welfare of the parish's resources, as well as overseeing the work of the parish's staff and volunteers. All parish priests, whether they are pastors or not, exercise this responsibility by taking a leadership role in various committees and

FAITH ACTIVITY

Ministry in the New Testament
Look up each of the following passages and relate them to the ministerial orders in the Church or to various aspects of priestly ministry:
Matthew 18:18, 28:19–20;
Luke 22:17–20; John 20:21–23;
Acts 15:1–6; 1 Timothy 3:1–13.

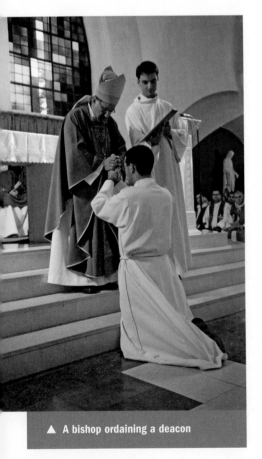

FAITH ACTIVITY

Conduct an Interview With a partner, interview a bishop, priest, or deacon about the day he was ordained and what he found most meaningful and moving about the liturgical celebration. Ask him what is most rewarding about this ministry today. Report your interview results to the class.

councils that every parish typically has. The priest shows moral leadership as well, both in the parish and in the local community, when he takes stands on important issues and works to achieve priorities that correspond to the Church's mission and the Gospel's vision of God's Reign.

- **Sanctifying** The priest's responsibility to lead his people to follow Christ and respond to the Holy Spirit is done primarily as he presides over prayer and celebrates the sacraments within the parish community. But he also accomplishes this ministry in other ways—through his offering of pastoral counsel and spiritual direction, by the witness of his own personal holiness, and by the many ways that he calls people to conversion.

The Ministry of Deacons The *Catechism*, quoting Vatican II, underlines that deacons are ordained "not unto priesthood, but unto the ministry[1]" (CCC, 1569). Their ordination is done through a sacramental act, but they are ordained to diaconal service rather than to priestly ministry. Deacons, like priests, depend on the bishop's pastoral authority as they exercise their ministries of word, worship, pastoral governance, and the service of charity and work on behalf of justice. In their ordination, they do not receive the ministerial priesthood but are called to a ministry of service for the good of the Church, under the direction of their bishop.

> We beseech you, Lord:
> look with favor upon this servant of yours
> who will minister at your holy altar
> and whom we now humbly dedicate to the office
>   of deacon.
>
> Send forth upon him, Lord, we pray, the Holy Spirit,
> that he may be strengthened
> by the gift of your sevenfold grace
> for the faithful carrying out of the work of the ministry.
>
> *From the Prayer of Consecration, Rite of Ordination of a Deacon, 21*

We can get a glimpse of the heart of a deacon's identity and mission by looking in the Acts of the Apostles at the story of the first deacon, Stephen (*6:1—7:60*). We see there that the ministry of the deacon was a response to certain needs that arose and were identified in the community. In order to meet those needs, the Apostles discerned candidates who were "men of good standing, full of the Spirit and of wisdom" (*Acts 6:3*). Prior to beginning their ministry, Stephen and the others chosen with him were first brought to the Apostles "who prayed and laid their hands on them" (*Acts 6:6*). Thereafter, in addition to his ministry of charity among the widows of the Greek-speaking Christians, Stephen preached the Good News of Jesus and "did great wonders and signs among the people" (*Acts 6:8*). When his ministry aroused the anger of certain

▲ A bishop ordaining a deacon

Jewish leaders, Stephen steadfastly continued to proclaim his faith in Jesus, eventually paying the price of his witness with his life and becoming the first martyr of the Church.

From this nucleus of the ministry of the first deacon, the Church across the centuries has experienced countless variations of the same essential elements: ordination at the hands of the bishop, a primary commitment to the ministry of service, and a proclamation of the Gospel through word and personal witness. In the next section we will consider in more detail how the order of deacons continues to grow and develop in our own day. However, it is helpful to remember its roots in the New Testament and the core dimensions of diaconal service that Stephen lived out.

GROUP TALK

1. What qualities and characteristics do you think a deacon should possess? Why?

2. What qualities and characteristics do you think a priest should possess? Why?

3. What qualities and characteristics do you think a bishop should possess? Why?

Who Can Ordain and Who Can Be Ordained

Only a bishop is invested with the authority to ordain a man to the three degrees of the sacrament—bishops, priests, and deacons. Ordinarily, in order to show that episcopal ordination involves entrance into the College of Bishops, at least three ordaining bishops confer the sacrament on a bishop-elect. Customarily, a single bishop does the ordination of priests and deacons, although there is nothing to prevent other bishops from assisting.

No one has a personal "right" to ordination. It always comes as a call from God, a grace from above. Church hierarchy alone has the responsibility and the right to discern who is called to receive the Sacrament of Holy Orders. In the Roman Catholic tradition, the decision to ordain only baptized men, not women, who have completed years of preparation is not the result of an arbitrary decision of the Pope. Rather, it is the result of prayerful discernment over many centuries, based on the example of Jesus himself, guided by the Holy Spirit, and done in humble obedience to the Lord's will for his Church. The rigorous care that is exercised about the suitability of candidates for Holy Orders is evidence of the prudence and great care with which the Church seeks to follow the Lord's command to find suitable workers for his harvest. (See *Matthew 9:35–37*.)

✓ Quick Check

1. What is apostolic succession?
2. What is the relationship between an individual bishop and the College of Bishops and the Pope?
3. What are three main ways priests act as coworkers with their bishops?
4. Who is able to confer the Sacrament of Holy Orders and who is able to receive it?

The Consecrated Life

Everyone baptized shares the call to follow Jesus in a life of holiness. We have seen that some of the faithful answer a call to ministry through Holy Orders, while others live out their call as members of the lay faithful and the common priesthood of all believers. Among both the ordained and the laity, there have been believers throughout history who have felt a particular desire to live out their discipleship by means of what is called the "consecrated life." The *Catechism* defines the consecrated life as the "state of life which is constituted by the profession of the evangelical counsels…" (*CCC*, 914).

Early on in the Church's existence, the eremitic (hermit's) life developed among those who chose to separate themselves from the world in a radical way. Some professed the three evangelical counsels of poverty, chastity, and obedience; and some did not. Also from the early centuries some followers of Christ chose to live consecrated lives as virgins and widows.

Today, when one speaks of the consecrated life, the most common are the religious life, secular institutes, and societies of apostolic life.

- **Religious Life:** This life includes religious women (sisters and nuns) and men (brothers and monks, some of whom are priests) who belong to a "religious institute," or religious "order" such as the Benedictines, Franciscans or Jesuits—to name a few. They follow a common rule of life under a superior and usually live in community. Members of a religious institute are required to make vows. A vow is a promise made to God freely concerning a possible and better good. The members of a religious institute pronounce public vows, which include poverty, chastity, and obedience.

- **Secular Institutes:** The *Catechism* describes these as "an institute of consecrated life in which the Christian faithful living in the world strive for the perfection of charity and work for the sanctification of the world especially from within[2]" (*CCC*, 928). Members of such groups "commit themselves to the evangelical counsels by sacred bonds and observe among themselves the communion and fellowship appropriate to their 'particular secular way of life'[3]" (929). For links to two secular institutes in the United States, The National Fraternity of the Secular Franciscans and the Third Order of Preachers, visit **www.harcourtreligion.com.**

- **Societies of Apostolic Life:** The *Code of Canon Law* (731.1) describes these groups in the following way: "Societies of apostolic life resemble institutes of consecrated life; their members, without religious vows, pursue the apostolic purpose proper to the society and, leading a life in common as brothers or sisters according to their proper manner of life, strive for the perfection of charity through the observance of the constitutions." In some of the constitutions of these institutions the members commit to embrace the evangelical counsels as well. The best known examples of these in the United States are Maryknoll and the Society of San Sulpice (Sulpicians).

FAITH ACTIVITY

Gifts in Community If your school, parish, or local hospital or Catholic University is staffed by a religious order, research what their particular charism is. Reflect on how their charism is visible in the life of the community. If not, research orders that may have been there in the past and reflect on how their charism has carried on.

In previous chapters, we have seen how each of the sacramental rituals is a kind of commitment statement that spells out the transformation required of those who participate in it. Sometimes, the connections between liturgy and life are fairly obvious; other times, the implications are subtle and require more careful examination. In the case of Holy Orders, the rites for ordaining bishops, priests, and deacons explicitly mention many of the ways that celebration of the sacrament is meant to transform the recipient.

Even the etymology of the word *ordination* makes it clear that this sacrament is about setting a person apart for a very specific ministerial role within the Church. The *Catechism* explains that in Roman antiquity the word *order* (*ordo*) designated an established governing body, and that the word *ordinatio* referred to the rite incorporating a person into a specific "order" within the Church (*CCC*, 1537–38). In addition to the order of bishops, priests, and deacons, other orders such as catechumens, virgins, spouses, and widows existed. The word *ordination* is used today to refer to only one sacrament. However, its root concept of being incorporated into a specific group, with designated functions in the Church, helps us to understand how the rite impacts the identity of the individual being ordained.

Bishop Daniel's Transformation

In the story at the beginning of the chapter, Bishop Daniel was keenly aware of how the celebration of an ordination liturgy changes a person's status in the Church. Most importantly, he knew that his ordination as a bishop was about an interior call for him to serve as an ever more faithful disciple of Jesus. One of the ways that he had been preparing himself spiritually for his new ministry was by reading the Rite of Ordination of a Bishop. One section in particular had struck him, a passage from the Homily (18) that the ordaining bishop would address to him before conferring the sacrament. It read, in part:

> The title of Bishop is one of service, not of honor, and therefore a Bishop should strive to benefit others rather than to lord it over them.

Daniel knew that in his new role as bishop many people would look up to him, show him signs of respect and honor, and regard him as one who exercised a very real authority over many people's lives. Yet, he also knew that if he was to be a sign of Christ to his people, he must excel in humility—not power—and lead by loving, serving, and caring for his flock, just as Jesus had. The magnitude of the challenges ahead made him very much aware of his humanity and how much he would need to rely on the Holy Spirit to guide him and to strengthen him.

Most Catholics only see their bishop when he makes a visit to their local parish for Confirmation or some other special celebration, or when they gather with people from other parishes on a diocesan-wide occasion. But the ministry of bishop involves a great deal more than visiting parishes and presiding at major celebrations. One of the chief responsibilities of a bishop is to nurture and support his coworkers—the priests, deacons, and lay ministers who carry out the day-to-day work of the Church. Since these are his key helpers, he must oversee their placement in ministerial assignments, that they are adequately prepared to carry out their ministries, and that they are supported, cared for and helped to grow in their ministries. A bishop also meets with many groups who help him to lead the diocese more effectively. Some of the most important of these groups are a Pastoral Council that advises him on the spiritual needs of the diocese, a Council of Priests who share his concerns for all aspects of the diocese at large, and a Finance Council that advises him on financial matters.

In addition to his responsibilities for the internal life of the diocese, a bishop must also relate to many others beyond the local Catholic community. He is involved in relationships with the leaders of other Christian denominations, as well as interfaith leaders. In order to promote Catholic values in society, a bishop must also be in contact with civic and political leaders. In that capacity he witnesses to Gospel values on behalf of the Church's social teachings, addressing a vast array of contemporary issues.

As a member of the College of Bishops, a bishop must also support and foster unity among his brother bishops in the national conference of bishops and in the worldwide episcopacy. He also relates in important ways with the Pope and his advisors in Rome, implementing their directives for the good of the Church, and entering into dialogue with various Vatican leaders to promote a spirit of communion among all of the local churches throughout the world.

Given the scope of a bishop's ministry, it is little wonder that Bishop Daniel was sobered by the responsibilities he was called to undertake at his ordination.

FAITH ACTIVITY

The Ministry of Bishops Read a recent issue of your diocesan newspaper or search your diocesan Web site to find examples of how your bishop is living out his ordination. Note in what ways he is leading others to transformation and conversion.

In the Person of Christ

One of the phrases frequently found in official Church documents is the reminder that ordained priests act "in the person of Christ." In an important Apostolic Exhortation on priestly formation (*I Will Give You Shepherds*), Pope John Paul II commented on the significance of the sacramental ordination of priests. It is, he said, an action of the Holy Spirit that joins them to Christ in a special way and that is the abiding source of the spiritual power of their ministry. He comments:

> In the Church and on behalf of the Church, priests are a sacramental representation of Jesus Christ...proclaiming his word, repeating his acts of forgiveness and his offer of salvation—particularly in baptism, penance and the Eucharist, showing his loving concern to the point of a total gift of self for the flock...In a word, priests exist and act in order to proclaim the Gospel to the world and to build up the Church in the name and person of Christ the head and shepherd.
>
> *I Will Give You Shepherds*, 15

Priests "exist and act," the Holy Father says, "in the name and person of Christ." These are very awesome words, and they remind us why sacraments are sometimes called "holy mysteries." The transformation of an ordinary human being through the Sacrament of Holy Orders into one who is a sacramental embodiment of Jesus Christ himself is truly an amazing aspect of our faith. Yet, this mystery of faith is lived out in very ordinary ways in the midst of the Church community. A parish priest's life is shaped decisively by the ministry he performs in Christ's name.

In the Prayer of Consecration for a priest, the bishop mentions that the priest's ministry touches the people he serves. They are:

- renewed in waters of rebirth

- nourished from the altar

- sinners reconciled

- sick raised up.

These phrases capture ever so briefly the joys of priestly ministry. It is a humbling yet exhilarating experience for a priest to be an agent of God's healing and forgiveness, standing in solidarity with people who look to him for comfort and courage, presiding at Eucharist, and preaching the Gospel.

A typical parish priest's day may start out with quiet prayer, followed by celebration of daily Mass for a handful of parishioners. His morning might include visits to the sick who are homebound or those in the hospital. He will offer them the Sacrament of Anointing, pray with them, hear their Confession and give them Holy Communion. He might also offer comfort to worried loved ones, or say a word of encouragement to exhausted spouse-caregivers, promising to have the parish's outreach ministers make contact to offer concrete support and assistance of various kinds. Later in the morning he might meet with a local ecumenical clergy group to discuss proposed common action in support of a local initiative on behalf of the poor, and lunch might be with a Catholic businessman, a parishioner, who has asked for advice on some troubling ethical issues at his office.

The parish priest's afternoon might be his first chance to work at his desk, answering correspondence, preparing remarks he will make in a few days to a high school religion class, and working on the agenda for the liturgy committee meeting the following evening. Later in the afternoon, two second graders will have appointments—one to make his First Confession, and the other who will come with his mother for an interview in preparation for his First Eucharist.

Dinner might be a hurried bite to eat alone in the Rectory, or perhaps a bit more leisurely meal with a family in the parish who want him to meet their visiting relatives from abroad. In any event, dinner cannot be too lengthy an affair, since his evening will involve perhaps a meeting with a parish committee or interviews in his office, meeting an engaged couple to prepare for their wedding, or counseling a young woman in a personal crisis who is asking where God is to be found in her life. If he is lucky, the priest will still have some energy when he gets home to read a chapter or two of a theology book he's wanted to catch up with, or perhaps read next Sunday's Scriptures and begin to think about what he will say in his homily. His day has been filled to the brim, but this typical parish priest will still need to end his day in prayer, reminding himself and thanking God that his greatest blessing has been to act "in the person of Christ" in so many different ways to all those whom he has encountered that day.

They come not to be served, but to serve.

We can learn so much about the ministry of those in Holy Orders by looking carefully at the text of the ritual in which they are ordained for service in the Church. From the instruction (homily) that is contained in the Rite of Ordination for Deacons, we can gain a very moving picture of the ministry for which their ordination prepares them.

> Strengthened by the gift of the Holy Spirit, they will help the Bishop and his priests in the ministry of the word, of the altar, and of charity, showing themselves to be servants of all. As ministers of the altar, they will proclaim the Gospel, prepare the sacrifice, and distribute the Lord's Body and Blood to the faithful. [They will] exhort believers and unbelievers alike and . . . instruct them in holy doctrine. They will preside over public prayer, administer baptism, assist at and bless marriages, bring Viaticum to the dying, and conduct funeral rites . . . they will perform works of charity in the name of the Bishop or pastor . . . you will recognize them as disciples of him who came not to be served, but to serve.

Rite of Ordination of a Deacon, 14

Deacons share in the Sacrament of Holy Orders, and their ordination calls them to important tasks of service in the Church. The Church currently has two kinds of deacons: *transitional* deacons who are on a path to priestly ordination and *permanent* deacons, who are not seeking priestly ordination. The Church's current discipline allows permanent deacons to be married if they are married at the time of their ordination; if they are single at that time, or if they are widowed after their ordination, they must remain single.

The bishops of the United States have been quick to act on the restoration of the permanent diaconate after the Vatican Council. At the present time, of the more than 30,000 permanent deacons throughout the world, more than a third of them minister in the United States. The ministry of deacons is dependent on the bishop whom they assist in the pastoral care of the local Church in various ways. The variety of ministries

FAITH ACTIVITY

Ministry in Your Parish With several classmates, research ordained and lay ministries in your parish. Visit the parish Web site, review a weekly bulletin, and possibly schedule an appointment with someone who works in your parish office. Find out the major parts of your parish priests' ministry, if you have a permanent deacon and what his ministry involves, and the role of the parish staff. Note which items you think are the most important and why.

in which permanent deacons serve is as broad as the life of the Church herself. Above all, theirs is a ministry of service—at the altar, as teachers, and in active works of charity. They serve in both full- and part-time positions, some as paid workers and some without monetary compensation. Many are married; some remain celibate. Permanent deacons are to be found in chancery offices, parishes, in hospital and prison chaplaincies, working in soup kitchens, and as teachers of theology.

In this section we have considered the commitments that the ordained undertake in their respective ministries of service. In the next section we will explore how the Church has reflected on the Sacrament of Holy Orders and how the ordained share in the priestly ministry of Christ himself.

Quick Check

1. What are the different roles a bishop has in his diocese?
2. What is meant by the phrase "in the person of Christ"?
3. How is a typical day in a parish priest's life a continuation of Christ's work?
4. What are the various aspects of the ministry of deacons?

GROUP TALK

1. Discuss the restored ministry of the permanent diaconate. What do you know about it, and why do you suppose the United States has so many more permanent deacons than other countries, even those with much larger Catholic populations?

2. Share a story of someone you know who is ordained. How has his life of dedication and holiness helped you live a life of holiness?

Ever Ancient, Ever New

The substance of our faith does not change. It comes to us as a gift of God, a divine revelation of truth that is not subject to change. However, as we have seen with each of the sacraments that we have studied, the Church is constantly deepening her understanding of the faith that has come down to us from the Apostles. Ritual forms in which we celebrate our faith in God have timeless, unchanging elements. And they also include expressions that develop and change over time. *What* the Church believes today may be the same as the faith of the Apostles; but *how* the Church understands and celebrates that faith has deepened and will continue to do so with the passage of time, as she strives to proclaim a living and ever-fresh Gospel to each successive generation.

In the renewal of the liturgy and revitalization of the ancient faith that was mandated by the Second Vatican Council, the bishops of the world wished to revitalize the way that the Church celebrates her ageless faith. The Council's stated aim was an *aggiornamento*, an updating of her life in order to bring the Gospel more effectively to contemporary people who search for meaning and truth to guide their lives. In order to do this, the bishops highlighted particular themes and gave new emphasis to certain perspectives that seemed to speak more effectively to people today.

We have noted already, for example, how the theme of the Paschal Mystery of Christ received renewed emphasis in the way that the liturgy and the sacraments are presented in the teaching of the Council. In similar fashion, the concept of the People of God was used very effectively in documents that reflected on the Church's nature and her mission in today's world. In this section we will learn about how the Vatican Council used the three linked concepts of priest-prophet-king to deepen its understanding of the Sacrament of Holy Orders.

Origins of the Priest-Prophet-King Theme

Old Testament The Old Testament links the three divine vocations of priest-prophet-king. An anointing marks each role as a consecration for mission.

Evidence for ritual anointings of priests for their mission is quite strong and appears early in the Old Testament. In the Book of Exodus, Moses gives direction for an ordination ritual to be used with Aaron and his descendants:

Now this is what you shall do to them to consecrate them, so that they may serve me as priests . . . You shall take the anointing-oil, and pour it on [Aaron's] head and anoint him . . . You shall then ordain Aaron and his sons.

Exodus 29:1, 7, 9

Similar passages describe the anointing of priests in the Books of Leviticus (*6:13; 8:12; 21:10*) and Numbers (*3:3*).

Prophets were also described as being anointed for their mission, as this text from 1 Kings 19:16 shows: "[The Lord said to Elijah] you shall anoint Elisha son of Shaphat of Abel-meholah as prophet in your place." More famous still is the passage from the Book of Isaiah describing his prophetic call, "The spirit of the Lord GOD is upon me, because the LORD has anointed me . . ." (*61:1*). Even the patriarchs were referred to as "anointed prophets" (*1 Chronicles 16:22; Psalm 105:15*). It is possible, however, that in the Old Testament the anointing of prophets was more of a metaphorical way of speaking about the divine authorization of their role than a reference to any physical ritual.

Clear evidence exists to show that kings in Israel were ritually anointed with oil. The First Book of Samuel describes how the prophet Samuel anointed David as king: "Then Samuel took the horn of oil, and anointed him in the presence of his brothers; and the spirit of the LORD came mightily upon David from that day forward" (*16:13*). The Old Testament also contains descriptions of the anointing of Saul (*1 Samuel 10:1*), Solomon (*1 Kings 1:39*), Jehu (*2 Kings 9:6*), Joash (*2 Kings 11:12*), and others.

FAITH ACTIVITY

Anointed Missions Identify organizations in your school that either already, or could present, opportunities for you and your fellow students to live out the roles of prophet, priest, and servant-leader. Consider how these roles are fulfilled in these organizations. Write a letter to your school newspaper or an e-mail to its Web site describing the opportunities that are available in your school.

New Testament The authors of the New Testament often used themes from the Old Testament as a way to explain to their communities that Jesus was the fulfillment of all that was foretold by the Scriptures. Other than the anointing by a woman in Bethany just prior to his death, there is no historical evidence that Jesus ever underwent any ritual anointing. Yet, his disciples freely used the metaphorical sense of anointing in describing him as the Anointed One who was priest, prophet, and king.

Only the Letter to the Hebrews (*3:1*) explicitly calls Jesus the High Priest. Here the author develops at great length the idea that Jesus has surpassed and summed up in his person all that the Old Testament priesthood foreshadowed. Although they do not specifically use the word "priest" as a title for Jesus, other New Testament authors refer to what Jesus did by describing his ministry in terms of priestly functions. They referenced such things as offering sacrifice, interceding on our behalf, expiating for our sins, and so forth.

We find in the New Testament explicit mention of Jesus a prophet, or rather, The Prophet. The Samaritan woman at the well says, "Sir, I see that you are a prophet" (*John 4:19*), and Jesus' disciples tell him that the people regard him as "one of the prophets" (*Matthew 16:14*). Even Jesus referred to himself as a prophet. (See *Matthew 13:57*; *Mark 6:4*; *Luke 4:24*.) In the Sermon on the Mount in Matthew 5—7, Jesus is presented as the greatest of all of the prophets, the one who has surpassed even Moses as the giver of the New Law.

When it comes to the term of king, the New Testament again shows some reticence about using this title in reference to Jesus, most likely because of the political overtones of the term. For the most part Jesus avoided using the title outright, though he did acknowledge it during his exchange with Pilate in John 18—19. In the minds of the Jewish people, however, the image of a shepherd-king who was to come, held great resonance. It was a reference to the reign of King David. So, by calling himself the Good Shepherd, Jesus was subtly but pointedly acknowledging that he was the king who would finally and definitively care for God's people.

GROUP TALK

Discuss the following in small groups.

1. What are some examples from Jesus' life of his being priest, prophet, and servant-king?

2. How did people of Jesus' day—his followers, those he healed, those who did not support him—react to Jesus in these roles?

3. What contemporary issues or concerns do you think are in most need of Christians living out their priestly, prophetic, and servant-leader roles?

Christian History Very early in the Church's history, the followers of Jesus were also called "anointed ones" or "Christians." (See *Acts 11:26*.) Soon the mission of Jesus' followers began to be discussed also in terms of the triad priest-prophet-king. We see an example of this in the writings of John Chrysostom (c. 347–407). Commenting on our being anointed and sealed in our Christian initiation, Chrysostom explains that God has made us "at once prophets and priests and kings, for . . . we have now not one of these dignities, but all three preeminently" (*Homily 3 on Second Corinthians*, 5). The use of this triad to describe those in ordained ministry does not appear in any significant way until the era of the Reformation, notably in the Council of Trent's teaching on priestly ordination, but also in the work of Protestant Reformers such as John Calvin. The first application of this framework to bishops does not appear in official Catholic teaching until the First Vatican Council in the 19th century.

The Priest-Prophet-King Theme at Vatican II

In our chapter on Baptism, we noted the prayer of anointing that uses this imagery in connection with every Christian. We discussed there the responsibilities that flow from our Baptism in light of those roles. In Chapter 2 of their important document on the nature of the Church (*Dogmatic Constitution on the Church*), the bishops at the Second Vatican Council used the framework of these same three roles to teach about the entire People of God. In Chapter 3, they used the triad to discuss the ministry of bishops and priests, and in Chapter 4, again they used the same threefold categories to talk about the mission of the laity.

By choosing to use the same threefold framework to discuss both the laity and the hierarchy, those in Orders are situated *within* the entire People of God, rather than being seen as set-apart. One can see the impact of this perspective in the way that the *Catechism* describes Holy Orders as one of the sacraments "at the service of communion" (CCC, 1211). Holy Orders, like the Sacrament of Matrimony, is thus presented as a ministry of service, a particular calling within the larger mystery of the Church, and not as if those in Holy Orders were the ones to whom the Church truly belongs.

One might ask whether describing both the laity and the ordained as a "priestly" people causes confusion. However, Church teaching has been clear and consistent in recognizing that while both the laity and the ordained share in Christ's priestly identity, they do so in distinctly different ways. The priesthood of the faithful and the ministerial priesthood of the ordained "differ from one another in essence and not only in degree" (*Dogmatic Constitution on the Church*, 10). The bishops go on in the same paragraph to explain further the way that each of these share in the one priesthood of Christ.

> The ministerial priest, by the sacred power he enjoys, teaches and rules the priestly people; acting in the person of Christ, he makes present the eucharistic sacrifice, and offers it to God in the name of all the people. But the faithful, in virtue of their royal priesthood, join in the offering of the Eucharist. They likewise exercise that priesthood in receiving the sacraments, in prayer and thanksgiving, in the witness of a holy life, and by self-denial and active charity.

Dogmatic Constitution on the Church, 11

Vatican II's use of this three-fold theme has now firmly rooted the imagery of priest-prophet-king in our understanding of the meaning of Holy Orders: "Bishops, therefore, with their helpers, the priests and deacons, have taken up the service of the community, presiding in place of God over the flock, whose shepherds they are, as teachers for doctrine, priests for sacred worship, and ministers for governing" (*Dogmatic Constitution on the Church*, 20). In the Council's documents on the episcopal office (*Ministry and Life of Priests*) and on the priesthood (*Pastoral Office of Bishops*), the same framework is again used. One significant evolution in the Council's use of this imagery was their description of the royal function in terms of both governance and pastoral ministry. Thus, the bishops (and their coworkers) act in the person not only of Christ the King but also Christ the Good Shepherd. By joining the two concepts of king and shepherd, Vatican II demonstrated that it was above all a *pastoral* Council, preoccupied with the pastoral effectiveness of those who minister in the person of Christ the Good Shepherd.

FAITH ACTIVITY

Your Local Bishop Every bishop has a Coat of Arms and motto for his ministry. Look at your diocesan Web site to find out what your bishop chose as his Coat of Arms and motto for his ministry.

GROUP TALK

The example of the Good Shepherd is one who came not to be served but to serve, and to seek out the lost.

1. The bishops at Vatican II expanded the teaching about the role of the bishop as king to include the biblical image of shepherd. Talk about why you think they did this and how it is significant.

2. Discuss what priority serving those in need and seeking the lost has in your parish and school. How does the parish community share in this ministry with the ordained?

Quick Check

1. How does the Old Testament link anointing with images of priests, prophets, and kings?
2. How does the New Testament link the images of priest, prophet, and king with Jesus?
3. Why were the followers of Jesus from very early on described as sharing in the priestly, prophetic, and royal dimensions of his ministry?
4. What is the importance of using the priest-prophet-king theme in discussing ordained ministry?

›Person of Faith

Saint Lawrence (c. 225?–258)

Precise details about the lives of the early saints are sometimes hard to come by, since biographers of the Church's early centuries seemed to be not as concerned about historical accuracy as those of today. They often wove together facts, stories, and legends that fit what was known about a saint. Their work tended to be more to impress, inspire devotion, and foster imitation than to describe precise details of a saint's life. This style of writing is sometimes at odds with our modern sensibilities. However, many such stories of the saints capture a genuine truth about their holiness and faith, even if some details may be historically uncertain or inaccurate.

In the case of Saint Lawrence, one of the most famous saints of the Roman Church, we have more reason to believe in the accuracy of details about his martyrdom than is the case with many others. We do not know much about his early life, other than that he was born in Huesca, Spain, in the year A.D. 225. We know that later he was one of the seven archdeacons of the church in Rome during the pontificate of Pope Sixtus II (257–258). According to the historical record, Sixtus had instructed Lawrence in the Christian faith before he became bishop of Rome, and it was after his ordination in 257 that Sixtus II made Lawrence a deacon and appointed him to oversee the temporal assets of the Roman Church. During this period of the Church's history, men often remained deacons for their entire lives, with no aspirations to the priesthood. Their ministry was focused especially on the works of charity, caring for the needs of the poor and the sick. In both prestige and influence, deacons held a much more significant position in the Christian community in Rome than is generally the case today.

In the year 257, the Roman Emperor Valerian unleashed a persecution against the Christians, seizing the properties of many wealthy nobles and putting bishops and priests to death. Among those captured in this persecution were Pope Sixtus II and several of the deacons who served with him. On August 6, 258, Sixtus and his fellow deacons were crucified. A pious legend reports that Lawrence met the Pope on the way to his death, and Sixtus prophesied that Lawrence would join him in glory four days later. More reliably, Saint Ambrose reports that the prefect of Rome demanded of Lawrence that he turn over to the Emperor the riches of the Church. Lawrence asked for three days' time so that he could gather those riches together. When his request was granted, he worked feverishly over the next three days distributing to the poor of Rome as many of the riches of the Church as he was able in order to prevent them from being seized. The story is then embellished by accounts that describe him confronting the Emperor, accompanied by a horde of the poor and lame of the city. When Valerian demanded the wealth of the Church, Lawrence reputedly pointed to the miserable crowd that accompanied him and said, "Here are the riches of the Church." This so infuriated the Emperor that he ordered Lawrence burned to death on the spot. Legend says that he was placed on an iron grill, and that as the flames consumed his body he told his persecutors to turn him over, since he was done on one side. His death is marked on August 10, which is his feast day. He was buried in one of the catacombs on the Via Tiburtina, and less than a century later Constantine built a small chapel over his grave. A church was built there by Pope Pelagius II in the sixth century. In the thirteenth century, Pope Honorius III constructed the basilica of San Lorenzo that still stands today. Another church in Rome, San Lorenzo in Panisperna, is built over the place where his martyrdom is purported to have taken place.

Saint Lawrence is one of the few martyrs and saints whose names are included in the Roman Canon (today's Eucharistic Prayer 1). Several historical records attest to his martyrdom and substantiate great devotion to him from the period shortly after his death. He remains today a patron of the city of Rome and is still venerated as an example of selfless charity and devotion to the poor and afflicted. Like Saint Stephen, one of the first deacons and the Church's first martyr (whose death is described in Chapter 7 of the Acts of the Apostles), Saint Lawrence stands as an inspiring example for deacons of every age who spend their lives in service of others.

REFLECT

1. How is the life of Saint Lawrence associated with the Sacrament of Holy Orders?

2. Name some deacons or other ordained people you have known or know about. How did their lives model the Sacrament of Holy Orders? Which ordained people can you most identify with as role models?

3. How does Saint Lawrence serve as an example for our lives?

Prayer

From the *Mass of Saint Laurence, Old Sarum Rite Missal, 1998,* Saint Hilarion Press

With the robe of joyfulness, alleluya,
Our Lord hath this day clothed His soldier, Laurence.
May Thy faithful's joyous assemblage clap their hands
More cheerfully than they have heretofore.
Today the noble martyr offered pleasing sacrifice to God,
Today he, being grievously tested,
Endured unto the end the torment of his fire;
And shrank not from offering his limbs to punishments most grievous.
Before the ruler he is summoned,
And settlement is made upon the Church's hidden holdings.
But he by words enticing is unmoved, and is unshaken
By the torments of the ruler's avarice.
Valerian is laughed to scorn,
And the Levite's liberal hand,
When he is asked for payments,
Giveth to the gathered poor.
For he was their minister of charity,
Giving them abundance from his means.
Therefore the prefect is enraged,
And a glowing bed made ready.
The torment-bearing instrument,
The gridiron of his suffering,
Roasteth his very viscera,
But he laugheth it to scorn.
The martyr sweateth in his agony,
In hopes of crown and recompense
Which is allotted those with faith,
Who struggle for the sake of Christ.
The court of heaven rejoiceth
For his warfare-waging,
For he hath prevailed this day
Against the lackeys of wickedness.
That we, then, may attain the gift of life,
By this our patron, be glad, O our choir,
Singing in the church upon his feast-day
A joyful alleluia.

Study Guide

▶Check Understanding

1. Describe how Jesus' actions established the tradition of calling and sending forth leaders for the Church.

2. Name the essential parts of the Sacrament of Holy Orders.

3. Discuss elements of the ritual of ordination that have changed over time.

4. Highlight what elements all three Ordination Rites (bishop, priest, deacon) have in common.

5. Define *apostolic succession*.

6. Explain the relationship between an individual bishop and the College of Bishops and the Pope.

7. List the three overarching ways priests act as co-workers with their bishops.

8. Recall who is able to confer the Sacrament of Holy Orders and who is able to receive it.

9. Summarize the different roles a bishop has in his diocese.

10. Explain what is meant by the phrase "in the person of Christ."

11. Give examples to show how a day in a parish priest's life is a continuation of Christ's work.

12. Describe the various aspects of the ministry of deacons.

13. Trace the Old Testament background of the linkage of anointing with images of priests, prophets, and kings.

14. Highlight the New Testament linkage of the image of priest, prophet, and king with Jesus.

15. Explain why the followers of Jesus very early on were described as sharing in the priestly, prophetic, and royal dimensions of his ministry.

16. Summarize the importance of using the priest-prophet-king theme in discussing ordained ministry.

▶Apply and Develop

17. The *Constitution on the Sacred Liturgy* says the aim above all else in the liturgical reform should be the full, conscious, and active participation of all the faithful in the celebration. Write an essay evaluating how well you believe the revised Ordination Rites accomplish this aim.

18. Choose either the Rite of Ordination for a bishop, priest, or deacon. Write an essay showing how the prayers and rituals of the rite reflect the ministry of that order.

19. The *Catechism,* 1569, says that the "imposition of hands [of deacons is] 'not unto the priesthood, but unto the ministry.'"[4] Explain what this means by comparing and contrasting the ministry of deacons with that of bishops and priests.

20. Imagine you've been asked to give a presentation to your bishop and the priests and deacons of your diocese. Your purpose is to give them concrete suggestions on how they could help people your age who are searching for meaning and truth. Be sure to make connections to stated roles and ministries of bishops, priests, and deacons.

▶Key Words

See pages noted for contextual explanations of these important faith terms.

aggiornamento (p. 209)

apostolic succession (p. 197)

cathedra (p. 190)

consecrated life (p. 202)

crosier (p. 190)

major orders (p. 193)

minor orders (p. 193)

miter (p. 190)

permanent deacon (p. 207)

presbyterium (p. 199)

secular institutes (p. 202)

Society of Apostolic Life (p. 202)

transitional deacon (p. 207)

Jesus said, "So they are no longer two, but one flesh. Therefore what God has joined together, let no one separate."

Matthew 19:6

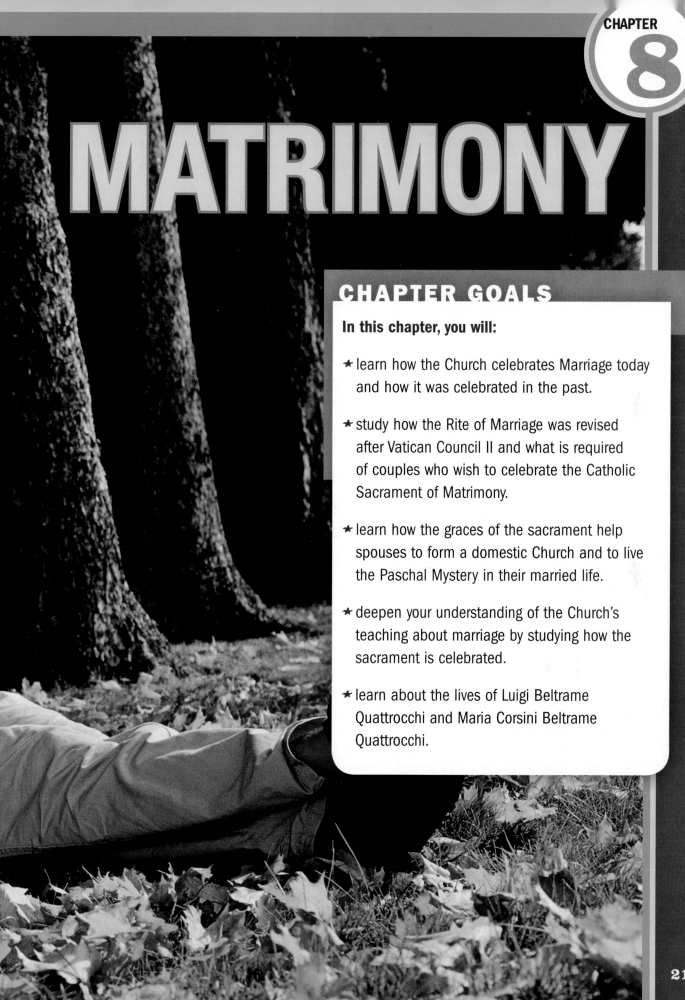

MATRIMONY

CHAPTER GOALS

In this chapter, you will:

★ learn how the Church celebrates Marriage today and how it was celebrated in the past.

★ study how the Rite of Marriage was revised after Vatican Council II and what is required of couples who wish to celebrate the Catholic Sacrament of Matrimony.

★ learn how the graces of the sacrament help spouses to form a domestic Church and to live the Paschal Mystery in their married life.

★ deepen your understanding of the Church's teaching about marriage by studying how the sacrament is celebrated.

★ learn about the lives of Luigi Beltrame Quattrocchi and Maria Corsini Beltrame Quattrocchi.

Hoa and Bill's Story

Hoa's parents, who were refugees from Vietnam, had brought her to this country when she was only a baby. The deep Catholic faith that sustained them during periods of active persecution in Vietnam—and later in their flight to freedom in the United States—was at the center of the family values that they passed on to Hoa. She, in turn, genuinely practiced her Catholicism as she grew up and later went off to college. After dating a number of young men who were not church-goers, Hoa was quite relieved when she finally met Bill, an active Catholic who placed a lot of importance on his faith.

Hoa was raised in the United States nearly her whole life. Yet, she was also thoroughly immersed in Vietnamese family and cultural values. These values were sometimes starkly different from Bill's expectations regarding married life. But the extra effort required to communicate and develop mutual understanding of one another's viewpoints had strengthened their relationship. They approached their upcoming marriage with confidence and a deep peace.

Hoa and Bill had taken Father Jennings' suggestion to welcome their guests at the church door as a couple, rather than waiting apart in sacristy or parlor. It made sense to them to do this together—to act as hosts extending hospitality to their guests, right from the start. Since Hoa's father was deceased, they had also agreed to depart from the customary entrance of bridesmaids and bride with her father, in favor of a more liturgical beginning to the celebration.

When everyone was ready, Father Jennings greeted the guests warmly and encouraged them to participate fully in the celebration. Then he walked to the back of the church where both bride and groom were waiting at the door with their families and the rest of the wedding party. After Father Jennings greeted Hoa and Bill with words of welcome and encouragement, the processional music began, and a cross-bearer, followed by acolytes carrying candles, started down the aisle. Others followed in procession—lectors, the two witnesses, and Father Jennings. Behind him came Hoa and Bill with their families. As they reached the sanctuary steps, the families shared hugs and well wishes. Then the bride and groom entered the sanctuary with Father Jennings.

The traditional Vietnamese marriage rituals are non-Christian, so Hoa and Bill left those until the reception. They had spent a considerable amount of time with Father Jennings to understand the Catholic marriage ceremony and the choices they could make among the prayers and readings available. They wanted to be certain that every aspect of the celebration reflected the love that they knew had come to them as a gift of God. As they listened intently to the Scripture readings, Hoa and Bill both sensed the sacredness of the moment they were sharing. They probably would not have expressed it in this way, but they both recognized that God was speaking to them at that very moment, and they knew that something deep was happening within them that would change their lives forever.

As the Liturgy of the Word concluded with Father Jennings' homily, he called Hoa and Bill forward, along with their two witnesses. After making introductory remarks, he questioned Hoa and Bill about their freedom in making this choice, about their faithfulness to each other, and their willingness to accept children and raise them in the church. Then he invited them to join hands and exchange their vows. Father Jennings received their consent with the reminder that what God had joined must never be divided.

The blessing and exchange of rings happened next, followed by the General Intercessions. The Mass continued as usual then, with the addition of the Nuptial Blessing after the Our Father.

GROUP TALK

Compare the marriage ritual of Hoa and Bill to weddings that you have attended. What are the similarities? What are the differences?

The Church Celebrates a Sign of God's Love

The Church taught solemnly at the Council of Trent that, "the sacraments of the new law . . . were all instituted by Jesus Christ our Lord[1]" (CCC, 1114). However, understanding in what sense Christ instituted each of the seven sacraments is not a simple matter. It would be a misunderstanding of the historical record to suggest, for example, that Jesus handed to the Apostles a comprehensive set of detailed instructions regarding exactly how these seven rituals—now called sacraments—should be celebrated in the Church after his death and Resurrection. Similarly, it would be wrong to say that Jesus simply left it up to the Church to devise rituals to remember him and continue his work.

As the *Catechism* explains, a much more complex interaction was at work. It involved the historical ministry of Jesus and his explicit commands, the abiding presence of the Holy Spirit who guides the Church throughout history, and the gradual discernment of the Church regarding how to remain faithful to the Lord's saving work in word and sacrament.

> The mysteries of Christ's life are the foundations of what he would henceforth dispense in the sacraments, through the ministers of his Church, for 'what was visible in our Savior has passed over into his mysteries.'[2] . . . [T]he Church, by the power of the Spirit who guides her 'into all truth,' has gradually recognized this treasure received from Christ and, as the faithful steward of God's mysteries, has determined its 'dispensation.'[3] Thus the Church has discerned over the centuries that among liturgical celebrations there are seven that are, in the strict sense of the term, sacraments instituted by the Lord.
>
> *Catechism of the Catholic Church, 1115, 1117*

We have seen that for some sacraments, for example, Baptism and Eucharist, the very first generation of disciples recognized the Lord's command to continue his saving work in and through specific rituals whose outlines have changed very little across the centuries. It is quite a different story when one studies the history of the Sacrament of Matrimony, one of the two Sacraments at the Service of Communion.

GROUP TALK

1. How does the Church continue through the sacraments Jesus' work of welcoming, feeding, forgiving, healing, and serving?

2. How does each of the sacraments help us remain faithful to Christ and his mission and work?

3. How has your attitude toward participating in the sacraments changed during this course?

Changing Forms, but an Unchanging Bond of Love

The Gospels record how Jesus' presence sanctified the wedding at Cana and how he taught about the sanctity of marriage on more than one occasion. (See *John 2:1–11; Matthew 5:27–32; 19:3–12*.) Likewise, Saint Paul frequently taught about marriage, recognizing that it must be made part of God's saving plan for believers. In one very famous passage, he even described marriage as a mystery, or sacrament, of Christ's love for the Church. (See *Ephesians 5:32*.)

We can find virtually no historical evidence from the earliest centuries of any special rituals used by the Christian Church as part of what we today would call a marriage ceremony. Indeed, in the earliest Christian centuries, spouses were married according to the prevailing civil customs. When Christians married in this way, they were "married in the Lord." Many such marriages happened in the home. The absence of historical records does not mean, however, that the Church was not involved in forming prayers for those who wished their civil marriage to receive God's blessing.

Gradually, we do find historical evidence indicating that the Church "discerned over the centuries" the value and even importance of surrounding civil marriage with sacred ritual (*CCC*, 1117). The first such evidence of prayers and blessings, specifically on the occasion of weddings, dates from as early as the fourth century.

By the seventh and eighth centuries we have records of the exchange of consent happening in the presence of an official of the Church and of Mass prayers on the occasion of marriages. Eventually, as the Church in the Middle Ages assumed many of the functions previously done by civil society, the witnessing and recording of marriages themselves were a regular part of the Church's responsibility.

By the start of the second millennium, the Church was increasingly involved in the celebration of marriages. Church authorities regulated many of its legal aspects. A number of different marriage rituals developed in various regions, and a significant degree of diversity tied to local customs prevailed.

As late as the *Roman Ritual* published in 1614, after the Council of Trent, there was room still for local customs to be incorporated into the celebration of marriage. However, the rite found in the *Roman Ritual* of 1614 became the standard that was used, for the most part, right up until the reform of the Second Vatican Council.

Reform and Renewal

A major reform of the Rite of Marriage was published in 1969. Many of its changes parallel emphases and adaptations made in the other revised rites.

- For example, the previous Rite of Marriage placed the exchange of consent between the couple before the introductory rite. Now, as with the other sacramental rites, the marriage liturgy happens following the Liturgy of the Word.

- In addition, the new rite contains a great many options to choose from in all of the important prayer texts, including the presider's Mass prayers as well as each of the segments of the marriage rite itself.

- The lectionary also offers a much richer collection of scriptural texts that show the breadth of the Church's reflection on the mystery of Matrimony across the scriptural era. This encourages the couple's active participation by giving them the chance to make the selection among these many options.

In 1990, the Vatican released a slightly revised second edition of the Rite of Marriage. It contained minor changes in some of the texts and ritual actions, but did not depart in any significant way from the basic ritual structure of the earlier edition.

FAITH ACTIVITY

Conduct an Interview Interview a Catholic couple about how their wedding was celebrated. Then write a brief description comparing it to Hoa and Bill's ceremony described in this chapter. Note what elements you see as particularly meaningful.

Different Rites One of the most significant changes in the post-Vatican II ritual is the creation of different rites for use in different circumstances: one for the marriage of two Catholics, another for the marriage between a Catholic and a baptized Christian, and a third for marriage between a Catholic and an unbaptized person.

Only the Marriage between two baptized persons is considered sacramental, since an unbaptized person is not capable of receiving a sacrament. The revised ritual provides a Rite for Marriage to take place within a Mass, as well as a separate Rite for Marriage outside of the Mass, but with a Liturgy of the Word. For pastoral reasons, a marriage within a Mass is usually recommended only between two Catholics, for it highlights the connection of all the sacraments to the Paschal Mystery. A Marriage within Mass between a Catholic and a baptized non-Catholic is only permitted when the bishop allows, and Communion is not given to the non-Catholic party. All of these rites, however, are full, rich liturgical experiences meant to be celebrated in a church in the midst of the assembly.

Prior to Vatican II, only marriages between two Catholics were allowed a full church wedding, while other "mixed marriages" were done with only minimal ritual in a private ceremony, apart from the church. Now, current discipline requires that every Catholic wedding be performed in a church, unless there is a compelling pastoral reason for the bishop to make an exception to this rule. Also, with a Church dispensation, Catholics may be married in a non-Catholic church and still have the marriage recognized by the Catholic Church as valid. While this option is not encouraged for Catholics, it does meet the pastoral realities of some couples where the non-Catholic spouse is resistant to the marriage taking place in the Catholic Church.

FAITH ACTIVITY

Popular Customs In small groups, make a list of some of the popular customs associated with celebrating marriages in our culture. Divide them into two columns: those with religious significance and those with no particular religious meaning. Discuss your lists and identify those you find most meaningful.

✓ Quick Check

1. How did Jesus show his desire to sanctify marriage as a sacrament?
2. How was marriage celebrated between Christians in the early centuries?
3. What is the earliest historical evidence of how the Church celebrated the religious dimension of marriage?
4. What were the major changes in the Rite of Marriage after Vatican II?

Preparing to Celebrate the Sacrament

The actual Marriage ritual is surprising in its simplicity. But a careful examination of what happens in that ritual reveals that it is a very powerful expression of the requirements of those who wish to celebrate a sacramental union.

Celebrating the Sacrament During Mass	
Entrance Rite	Procession to the Altar
Liturgy of the Word	Old Testament Reading Psalm Response New Testament Reading Gospel Proclamation Homily
Rite of Marriage	Introductory Remarks Questions of the Couple Exchange of Consent Blessing & Exchange of Rings General Intercessions
Liturgy of the Eucharist	Preparation of Altar & Gifts Eucharistic Prayer Our Father Nuptial Blessing Sign of Peace Communion Prayer After Communion
Concluding Rite	Solemn Blessing Dismissal

The questions asked by the priest clearly indicate for us what is expected of the couple:

> N. and N., have you come here freely and without reservation to give yourself to each other in marriage?
>
> Will you love and honor each other as man and wife for the rest of your lives?
>
> Will you accept children lovingly from God, and bring them up according to the law of Christ and his Church?

Rite of Marriage, 24

The words of the consent given, or vows exchanged, by the couple also highlight some important elements of a Christian Marriage.

> I, N., take you, N., to be my wife/husband.
> I promise to be true to you
> in good times and in bad,
> in sickness and in health.
> I will love you and honor you
> all the days of my life.

Rite of Marriage, 25

Connecting the Rite and Symbol to Everyday Life

Reflect on the following questions.

· Why do you think the Liturgy of the Word comes before the consent to marry in the Marriage ritual? What does this say about the role of Scripture in married life?

· Discuss the questions that the priest asks of a couple prior to their exchange of vows. Are there any other questions you feel might be added in today's world?

· What are some practical ways, in the sense of caring, that the vows are lived out in daily life?

· How can you be true to those who mean the most to you? How do you honor your family? In what ways can you support family and friends through difficulties?

So, from the text of the Rite, we see that the Church understands that marriage must include these elements:

- the couple's consent must be freely given and unconditional

- they must intend to enter into a communion of life and love with each other in a way that is mutual and definitive

- they must intend to be faithful to each other in an exclusive relationship

- they must be open to the gift of children, should God so bless them; the Catholic party must promise to share his or her faith with the children by having them baptized and raising them Catholic.

Properly Disposed

As we have seen in previous chapters, Catholics who participate in the sacraments are expected to be properly disposed and well prepared in order that they participate fully and authentically in the ritual. We have seen earlier that this was an important concern of the bishops at the Vatican Council as they formulated the guidelines contained in the *Constitution on the Sacred Liturgy.*

Pastoral practice generally identifies certain minimum requirements for receiving a sacrament, as well as the fuller and richer developmental and faith characteristics that promote a more fruitful reception of the sacrament. For example, the Catholic Church emphasizes the communal and public nature of the marriage commitment, which is why marriages happen before the Church's minister and two witnesses, and ordinarily as part of a gathering of the Church community. But the ultimate goal when celebrating a wedding is much more than meeting these bare minimum requirements. The Church truly desires that couples have the proper attitudes of mind and heart so that they are ready to receive as fully as possible the graces of the Sacrament of Matrimony.

Well Prepared

Catholics see marriage as a sacred reality, something given to humanity by God himself at creation, both to enrich the couple through their mutual love and to bring offspring into the world by the sharing of their love. We also know that Jesus raised marriage to the special dignity of a sacrament—by making it a sign that reminds us of the loving union that exists between him and his Church. In order to help couples understand just what a gift of God's grace a Christian Marriage is meant to be, the Church offers multiple opportunities to prepare for this sacrament.

Remote Preparation The most basic preparation for marriage happens within a Christian family, within a faith-filled household. By virtue of one's life in a family where parents model what it means to live as disciples of Jesus—where spouses reverence and nourish each other in ways that allow the grace of married love to flourish between them—children naturally absorb what the Sacrament of Matrimony is all about. They learn how one ought to live the sacrament within the context of faith. When parents make their home a place of faith, of love, and of Christian service, children are taught how to live as disciples of Jesus in the ordinary ways of everyday life. When parents introduce their children to family prayer, reading of the Scriptures, caring for those less fortunate, training children in virtue and in

healthy attitudes toward the body and human sexuality—all of these contribute to forming attitudes of mind and heart that ultimately make children better prepared for a successful Christian Marriage.

Remote preparation for marriage also takes place during catechetical instruction. When young people learn the basic truths of their faith and receive moral formation in light of the Ten Commandments and the Beatitudes, they are being gradually prepared to approach marriage as faith-filled young adults. All aspects of religious education and practice as we grow toward adulthood contribute in a real way to helping us prepare to live our life's vocation in Marriage—or in whatever other state God calls us to live—as faithful disciples of Jesus. Even this course that you are taking now on the sacraments is helping you to understand better many aspects of your faith that will allow you to participate in the sacraments in a more fruitful and grace-filled manner.

Immediate Preparation When a couple gets engaged and approaches their pastor about being married in the Catholic Church, their immediate preparation for the sacrament begins. Certain routine formalities must be met, such as obtaining a civil wedding license, getting copies of Baptism certificates, and filling out other paperwork required by Church law.

In addition to these more administrative-type marriage requirements, a vitally important spiritual preparation is involved. Most dioceses and parishes have guidelines in place for this type of preparation. A number of programs available—such as Engaged Encounter, Pre-Cana, Foccus, Sponsor Couple, and others—provide a structure allowing couples to explore many important topics that contribute to marital success. Typical among these topics include consideration of couple communications, finances in marriage, in-laws, parenting, natural family planning, couple spirituality, as well as other issues. Frequently parishes provide sponsoring couples, married couples from the parish, who support and facilitate the preparation of engaged couples for marriage. Another important part of marriage preparation is preparing for the ceremony. The ritual for marriage has many options of texts, readings, music, and so forth from which the couple can choose; and when this is done with an attitude of faith, it can be very spiritually rewarding.

FAITH ACTIVITY

Local Practice Find out how couples are prepared for marriage in your parish. In a group, compare notes on any differences in approach and discuss what you think are the strong/weak points. If you were asked to suggest additional requirements, what might those be?

A Covenant Relationship

Because of the Catholic understanding of Marriage as a rite and sacrament, preparation in the Church addresses our theological and spiritual understandings of marriage as well. One of the most basic of these is that marriage is a covenant, a sacred contract between two persons, in which Christ becomes present to the spouses and in their love relationship in a very special way. Matrimony is a sacrament because it is a sign of Christ's presence and saving grace in the lives of Christian spouses.

The Scriptures are filled with stories about covenant relationships between God and those whom he called to enter into an intimate relationship of love with him. The names of Noah, Abraham, Moses, and many of the prophets are connected to stories of God's gracious initiative, offering to enter into a protective relationship with his people, if only the people will promise in return to be faithful to him and him alone. The Old Testament even uses the image of the marriage relationship to explain something of the intensity and intimacy of the covenant relationship that God wishes to have with us. The Book of Hosea is a prime example of this.

Jesus, of course, gave us the fullest meaning of what covenant love is all about when he established the new covenant. Just as he raised the meaning of covenant to a new level by his sacrificial death and life-giving Resurrection, so he has raised the natural meaning of marriage to a supernatural significance. This is why the Church recognizes it as one of the seven sacraments and teaches that marriage is based on the consent of both parties who form a covenant of faithful and fruitful love by choosing to give themselves to each other mutually and definitively.

The natural meaning of marriage is written into human nature itself. It is sometimes discussed in terms of the natural law intended by the Creator that governs how marriage should be lived by every human being. Marriage preparation programs typically cover these natural-law aspects of Church teaching, as well as some of our understandings of marriage that are specifically part of our Catholic faith. Among these are the following:

- God created humans to be in a male-female relationship and union of love, a union that is the most basic form of human communion. In that context sexuality is seen as a gift of God and as intrinsic to our dignity as human persons.

- Marriage is meant by God to be an exclusive relationship; polygamy is not part of God's plan. Adultery and open marriages are also contrary to God's law and a grave offense against the dignity of marriage. Chastity, modeled by Christ himself, is an obligation of every person, whatever his or her state in life.

- Marriage is a permanent commitment. The marriage between two Christians forms a spiritual bond that is indissoluble. Divorce is not permitted, and those who divorce and remarry without a Church annulment live an imperfect communion with God's law. As such, they are not permitted to share in the Eucharist, although they are still members of the Church and are encouraged to participate in every other way possible in the Church's life.

- Spouses must be open to the gift of fertility if God wishes to bless them with children. That is why the Church teaches that spouses may not use any artificial means of birth control, even if the couple's intentions, such as the responsible regulation of births, are legitimate.

- As a sacrament, Matrimony gives to spouses the grace to love each other with a measure of Christ's love. Their human love is sanctified, or made holy, by Christ's presence. The sacramental graces of marriage strengthen the spouses' indissoluble unity and help them on their spiritual journey toward heaven.

GROUP TALK

1. How do the Church's teachings on marriage support and enlarge upon the teachings of the dignity of the person?

2. Discuss some specific ways that our culture gives us messages that do not support the indissolubility of marriage. How can we promote the "now and forever" aspect of Christian Marriage?

3. In various parts of the world, polygamy is considered a legitimate form of marriage. Discuss the issues that are raised when a person in that culture converts to Catholicism and wishes to be "married in the Church."

Mixed Marriages This refers to a Catholic marrying a baptized non-Catholic, and not to interracial marriages as the phrase is so often used. If a Catholic is marrying a baptized non-Catholic, special permission to do so must be granted by the bishop; the Catholic party must promise to have the children baptized and raised Catholic. This requirement is usually the couple's first introduction to the challenges posed by a mixed marriage. When a Catholic marries a non-baptized person, the marriage is one with a disparity of cult. Special dispensation is required.

Although there are many examples of very successful mixed marriages, it is important to recognize that such unions inevitably come with added challenges. Marriage is such an intimate sharing of a couple's lives that it can be problematic when a spouse does not share one's deeply held religious convictions. In addition, the practical difficulties are multiplied when it comes to questions of church attendance, religious formation for children, and so forth. Couples in mixed marriages need to especially work to foster communication, understanding, and respect for each other's religious values and viewpoints. During the preparation process, supplemental resources often are offered to acquaint the non-Catholic party with the basic beliefs and practices of their Catholic spouse. The Catholic party is usually encouraged to meet with their partner's minister as well, in order to become more familiar with the religious background and values of their future spouse.

GROUP TALK

Catholics today are just as likely to marry someone who is not Catholic as they are to marry a Catholic.

1. If you were to marry, how important would it be to you to marry someone with a faith similar to yours?

2. If you were to marry, what values do you see yourself bringing to the marriage based upon your faith?

☑ Quick Check

1. What are the main parts of the Rite of Marriage celebrated during Mass?
2. What questions are asked of the couple before they give their consent to be married?
3. What is meant by remote and immediate preparation for marriage?
4. What is the importance of covenant to our understanding of Christian Marriage?

Matrimony 231

A Commitment to Faith-Filled Love

Throughout this book, we have seen that participation in the liturgy of a sacrament carries with it very specific responsibilities or commitments for how one must live life in the world. The sacraments are about the transformation of our natural selves into graced selves. In other words, they celebrate our conversion to Christ, our ongoing transformation into progressively more faithful disciples of Jesus and members of his Body, the Church.

In some instances we have seen that the sacrament calls for a very broad and all-encompassing response to discipleship, as is the case with Baptism. In other cases the sacrament celebrates a very specific, focused way of living our faith, such as in the Anointing of the Sick. Matrimony is one of the sacraments whose ritual transforms us in a particular fashion. Even in a secular setting, marriage is recognized as an event that changes two people. Civil society grants all sorts of legal rights and protections to people once they are married—rights and protections that do not exist prior to the marriage ceremony. There is a similar kind of new reality that a couple experiences when they celebrate the Sacrament of Matrimony. Henceforth, they respond to and live Christ's grace in their lives in a new and different way.

The *Catechism* summarizes in very broad terms how Marriage transforms a couple. The following are paraphrased effects of the sacrament from the *Catechism* (1661):

- It deepens their love for one another by sharing the love with which Christ loved the Church.

- It strengthens their unity and helps their union to be indissoluble.

- It helps spouses grow in holiness.

In the remainder of this section we will look more closely at two themes that illustrate in very fundamental ways how the grace of this sacrament transforms the everyday lives of a Christian married couple—the domestic Church and the Paschal Mystery.

1. What are some of the movies and television shows that are popular today? Choose three and discuss how they portray marriage.

2. How does this compare with a marriage intended to manifest God's unconditional love for all of us and Christ's love of the Church?

The Domestic Church

The idea of the family as the Church-in-miniature, the domestic Church, is a very ancient one. The bishops at the Second Vatican Council—in their Dogmatic Constitution on the Church—used this traditional way of speaking as they described the various different members who make up the People of God.

> The family is, so to speak, the domestic Church. In it parents should, by their word and example, be the first preachers of the faith to their children; they should encourage them in the vocation which is proper to each of them, fostering with special care vocation to a sacred state.
>
> *Dogmatic Constitution on the Church*, 11

A number of years after the close of the Council, Pope John Paul II wrote an Apostolic Exhortation, *The Family in the Modern World,* in which he returned to this idea and used it very extensively to reflect on the vocation of couples in the Sacrament of Matrimony. He called the family "a living image and historical representation of the mystery of the Church" (49). He also wrote about the Christian family's share in the mission of the Church "in a way that is original and specific . . . as an 'intimate community of life and love,' at the service of the Church and of society" (50).

The Holy Father then developed his teaching about the family as the domestic Church in light of the familiar triad of priest-prophet-king that we have discussed in the chapters on Baptism and Holy Orders. In applying this framework to the domestic Church, he described the family as a believing and evangelizing community, a community in dialogue with God, and a community at the service of humanity.

A Believing and Evangelizing Community The very beginning of marriage, the actual celebration of their wedding liturgy, is a couple's first "profession of faith," a prophetic proclamation of the place that they wish God to have at the heart of their relationship. That profession of faith continues throughout their marriage as they welcome God who comes to them in and through the events, problems, joys, difficulties, and circumstances of everyday life. Parents—by their example and by their instruction of their children in the basics of Christian faith—fulfill their prophetic mission of proclaiming the word of God within the domestic Church.

In his Apostolic Exhortation on evangelization, *On Evangelization in the Modern World,* Pope Paul VI captures the heart of how the domestic Church becomes a center of **evangelization.**

> The family, like the Church, ought to be a place where the Gospel is transmitted and from which the Gospel radiates. In a family which is conscious of this mission, all the members evangelize and are evangelized. The parents not only communicate the Gospel to their children, but from their children they can themselves receive the same Gospel as deeply lived by them. And such a family becomes the evangelizer of many other families, and of the neighborhood of which it forms part.

On Evangelization in the Modern World, 71

FAITH ACTIVITY

A Radiating Light Identify ways that you have seen the Gospel radiate in the lives of families you know. Be specific. Share the list in a group. Brainstorm reasons why families might resist radiating the Gospel. Use both lists to write a shared mission statement for families.

The kind of evangelization that the Pope referred to in his exhortation is nothing exotic or out of the ordinary. He is pointing out the power of the everyday witness of Christian living that parents and children give to one another by their lives of goodness and holiness. Simply to live as a faithful Christian day-in and day-out is an extremely effective form of evangelization. Such witness spreads the Good News of the Gospel more powerfully than any other means possible.

A Community in Dialogue with God By virtue of their Baptism, Christian spouses are joined to Christ the High Priest as a priestly people. In the domestic Church spouses exercise their priestly role by working to make themselves, one another, and their children holy. In his Letter to the Romans, Saint Paul urged the Christian community to offer up their everyday lives to God as if they were priests conducting a religious ceremony.

I appeal to you therefore, brothers and sisters, by the mercies of God, to present your bodies as a living sacrifice, holy and acceptable to God, which is your spiritual worship.

Romans 12:1

One of the primary effects of the Sacrament of Matrimony is the **sanctification** of the spouses who are joined together in Christ's love. Marriage is meant to make both husband and wife more faithful disciples of the Lord Jesus. They grow in holiness by carrying out the responsibilities that are theirs in the vocation that is unique to their state in life.

As parents, Christian spouses are called to care for the physical and spiritual needs of their children. They lead their children in the way of holiness by teaching them to love God and introducing them to the dialogue with God that we call prayer. Participation in the Church's sacramental life has a high priority. The Eucharist, which is the source of the Church's life, must also be the source of the spiritual life of the domestic Church. In addition, the need for ongoing conversion to discipleship must be supported and nourished by the family's regular participation in the Sacrament of Penance.

Family prayer together should be at the heart of the domestic Church's life. This includes prayers such as the Liturgy of the Hours, observance of seasonal feasts, private devotions, and individual prayer of all sorts. Pope John Paul II made this remarkable assertion.

> the Christian family's actual participation in the Church's life and mission is in direct proportion to the fidelity and intensity of the prayer with which it is united with the fruitful vine that is Christ the Lord.
>
> *On the Role of the Christian Family in the Modern World*, 62

A Community at the Service of Humanity We have discussed in earlier chapters how we participate in Christ's kingship by sharing his model of service. Just as the Good Shepherd guides the flock by showing care for its welfare on every level, so the domestic Church must be a place where all of the needs of the human family are a matter of concern and responsive action. Christian spouses must make their homes a place where those who are in need are loved, cherished, and made to feel welcome. The family must be a unit of society that does the works of both charity and justice. But parents must not only lead their children by example. They must also instill in them a spirit of compassion and train them in how to act on that compassion in practical ways. It is in the domestic Church that children are given their first moral formation, taught about the Beatitudes, the corporal and spiritual Works of Mercy, and introduced to Jesus' Great Commandment to love neighbor as well as God.

The Paschal Mystery

Saint Paul calls marriage a "great mystery" because it is an image of Christ's love for the Church. In the same passage, he admonishes husbands to "love your wives, just as Christ loved the church and gave himself up for her" (*Ephesians 5:25*). Every sacrament in its own way invites us to live more deeply this fundamental mystery rooted in our Baptism—the Paschal Mystery, by which we share in the dying and rising of Christ Jesus.

In *On the Role of the Christian Family in the Modern World* the Holy Father makes specific the connection between the grace of marriage and the Paschal Mystery: "By virtue of the mystery of the death and Resurrection of Christ, of which the spouses are made part in a new way by marriage, conjugal love is purified and made holy" (56). The "new way" that spouses are made part of the Paschal Mystery is that they must learn to die to their old selves in order to find new life in their marriage. Saint Paul describes it this way.

. . . you have stripped off the old self with its practices and have clothed yourselves with the new self . . . As God's chosen ones, holy and beloved, clothe yourselves with compassion, kindness, humility, meekness, and patience. Bear with one another and, if anyone has a complaint against another, forgive each other; just as the Lord has forgiven you, so you also must forgive. Above all, clothe yourselves with love, which binds everything together in perfect harmony.

 Colossians 3:9–10, 12–14

GROUP TALK

1. What do you think of Saint Paul's instruction for clothing ourselves in Christ, dying to self, and rising to new life in the Lord?

2. Which parts of Saint Paul's advice do you think are most needed in today's world?

3. What advice do you feel is most important for successful marriages? Loving families? Your relationships with peers?

In Ordinary Circumstances Saint Paul's words are very moving, and they describe in eloquent terms the process by which we grow in holiness. However, they refer to the basic, everyday realities of married life. Spouses live out the mystery of dying-rising in countless ways, bit by bit, throughout the years of their marriage. In the early years of a relationship, young spouses discover the difference between being single and married, of realizing that someone else's needs are as important as their own. As children are born and the demands of parenting increase, so do the ways in which dying to self becomes a daily fact of life for a married couple. There are the joys—the risings to new life—to be sure. But ask any parent, and he or she will tell you that the sacrifices made for children are a daily aspect of how the Sacrament of Matrimony helps them to live the Paschal Mystery.

Some couples also experience the Paschal Mystery in their relationship itself. Marriages can sometimes become problematic and conflictual, even for faith-filled spouses. Problems can arise in the best of relationships, and solving them inevitably requires of both spouses a new degree of dying to self in order that the relationship may be given new life. There are also the crosses of life that happen when illnesses and even death come in untimely fashion. There are moments of painful growth when jobs are lost and financial worries overwhelm a family. Betrayals from friends and even family can be a similar cross to bear. In other words, the entire spectrum of human life— what the Vatican Council called the "griefs and anxieties . . . of this age" (*Pastoral Constitution on the Church in the Modern World*, 1)—offer ample opportunities for spouses to live out the Paschal Mystery and find their "conjugal love purified and made holy" (*On the Role of the Christian Family in the Modern World*, 56).

When one considers the challenges that face a couple even under ideal circumstances, it becomes clear how important it is for Christian spouses to be open to the graces of the Sacrament of Matrimony and to grow constantly in their reliance on Christ and the power of the Holy Spirit at work in their relationship. Ultimately, of course, the Paschal Mystery is about deliverance from pain and peril, and this is equally true for married couples. Those who have lived the Sacrament of Matrimony over many years offer moving testimony to the joys that they have found as they have grown old together in the Lord. What may have seemed like unbearable crosses at the time are often regarded in retrospect as blessings in disguise, and spouses who have weathered life's storms together possess a peace and loving communion that is clearly a gift of God.

FAITH ACTIVITY

Support and Help Find out what resources are available through your parish or in your local community for couples who are struggling in their marriage. Share the resources you identify in a group, and then compile a master resource list that might be made available to those looking for help.

✓ Quick Check

1. What are the effects of the Sacrament of Matrimony?
2. What is the meaning of the phrase *domestic Church*?
3. What are some of the specific responsibilities of parents toward their children when making their home a domestic Church?
4. How is Christian married life a participation in the Paschal Mystery?

Liturgy Proclaims What We Believe about Marriage

One of the most important themes throughout this book has been the idea that the authentic faith of the Church is embedded in the Church's worship. Our liturgical rites are, in a sense, the faith of the Apostles being handed down to us from generation to generation. The sacraments enact and embody our experience of God and his saving mysteries. What the Church believes and teaches about each of the sacraments can be discovered, to a great extent, by a careful reading of the way we celebrate each of those sacramental rituals. This is why it's so important that the liturgy be celebrated faithfully, according to the Church's official rites, without unauthorized additions or deletions. It is also the reason why, while being open to cultural adaptation, the *Constitution on the Sacred Liturgy* requires that any adaptations "harmonize with [the liturgy's] true and authentic spirit" (37).

The way that Matrimony is celebrated has often reflected the influence of popular customs at the local level, perhaps more so than in other sacraments. This offers a particular challenge to the Church's faith, especially when those customs do not have any specifically Christian significance, or are even opposed to what our faith tells us is the true meaning of the sacrament. In the section that follows, we will examine some aspects of the Church's celebration of the Sacrament of Matrimony, highlighting certain dimensions of our faith that the rite embodies.

Toward a Deeper Understanding

The Entrance Rite The renewed ritual of marriage indicates that the liturgy begins with the priest going to the door of the church, where he greets the bride and groom, together, with words of welcome. Then all of the ministers, including the cross bearer, acolytes, incense bearer if needed, lectors, extraordinary ministers of Holy Communion, priest, and bridal party, enter the assembly in a solemn liturgical procession as the community sings the entrance song. The only members of the bridal party the rite mentions—in addition to the bride and groom—are "their parents and the two witnesses" (20).

This way of beginning a wedding differs in dramatic fashion from what we consider the "traditional" way that a wedding should begin: a bridal procession of female attendants that culminates with the father and his daughter processing alone down the aisle. The reason for this difference is that the Church looks upon the liturgy as a celebration of the entire Christian community. The Church regards the bride and groom as equal partners in the celebration of their marriage, while much of our popular culture regards a wedding as "the bride's day." In the liturgy any special focus on a single individual is generally discouraged. Rather, the focus is meant to be on our common worship of God as we celebrate a moment when those receiving the sacrament are being strengthened in love and faith.

GROUP TALK

Imagine what it would be like if all marriages of two Roman Catholics were to take place during the parish Sunday celebration of the Eucharist. Discuss the considerations and implications.

The Liturgy of the Word The only readings permitted in a wedding liturgy are those Bible passages contained in the Lectionary. The Lectionary readings suggested for the Rite of Marriage follow the familiar format of Old Testament, Psalm, New Testament, and Gospel. Some couples sometimes ask if they can substitute or add to biblical readings with favorite texts of their own—poems, passages from secular sources reflecting on their love for each other, even texts of popular songs. The reason this is not possible is that this would undermine the essential role that the Liturgy of the Word plays in each of the sacramental rites. The scriptural readings proclaim the faith of the Church and are meant to instruct us about and prepare us for the sacrament that is to be celebrated. Saint Paul reminds us in his Letter to the Romans that, "faith comes from what is heard, and what is heard comes through the word of Christ" (*10:17*). This truth is the foundation of our understanding that the sacraments "are precisely sacraments of faith, a faith which is born of and nourished by the word" (*Decree on the Ministry and Life of Priests*, 4).

FAITH ACTIVITY

Scripture Selection Look at the Scripture readings available in the Lectionary for the Rite of Marriage. If you were assisting a couple in their selection, which would you recommend and why?

One of the richest ways for a couple to prepare for their wedding is to read, pray over, study, and discuss with one another the more than three dozen passages contained in the Lectionary. There, one finds texts that reveal the mystery of divine love reflected in human love, inviting us to realize more deeply how a couple is invited to experience salvation in the midst of their marriage in Christ. A couple who focuses their spiritual preparation for their life together on the Scriptures to be proclaimed at their wedding will surely come to that day with hearts and minds open to the graces that God wants to shower upon them in their marriage.

The Rite of Marriage Many of our sacraments have ritual elements that call for a kind of examination and testing of those who seek the sacraments. The clearest example of this is the requirement that one make the baptismal promises before being baptized. In the ordination liturgy there are questions addressed to the candidate for bishop, priest, or deacon that must be answered before the laying on of hands and ordination prayer. Here, as the actual Rite of Marriage begins, there is an equivalent questioning of the bride and groom regarding their intentions. The presider begins by addressing issues that are related to the Church's teaching about the essential requirements for valid marital consent: freedom, faithful commitment to each other, and openness to children.

By this public examination of the bride and groom, the Church demonstrates how seriously she weighs the importance of being properly disposed before a couple may celebrate the Sacrament of Matrimony. As humans we have a God-given, natural right to marriage. However, in order to celebrate the sacramental expression of that right, a couple must demonstrate a standard of readiness that reflects the Church's understanding of Christ's design for Christian Marriage. In an individualist culture such as our own, this careful examination of the couple's readiness underlines the Church's conviction that marriage is a public reality with social consequences, not just a private arrangement made between two individuals. It also proclaims to all who are present the essential dimensions of what Christ intended a sacramental marriage to embody. In our culture that so often denies that these values are essential for successful marriage, the liturgy reminds us what the faith of the Church teaches.

A similar teaching occurs by virtue of the vows that the bride and groom exchange. This exchange of consent is the essential element required for a valid marriage, and the words contain the heart of what the Church believes Christ wishes for married couples—a love relationship that is unconditional and indissoluble, just as God's love for us is irrevocable and unconditional. This is yet another reason why Christian Marriage is regarded as a sign of God's love for the Church, and why the Church insists that only such a commitment qualifies as a Christian Marriage.

We have seen in earlier chapters that a number of sacramental rituals have "explanatory rites" immediately after celebrating the essential element of the sacrament. An example from Baptism would be the anointing with chrism, candle, and white garment, or in Holy Orders, the conferral of chalice and paten at a priestly ordination. In the marriage rite, the blessing and exchange of rings serves this same purpose of expanding on the meaning of the sacrament by means of a symbolic expression. The ritual is simple yet profound, and stands out as the primary explanatory rite of the wedding liturgy. The words of both the presider in the blessing and of the couple as they exchange rings indicate that their rings are "a sign of love and fidelity."

The Nuptial Blessing The final element of the marriage ritual that we will note is the Nuptial Blessing that occurs after the Eucharistic Prayer and the Our Father (or, when the Eucharist is not celebrated, immediately after the General Intercessions). All three alternative Nuptial Blessings contain a very concise statement of key elements in the Church's theology of marriage, as well as what the Christian community hopes for in terms of the blessings of married life. The richness of this prayer makes it a fitting summary and illustration of the point we made at the beginning of this section, namely that "the liturgy proclaims what we believe about marriage."

FAITH ACTIVITY

A Continuing Sign Think about the ways married couples are signs of love and fidelity. What examples can we learn from couples about being true to God, others, and ourselves? Using images and words, create a visual representation of what it means to love and be true.

Holy Father, you created mankind in your own image
and made man and woman to be joined as
husband and wife
in union of body and heart
and so fulfill their mission in this world.

Father, to reveal the plan of your love,
you made the union of husband and wife
an image of the covenant between you and your people.
In the fulfillment of this sacrament,
the marriage of Christian man and woman
is a sign of the marriage between Christ and the Church.
Father, stretch out your hand, and bless N. and N.

Quick Check

1. What is unique about the Entrance Rite?
2. What is the significance of the Liturgy of the Word?
3. What is the importance of the public questioning of the bride and groom before they say their vows?
4. What is the significance of the exchange of rings between the couple?

Lord, grant that as they begin to live
    this sacrament
they may share with each other the gifts
    of your love
and become one in heart and mind as witnesses to your
    presence in their marriage.
Help them to create a home together
(and give them children to be formed by
    the Gospel
and to have a place in your family).

Give your blessing to N., your daughter,
so that she may be a good wife (and mother),
caring for the home,
faithful in love for her husband,
generous and kind.
Give your blessings to N., your son,
so that he may be a faithful husband
(and a good father).

Father, grant that as they come together at your table
    on earth,
so they may one day have the joy of sharing your feast
    in heaven.

We ask this through Christ our Lord.
Amen.

Rite of Marriage, 120

Cultural Marriage Customs

In the chapter on the Eucharist, we discussed the fact that the Second Vatican Council called for greater inculturation of the liturgy. We cited the example of adaptations made in the Eucharistic liturgy in Zaire. The process of cultural assimilation of the marriage liturgy has gone on long before Vatican II, for many centuries. One very good example of this process is found in Spanish-speaking countries where a great many native customs have long been incorporated into the wedding liturgy. Traditions popular in Mexico provide an excellent example:

- In some places in northern Mexico there is a tradition of giving a "ring of promise" long before the official engagement ring is exchanged.
- Sponsors, called *madrinas* or *padrinos,* are an important part of the wedding party, and there are often a large number of such persons with special roles to play in the ceremony. They enter in the entrance procession and occupy places of honor in the church.
- The *madrina de ramo* carries flowers for the Blessed Virgin Mary.
- The *madrina de laso* carries a jeweled or beaded rope that is placed around the couple as they say their vows.
- The *madrina de arras* holds thirteen gold coins that the bridegroom will present to the bride. These are a symbol of his commitment to care for his wife and that he places in her care all of his goods. The bride's acceptance of the coins shows her willingness to place her confidence and trust in her husband to care for her well-being.
- The *madrina de copas* carries wine glasses that will be used at the reception for the toast.
- Both *madrinas* and *padrinos* may carry religious articles such as a prayer book or a rosary.
- There is also a *madrina de velacion* who is specially chosen by the bride to be the person to whom she will turn for guidance throughout her marriage.
- There may also be someone in the procession carrying the *recuerdos,* gifts to be given to guests as a memento of the day.
- During the ceremony the priest blesses the couple with a cross, which they both kiss as a sign of their pledge of faithfulness to each other.
- The *laso* is a large loop of cord placed in a figure eight over the shoulders of the couple as they recite their vows. This symbolizes the love that binds them together.

FAITH ACTIVITY

Research Customs Investigate other ethnic Catholic wedding customs, along with their meanings. Present your findings to the class.

Persons of Faith

Luigi Beltrame Quattrocchi and Maria Corsini Beltrame Quattrocchi (1905–1951)

On October 21, 2001, Pope John Paul II for the first time in history beatified a married couple. Beatification is the step just prior to canonization in the process of declaring someone an official saint of the Catholic Church. This historic step was taken in the presence of three of the couple's four children, and it signaled the desire of the Holy Father to bring attention to the teaching of the Vatican Council that holiness is a universal call, directed to all the baptized, and not just to priests, monks, or nuns. Usually a saint's feast day is the date of his or her death. However, in view of the fact that the couple had two different dates of death, the Pope in another unprecedented move designated their wedding date, November 25, as their joint feast day. (The years of their marriage are in parentheses in the title above.)

Luigi Beltrame was born on January 12, 1880, in Catania and grew up in Urbino, Italy. His uncle, Luigi Quattrocchi, who was childless, asked the boy's parents if he and his wife could raise him, and they consented. This was the origin of Luigi's double surname, Beltrame Quattrocchi. He studied to be a lawyer and worked as a civil servant throughout a long career. His children reported in the process of his beatification that Luigi was not particularly religious until he met his wife, Maria Corsini, and married her in 1905. As their marriage progressed, he grew with her in holiness.

Maria Corsini was born into a noble Florentine family on June 24, 1884. She received a solid education, loved music, and became a professor and writer on educational topics, in addition to her many charitable activities and involvements in Catholic social action movements. One year after their marriage, she gave birth to her first child, Filippo

(1906). Two other pregnancies followed, and Stefania (1908) and Cesare (1909) were born next. In 1913, she became pregnant for the fourth time, and the doctors told her that there was only a five percent chance that she and the baby would survive what was predicted to be a very dangerous pregnancy. Despite the doctors' advice urging her to have an abortion, Luigi and Maria put their trust in God and refused the abortion. After what proved to be a very painful and difficult pregnancy, Enrichetta was born healthy in 1914.

The life of Luigi and Maria that followed was a very ordinary one that became the context for a deepening and extraordinary life of holiness. As a middle-class family of six, the household was comfortable but not immune to the stresses and hardships of the times. They lived through the First and Second World Wars, the Great Depression, and fascism. In his homily at their beatification, Pope John Paul II said of them, "Drawing on the word of God and the saints, the blessed couple lived an ordinary life in an extraordinary way. Among the joys and anxieties of a normal family, they knew how to live an extraordinarily rich spiritual life." Cardinal José Saraiva Martins, prefect of the Congregation for the Causes of Saints, said that they "made a true domestic church of their family, which was open to life, to prayer, to the social apostolate, to solidarity with the poor and to friendship."

Luigi and Maria developed the habit of daily participation in the Eucharist. It was reported that each morning he waited until after Mass to say "Good Morning" to her, indicating that only then had the day begun in earnest. They had an active family life, and dedicated themselves to raising healthy children with a love for God and neighbor. They followed sports, went on holidays together, and had a large circle of family and friends with whom they gathered regularly for meals and other celebrations. During the Second World War, their apartment in Rome became a regular shelter for Jews and other refugees. Maria and Luigi prayed the Rosary together every evening, and on the eve of every month's first Friday they observed a family holy hour. They were deeply spiritual, but not overly pious. The fruit of the deep spirituality that characterized their home was evident in the fact that three of their four children entered religious life. Enrichetta, the youngest, remained single to care for her aging parents until their deaths.

In addition to their devotion to work, home, and family, Maria and Luigi reached out in active ways in the works of charity and justice. Maria was involved in establishing the Catholic University of the Sacred Heart in Italy and served as a volunteer nurse for the Red Cross during the war in Ethiopia and the Second World War. Luigi collaborated with her in starting a scout group for boys in the poor sectors of Rome, and they were involved in several forms of marriage and family apostolates. On November 9, 1951, Luigi died at the age of 71 of a heart attack in their home in Rome. Maria survived him for 14 years as a widow and then died at the age of 81 on August 26, 1965, in Enrichetta's arms at their house in the mountains, at Serravalle.

REFLECT

1. How do the lives of Luigi and Maria Beltrame Quattrocchi serve as models for married couples?

2. Do you know of any couples who have lived just, holy, and spiritual lives? Without revealing personal details, describe how they have faced life's blessings and challenges together?

3. What can you do to promote the sanctity of marriage?

The Final Blessing from the Rite of Marriage (128)

(Responses are in parentheses.)

May almighty God, with his Word of blessing, unite your hearts in the never-ending bond of pure love. (Amen)

May your children bring you happiness, and may your generous love for them be returned to you, many times over. (Amen)

May the peace of Christ live always in your hearts and in your home.
May you have true friends to stand by you, both in joy and in sorrow.
May you be ready and willing to help and comfort all who come to you in need.
And may the blessings promised to the compassionate be yours in abundance. (Amen)

May you find happiness and satisfaction in your work.
May daily problems never cause you undue anxiety, nor the desire for earthly possessions dominate your lives.
But may your hearts' first desire be always the good things waiting for you in the life of heaven. (Amen)

May the Lord bless you with many happy years together, so that you may enjoy the rewards of a good life.
And after you have served him loyally in his kingdom on earth, may he welcome you to his eternal kingdom in heaven. (Amen)

Study Guide

▶Check Understanding

1. Explain in what way(s) Jesus indicated his desire to sanctify marriage as a sacrament.

2. Describe how marriage was celebrated between Christians in the early centuries after Christ.

3. Identify our earliest historical evidence of how the Church celebrated the religious dimension of marriage between believers.

4. Highlight the major changes in the Rite of Marriage after Vatican II.

5. Outline the Rite of Marriage celebrated during Mass.

6. Restate in your own words the questions asked of the couple before they give their consent to be married.

7. Summarize what is included in both remote and immediate preparation for marriage.

8. Explain the notion of covenant and how our Judeo-Christian tradition has used it so that it now sheds light on Christian Marriage.

9. List the effects of the Sacrament of Matrimony.

10. Discuss what the phrase *domestic Church* means.

11. Name some of the specific responsibilities of parents toward their children when they recognize that they must make their home a domestic Church.

12. Tell how Christian married life is a participation in the Paschal Mystery.

13. Describe the Entrance Rite and explain how it shows what Catholics believe about the Sacrament of Matrimony.

14. Explain the significance of the Liturgy of the Word in Catholic wedding ceremonies.

15. Describe the importance of the public questioning of the bride and groom before they say their vows.

16. Recall the significance of the exchange of rings between the couple at a wedding.

▶Apply and Develop

17. Compare and contrast the Church's involvement in marriage in the first century and today. Write an essay reflecting on the advantages of the way it is today.

18. Create a two-page handout that could be given to engaged couples preparing for marriage about the Church's understanding of marriage based on natural law and the new covenant.

19. Pope John Paul II described the family as a believing and evangelizing community, a community in dialogue with God, and a community at the service of humanity. Choose one of these phrases and support how the sacraments—Matrimony and others—can help a couple achieve this.

20. Study carefully the text of the Nuptial Blessing provided in the chapter. Then make a list of the Church's teachings about the Sacrament of Matrimony that are contained in the prayer.

▶Key Words

See pages noted for contextual explanations of these important faith terms.

domestic Church (p. 233)

evangelization (p. 234)

mixed marriage (p. 231)

sanctification (p. 235)

CATHOLIC SOURCE BOOK
Scripture

The Catholic Bible contains seventy-three books—forty-six in the Old Testament and twenty-seven in the New Testament.

The Old Testament

The Pentateuch
Genesis	Exodus	Leviticus	Numbers	Deuteronomy

The Historical Books
Joshua	2 Samuel	1 Chronicles	Nehemiah	Esther
Judges	1 Kings	2 Chronicles	Tobit	1 Maccabees
Ruth	2 Kings	Ezra	Judith	2 Maccabees
1 Samuel				

The Wisdom Books
Job	Proverbs	Song of Songs	Sirach (Ecclesiasticus)
Psalms	Ecclesiastes	Wisdom	

The Prophetic Books
Isaiah	Ezekiel	Amos	Nahum	Haggai
Jeremiah	Daniel	Obadiah	Habakkuk	Zechariah
Lamentations	Hosea	Jonah	Zephaniah	Malachi
Baruch	Joel	Micah		

The New Testament

The Gospels
Matthew	Mark	Luke	John

The Acts of the Apostles

The New Testament Letters
Romans	Philippians	1 Timothy	Hebrews	1 John
1 Corinthians	Colossians	2 Timothy	James	2 John
2 Corinthians	1 Thessalonians	Titus	1 Peter	3 John
Galatians	2 Thessalonians	Philemon	2 Peter	Jude
Ephesians				

Revelation

The Creeds

Nicene Creed

We believe in one God,
    the Father the Almighty,
    maker of heaven and earth,
    of all that is seen and unseen.
We believe in one Lord, Jesus Christ,
    the only Son of God,
    eternally begotten of the Father,
    God from God, Light from Light,
    true God from true God,
    begotten, not made, one in Being
      with the Father.
    Through him all things were made.
For us men and for our salvation
he came down from heaven:
by the power of the Holy Spirit
he was born of the Virgin Mary, and
    became man.
For our sake he was crucified under
    Pontius Pilate;
he suffered, died, and was buried.
On the third day he rose again
    in fulfillment of the Scriptures;
    he ascended into heaven
      and is seated at the right hand
        of the Father.
He will come again in glory
    to judge the living and the dead,
      and his kingdom will have no
      end.
We believe in the Holy Spirit, the Lord,
    the giver of life,
      who proceeds from the Father
      and the Son.
      With the Father and the Son he is
      worshiped and glorified.
    He has spoken through the Prophets.
We believe in one holy catholic and
    apostolic Church.
We acknowledge one baptism for the
    forgiveness of sins.
We look for the resurrection of the
    dead,
    and the life of the world to come.
Amen.

Apostles' Creed

I believe in God, the Father almighty,
    creator of heaven and earth.
I believe in Jesus Christ, his only Son,
    our Lord.
He was conceived by the power of the
    Holy Spirit
    and born of the Virgin Mary.
He suffered under Pontius Pilate,
    was crucified, died, and was buried.
He descended to the dead.
On the third day, he rose again.
He ascended into heaven,
    and is seated at the right hand of
      the Father.
He will come again to judge the living
    and the dead.
I believe in the Holy Spirit,
    the holy catholic Church,
    the communion of saints,
    the forgiveness of sins,
    the resurrection of the body,
    and the life everlasting.
Amen.

Catholic Church Traditions

The Universal Church

Eastern Church[1]	Antiochene Rite (West Syrian)	Syrian Church *sui iuris*[2]
		(Syro-)Maronite Church *sui iuris*
		(Syro-)Malankara Church *sui iuris*
	Chaldean Rite (East Syrian)	Chaldean Church *sui iuris*
		Syro-Malabar Church *sui iuris*
	Byzantine Rite (Constantinopolitan)	Melkite-Greek Church *sui iuris*
		Albanian Church *sui iuris*
		Bulgarian Church *sui iuris*
		Belarussian Church *sui iuris*
		Hellenic-Greek Church *sui iuris*
		Italo-Albanian Church *sui iuris*
		Hungarian Church *sui iuris*
		Russian Church *sui iuris*
		Ruthenian Church *sui iuris*
		Romanian Church *sui iuris*
		Ukrainian Church *sui iuris*
		Krizevci [Yogoslav] Church *sui iuris*
		Slovak Church *sui iuris*
		Georgian Church (not *sui iuris*)
	Alexandrian Rite	Coptic Catholic Church *sui iuris*
		Ethiopian Catholic Church *sui iuris*
	Armenian Rite	Armenian Catholic Church *sui iuris*
Western Church	Roman (Latin) Rite	Latin Church *sui iuris*

[1]These are Catholic Churches. There are many Orthodox churches that have similar names. Orthodox churches broke away from the Catholic Church; the churches listed here did not break away, or did break away but were later reunited.

[2]"Church *sui iuris*" is defined as a community of the Christian faithful joined together by its own hierarchy according to the norm of law and explicitly or tacitly recognized by the supreme authority of the Church (i.e., the Pope alone or an Ecumenical Council in union with him).

Liturgy

The Seven Sacraments

In the sacraments Jesus continues his saving work. During his life Jesus welcomed, fed, healed, and forgave people. Through the sacraments he continues to share God's life and love with his followers. Because the sacraments are founded on the ministry of Jesus and witnessed to in the early Church, we can find Biblical roots for the sacraments.

Sacraments of Initiation Three sacraments together complete initiation into the Church: Baptism, which begins new life in Christ; Confirmation, which strengthens that life; and, Eucharist, which nourishes that life and transforms the recipient to become more Christlike.

- Baptism—John 3:5; Matthew 28:19–20; Romans 6:3–11; Acts 19:1–7
- Confirmation—Acts 8:14–17, 9:17–19, 19:5; Titus 3:4–8
- Eucharist—John 6:1–15, 25–71; Matthew 26:26–28; Mark 14:22–25; Luke 22:7–20

Sacraments of Healing In the Sacraments of Healing God's forgiveness of sins and healing are given to those suffering physical and spiritual sickness.

- Reconciliation (also called the Sacrament of Penance, the Sacrament of Conversion, and the Sacrament of Confession)—John 20:19, 22–23; Mark 1:15, 2:5, 10; Luke 7:48, 15:18
- Anointing of the Sick—Mark 6:12–13, 16:17–18; Matthew 10:8; James 5:14–15

Sacraments at the Service of Communion In these sacraments, Catholics receive the grace to commit to and serve God and the community.

- Holy Orders—John 10:36; Acts 1:8, 2:4; 1 Timothy 4:14; 2 Timothy 1:6–7
- Matrimony—Matthew 19:6; John 2:1–11; 1 Corinthians 7:39; Ephesians 5:31–32

The Liturgy of the Hours

The Liturgy of the Hours is the Church's annual cycle of seasons and feasts that celebrates the Paschal Mystery. It begins on the First Sunday of Advent and ends on the feast of Christ the King.

Advent In this liturgical season, the Church devotes four weeks for the People of God to prepare to celebrate the coming of Christ at Christmas. The color for this season is violet, as a sign of anticipation and penance. On the third Sunday vestments may be pink, as the Advent wreath candle. This is joyful anticipation of the nearness of Christmas.

Christmas Christmas celebrates the Son of God becoming man, God visible in humankind. The color for this season is white. It celebrates Christ's first coming over 2,000 years ago, Christ's presence with us now, and the anticipation of his second coming at the end of time. This season includes the feast of the Holy Family and the feast of Epiphany. In the current liturgical calendar, The Churches of the West celebrate the birth of Christ on December 25.

Lent The forty days of Lent are a time of fasting, praying, and almsgiving. Lent begins with Ash Wednesday; ashes are blessed and put on the foreheads of Catholics as a reminder of their sinfulness and of penance. The color of this season is violet. Fasting, abstinence, and personal reflection on Baptism during Lent help prepare Catholics for the celebration of Easter and renewal of Baptismal Promises.

The Triduum The word *Triduum* means, "three days." Triduum starts with the celebration of the Lord's Supper on Holy Thursday, includes Good Friday and Holy Saturday, and ends with evening prayer on Easter Sunday. The color for Holy Thursday is white, the color for Good Friday is red, and there is no color on Holy Saturday. Because the Triduum specifically celebrates the life, death, and Resurrection of Jesus, it is the high point of the Church year.

Easter Season Easter, the feast of the Resurrection of Christ, is the greatest feast of the Church year. The Easter Season begins on Easter Sunday and lasts until Pentecost, fifty days later. The color for this season is white.

Ordinary Time This season occurs twice each Church year. The first, shorter period falls between Christmas and Lent; the second period accounts for most Sundays of the Church year, starting after the end of the Easter season and ending with the Feast of Christ the King, the Sunday before Advent begins. The color of this season is green. Ordinary Time focuses on everyday Christian life, during which we learn about Jesus' life and teaching from one of the Gospels.

Holy Days of Obligation

Catholics are required to attend Mass on Sunday unless serious reason prevents them from doing so. Catholics also must participate in Mass on certain holy days.

U.S. Holy Days of Obligation	
Holy Day	**Date**
Mary the Mother of God	January 1
The Ascension of the Lord	Forty days after Easter, or the Sunday nearest the end of the forty-day period
The Assumption of Mary	August 15
All Saints' Day	November 1
The Immaculate Conception of Mary	December 8
Christmas	December 25

Moral Life

Ten Commandments—the fundamental moral laws given by God to his people to help them live by the covenant; these laws apply to us today. They are also called the Decalogue, literally meaning "ten words."

1. I, the Lord, am your God: you shall not have strange gods before me.

- This teaches us to put God first in our lives, to place our hope and trust in him, to believe in him and all that he has revealed.
- We have a duty to nourish and protect our faith, as well as help it develop and grow.

2. You shall not take the name of the Lord your God in vain.

- This calls us to be careful about how we use the name of God, Jesus Christ, his Mother Mary, and the saints.
- It is not right to swear, using God's name to condemn someone else.

3. Remember to keep holy the Lord's day.

- This tells us to worship and praise God on Sunday.
- Participation in Mass on Sundays is so important that we are obligated to do so.
- We are also called to refrain from unnecessary work on the Lord's Day, and to avoid requiring things of other people that would make it difficult for them to observe the Lord's Day.

4. Honor your father and your mother.

- Respect and obey parents, guardians, and others who have proper authority.
- Show gratitude for all that parents and guardians do.
- Give emotional, moral, and material support to parents as they age, making sure they have what they need to maintain their lives and dignity.

5. You shall not kill.

- Respect and protect your life and the lives of others.
- Honor the dignity and gift of human life at all its stages, from conception to natural death.
- Counteract hatred and violence, both explicit and implied, and promote peace in all levels of society.

6. You shall not commit adultery.

- Be faithful to spouses, friends, and family.
- Respect God's gift of sexuality as integral to the human person.
- Learn to appreciate the gift of sexuality by practicing the virtue of chastity and self-mastery.

7. You shall not steal.

- Respect the things that belong to others.
- Share what you have with those in need and recognize that the earth's resources are intended for all people.

8. You shall not bear false witness against your neighbor.

- Be honest and truthful.
- Avoid bragging.
- Don't say untruthful or negative things about others.

9. You shall not covet your neighbor's wife.

- Don't lust after another person's spouse.
- Practice modesty in thoughts, words, dress, and actions.

10. You shall not covet your neighbor's goods.

- Rejoice in others' good fortune.
- Express gratitude for what you have—not envy of others' possessions.
- Don't be greedy or preoccupied with money or power.

Living the Beatitudes	
Blessed are the poor in spirit.	You depend on God rather than on things, and you believe that helping others is more important than acquiring things.
Blessed are those who mourn.	You are aware of the sufferings of others and walk with them in their grief; your grieving is not dominated by selfishness.
Blessed are the meek.	You are humble, patient, and gentle with yourself and with others.
Blessed are those who hunger and thirst for righteousness.	You stand up for what is right and for the rights of others; you work for a more just world and the fullness of God's kingdom.
Blessed are the merciful.	You readily forgive others from the heart, refusing to hold a grudge, and you forgive yourself as you seek God's forgiveness and the forgiveness of those you have hurt or harmed.
Blessed are the pure in heart.	You recognize God's image in yourself and in those around you, and you treat others with reverence.
Blessed are the peacemakers.	You live peacefully with others and promote peace between people and groups.
Blessed are those who are persecuted for righteousness' sake.	You make a stand for what you believe in, even when you suffer emotional or physical pain as a result of your decision.

Gifts of the Holy Spirit

Wisdom	This gift gives us the power to see things from God's perspective. We develop this gift as we meditate and contemplate on his presence, action, and guidance in our lives. This kind of reflection helps us clarify what we believe and guides us to make right judgments and good decisions. Through wisdom we have the power to love what is of God and to value all of his creation.
Understanding	This gift gives us a way to understand Jesus' teachings and the Tradition of the Church. It helps us get to the heart of revealed truth even when we do not fully understand its entire meaning. It gives us a real confidence in the revealed word of God and leads us to draw orthodox conclusions from Scripture and doctrine. It is the power to know how to live our lives as followers of Jesus and to apply the teachings of the Church to our lives.
Counsel (Right Judgment)	This gift helps us know what we should do in difficult situations. It helps us judge our own actions correctly. It is the power to know how to make right choices and good decisions that are consistent with Jesus' teachings. This gift often involves asking others for help and offering good, moral advice to others.
Fortitude (Courage)	This gift ensures a confident spirit of resolution, firmness of mind, and strong will to persevere knowing that God's providence (by which he guides his creation toward its perfection yet to be attained) will enable us to overcome all obstacles. It helps us persist in the practice of virtue even when we do fail or are persecuted for trying. It is the power to stand up for our beliefs and the values of Jesus' message especially when it is difficult.
Knowledge	This gift enables us to judge what is happening in relationships, the environment, and social situations. We are able to see God's providence in what happens in our lives. This gift is sometimes called the science or knowledge of the saints (see *Proverbs 30:3*) because those who have knowledge can distinguish between impulses and the inspiration of grace.
Piety (Reverence)	This gift places us in a right relationship with God. It enables us to see God as our loving Father. Pope John Paul II described it as a gift that opens our hearts to "tenderness toward God and our brothers and sisters . . . expressed in prayer." Through it we develop a loving obedience toward God. It is the power to see God's presence in all people and life experiences.
Fear of the Lord (Wonder and Awe)	This gift inspires us with awareness of God's majesty and the fact that he has created us in his image. Wonder and awe help us appreciate the mystery of the Trinity and respond with love and goodness to God's initiative of love by which he sent his Son to atone for our sins, and the love by which his Son, Jesus, freely offered himself for our salvation. Through this gift we know we have a spiritual dimension and are able to be in relationship with God. It is the power to recognize how awesome he truly is.

The Virtues

Virtues are good moral and spiritual habits that help us make good moral decisions, avoid sin, and strengthen character. There are two types of virtues: theological virtues and human (or moral) virtues.

Theological Virtues

The theological virtues are the foundational virtues of faith, hope, and charity. They are called the theological virtues because they are rooted in God, directed toward him, and reflect his presence in our lives. In Greek *theos* means "god."

- Faith means believing in him and all that he has revealed to us and what the Church proposes for our belief. It involves seeking to know and do God's will.

- Hope is trusting in God the Father, in everything that Christ has promised, and in the help of the Holy Spirit. It is the desire to achieve eternal happiness in heaven and to cooperate with the graces that make this desire come true.

- Charity (love) is the cornerstone of all virtues. "By charity, we love God above all things and our neighbor as ourselves for love of God" (*Catechism*, 1844). Charity places concern for God, especially shown through love of others, above everything else.

The theological virtues are gifts from God. They do, however, call for a response on our part. As identifying marks and positive character traits, the virtues show themselves in patterns of behavior exhibited over a long period of time. So, by living faithfully, hopefully, and lovingly, we cooperate with God's gifts of faith, hope, and charity.

Cardinal Virtues

Among the moral virtues, the four cardinal virtues are the principal virtues that help us lead a moral life by governing our actions, controlling our passions and emotions, and directing our behavior as disciples of Christ. With the help of God's grace, we develop the moral virtues through education, practice, and perseverance.

- Prudence helps us make practical, correct judgments about what to do and the right way to do it.

- Justice is giving God and people their due; it reminds us that all people have rights and should have their basic needs met.

- Fortitude is courage, strength when confronted with difficulties, perseverance in pursuing that which is good.

- Temperance is moderation, balance, and self-control.

These virtues are called *cardinal* based on the Latin root of the word *cardo,* which means, "hinge." The Christian moral life hinges on these four virtues working together smoothly, just as the hinges of a door keep it centered, stable, and workable.

Neglecting the cardinal virtues weakens our character. Used consistently, they strengthen our character and support our endeavors to live a good life.

The Precepts of the Church

Living Out the Precepts	
1. You shall attend Mass on Sundays and holy days of obligation and abstain from servile labor.	We are required to participate in the Eucharistic Liturgy on all Sundays and holy days of obligation.
2. You shall confess your sins at least once a year.	This is the minimum required of a Catholic. It is required of a Catholic only if one has committed an unconfessed mortal sin since one's last worthy confession. The reception of the Sacrament of Reconciliation continues the Holy Spirit's work of conversion and forgiveness and ensures that we are prepared to receive the Eucharist.
3. You shall receive Holy Communion at least once during the Easter season.	This, too, is a minimum requirement. It is hoped that most Catholics receive both Reconciliation and the Eucharist more than once a year. This precept, however, highlights the importance of the Easter season, for the feasts of Holy Week and Easter are the origin and center of the Catholic liturgy.
4. You shall observe the prescribed days of fasting and abstinence.	The Church prescribes certain days when we are to fast (eat only one full meal) or to abstain from eating meat. These days prepare us for liturgical feasts and help us practice control of our instincts and appetites.
5. You shall provide for the material needs of the Church according to your abilities.	There could be no liturgical life to support our moral life if there were no church buildings, liturgical vestments and objects, and parish personnel. Each Catholic is expected to contribute to the material needs of the Church as well as the needs of the larger community and the world.

Prayer

The Sign of the Cross

In the name of the Father,
and of the Son,
and of the Holy Spirit.
Amen

In nomine Patris,
et Filii,
et Spiritus Sancti.
Amen.

The Lord's Prayer

Our Father, who art in heaven,
hallowed be thy name;
thy kingdom come,
thy will be done on earth as it is in heaven.
Give us this day our daily bread;
and forgive us our trespasses
as we forgive those who trespass against
    us;
and lead us not into temptation,
but deliver us from evil.
Amen.

Pater noster, qui es in coelis:
sanctificetur nomen tuum;
adveniat regnum tuum;
fiat voluntas tua, sicut in coelo, et in terra.
Panem nostrum quotidianum da nobis
    hodie;
et dimitte nobis debita nostra,
sicut et nos dimittimus debitoribus nostris;
et ne nos inducas in tentationem;
sed libera nos a malo.
Amen.

Hail Mary

Hail, Mary, full of grace!
The Lord is with you;
blessed are you among women,
and blessed is the fruit of your womb,
    Jesus.
Holy Mary, Mother of God,
pray for us sinners,
now and at the hour of our death.
Amen.

Ave Maria, gratia plena,
Dominus tecum;
benedicta tu in mulieribus,
et benedictus fructus ventris tui, Jesus.
Sancta Maria, Mater Dei,
Ora pro nobis peccatoribus,
Nunc et in hora mortis nostrae.
Amen.

Glory to the Father

Glory to the Father,
and to the Son,
and to the Holy Spirit:
as it was in the beginning,
 is now,
and will be forever.
Amen.

Gloria Patri,
et Filio,
et Spiritui Sancto.
Sicut erat in principio,
et nunc, et semper,
et in saecula saeculorum.
Amen.

Act of Contrition (traditional)

O my God, I am heartily sorry for having offended you, and I detest all my sins, because of your just punishments, but most of all because they offend you, my God, who are all good and deserving of all my love. I firmly resolve, with the help of your grace, to sin no more and to avoid the near occasion of sin.

Act of Contrition (contemporary)

My God, I am sorry for my sins with all my heart. In choosing to do wrong and failing to do good, I have sinned against you whom I should love above all things. I firmly intend, with your help, to do penance, to sin no more, and to avoid whatever leads me to sin. Our Savior Jesus Christ suffered and died for us. In his name, my God, have mercy.

The Rosary

The rosary is called the *Psalter of Mary* because all fifteen of its mysteries, with their 150 Aves, correspond to the number of the psalms. Praying all fifteen decades at once is called the *Dominican Rosary.* The Rosary is the most well-known and used form of chaplet (a devotion using beads; from a French word meaning "crown" or "wreath"). There are other chaplets, such as those in honor of Saint Bridget of Sweden and in honor of Mary, the Immaculate Conception.

1. Sign of the Cross and Apostles' Creed
2. Lord's Prayer
3. Three Hail Marys
4. Glory to the Father
5. Announce mystery; Lord's Prayer
6. Ten Hail Marys
7. Glory to the Father

Repeat last three steps, meditating on the other mysteries of the rosary.

The Fatima invocation (recommended by Mary to the children at Fatima in 1917) is sometimes recited between decades: "O my Jesus, forgive us our sins. Save us from the fires of hell, and bring all souls to heaven, especially those who most need your mercy."

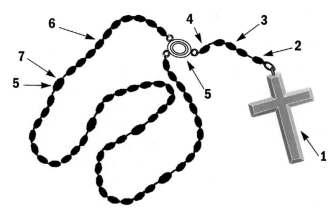

The Mysteries of the Rosary

Joyful Mysteries
(Mondays and Saturdays)

1. **The Annunciation** (humility)
   Isaiah 7:10–14; Luke 1:26–38

2. **The Visitation** (charity)
   Isaiah 40:1–11; Luke 1:39–45;
   John 1:19–23

3. **The Nativity** (poverty)
   Micah 5:1–4; Matthew 2:1–12;
   Luke 2:1–20; Galatians 4:1

4. **The Presentation** (obedience)
   Luke 2:22–35; Hebrews 9:6–14

5. **The Finding of Jesus in the Temple**
   (piety)
   Luke 2:41–52; John 12:44–50;
   1 Corinthians 2:6–16

Luminous Mysteries
(Thursdays)

1. **Baptism in the Jordan** (commitment)
   Matthew 3:13–17; Mark 1:9–11;
   Luke 3:21–22; John 1:29–34

2. **The Wedding at Cana** (fidelity)
   John 2:3–5, 7–10; John 13:14–15; Luke
   6:27–28, 37; Luke 9:23; John 15:12

3. **Proclamation of the Kingdom of God**
   (conversion)
   Mark 1:14–15; Luke 4:18–19, 21;
   Matthew 5:38–39, 43–44; Matthew
   6:19–21; Matthew 7:12; Matthew 10:8

4. **The Transfiguration** (promise)
   Matthew 5:14, 16; Matthew 17:1–2, 5,
   7–8; Luke 9:30–33; John 1:4–5, 18;
   2 Corinthians 3:18

5. **Institution of the Eucharist** (grace)
   John 13:1; Matthew 26:18; Luke 22:15–16,
   19–20; Matthew 5:14, 19–20;
   1 Corinthians 11:26; John 17:20–21;
   1 Corinthians 12:13, 26–27

Sorrowful Mysteries
(Tuesdays and Fridays)

1. **The Agony in the Garden** (repentance)
   Matthew 26:36–46; Mark 14:26–42;
   Luke 22:39–53; John 18:1–12

2. **The Scourging at the Pillar** (purity)
   Isaiah 50:5–9; Matthew 27:15-26;
   Mark 15:1–15

3. **The Crowning with Thorns** (courage)
   Isaiah 52:13–53:10; Matthew 16:24–28,
   27:27–31; Mark 15:16–19;
   Luke 23:6–11; John 19:1–7

4. **The Carrying of the Cross** (patience)
   Mark 8:31–38; Matthew 16:20–25;
   Luke 23:26–32; John 19:17–22;
   Philippians 2:6–11

5. **The Crucifixion** (self-renunciation)
   Mark 15:33–39; Luke 23:33–46;
   John 19:23–37; Acts 22:22–24;
   Hebrews 9:11–14

Glorious Mysteries
(Sundays and Wednesdays)

1. **The Resurrection** (faith)
   Matthew 28:1–10; Mark 16:1–18;
   Luke 24:1–12; John 20:1–10;
   Romans 6:1–14; 1 Corinthians 15:1–11

2. **The Ascension** (hope)
   Matthew 28:16–20; Luke 24:44–53;
   Acts 1:1–11; Ephesians 2:4–7

3. **The Descent of the Holy Spirit Upon
   the Apostles** (love)
   John 14:15–21; Acts 2:1–11; 4:23–31;
   11:15–18

4. **The Assumption** (eternal happiness)
   John 11:17–27; 1 Corinthians 15:20–28,
   42–57; Revelation 21:1–6

5. **The Coronation of Mary**
   (Marian devotion)
   Matthew 5:1–12; 2 Peter 3:10;
   Revelation 7:1–4, 9–12; 21:1–6

GLOSSARY

A–C

absolution—An essential element of the Sacrament of Penance in which the priest, by the power entrusted to the Church by Christ, pardons the sin(s) of the penitent. (*136*)

aggiornamento—Italian word for "updating" used by Pope John XXIII to describe the work of the Second Vatican Council. (*209*)

Apostolic Pardon—The special blessing given to the dying which grants a plenary indulgence. (*168*)

apostolic succession—The phrase used to describe that the authority to lead and teach the Church can be traced through the centuries from the Apostles to their successors, the bishops. (*197*)

catechumenate—The period of time between the Rite of Acceptance into the Order of Catechumens and the Rite of Election, when those seeking Baptism are instructed in the faith and grow in readiness for Baptism. It also refers to the entire process of formation in preparation for Baptism. (*41*)

cathedra—Latin term for the bishop's chair in his cathedral, the symbol of his teaching authority. (*190*)

Catholic social teaching—The body of official Church documents written by Church leaders in response to various social, political, and economic issues. (*56*)

character—An indelible spiritual sign imprinted on the soul in the non-repeatable Sacraments of Baptism, Confirmation, and Holy Orders. (*42*)

chrismation—Term used in Eastern rite churches for the sacrament called Confirmation in the West. (*72*)

common priesthood of the faithful—Term used to describe the share that all the faithful have in the one priesthood of Jesus Christ by virtue of being made members of the Body of Christ through their Baptism. (*53*)

communion of saints—All faithful Church members on earth, in heaven, and in purgatory; communion in holy things and among holy persons. (*122*)

confession—An essential element of the Sacrament of Reconciliation, which consists of telling one's sins to the priest. (*136*)

conscience—Refers to the act of judging based on one's knowledge of right and wrong. (*133*)

consecrated life—"The state of life which is constituted by the profession of the evangelical counsels [*LG* 44 § 4.]" (*CCC*, 914). (*202*)

contrition—An essential element of the Sacrament of Reconciliation, which consists of sorrow and hatred for the sin committed, together with a resolution not to sin again. (*136*)

crosier—The bishop's pastoral staff, shaped like a shepherd's crook. (*190*)

D–F

deposit of faith—Term used to refer to the divinely revealed truths entrusted to the Church for the salvation of all people. (*119*)

domestic Church—Phrase used at the Second Vatican Council (*Dogmatic Constitution on the Church*, 11) to describe the Christian family as the Church of the home—a specific embodiment of the larger reality of the Church. The family is the place where a community of believers carry on and experience the fundamental activities of the Church in the most basic way: through prayer and worship, sharing in the sacramental activity of the larger Church, proclaiming the word of God in evangelization and catechesis, and offering the witness of discipleship by doing missionary activity and the works of charity and justice. (233)

Eastern Churches—Families of Christian churches stemming from ancient times that reflect distinctive traditions of prayer, worship, and theology. (73)

epiclesis—A prayer asking for the sanctifying power of God's Holy Spirit. (149)

evangelization—The effort of bringing the Gospel, or "Good News" of the message and person of Christ to the whole world. This is to be done by proclamation and living testimony as Christ commanded. (234)

Extreme Unction—The name formerly used for the Sacrament of Anointing. (165)

Gifts of the Holy Spirit—Spiritual gifts given by the Holy Spirit that help people live God's love: wisdom, understanding, counsel (right judgment), fortitude (courage), knowledge, piety (reverence), and fear of the Lord (wonder and awe). (85)

grace—Our participation in the life of God. "Grace is *favor, the free and undeserved help* that God gives us to respond to his call to become children of God, adoptive sons, partakers of the divine nature and of eternal life" (*CCC*, 1996). (18)

Incarnation—The truth of faith that the Son of God assumed human nature and became man in order to accomplish our salvation in that same human nature. Jesus Christ, the Son of God, the second Person of the Trinity, is both true God and true man, not part God and part man. (15, 149)

inculturation—The adaptation of the liturgy by incorporating cultural expressions that help to express the authentic meaning of the Church's worship. (112)

indulgence—The remission before God of the temporal punishment due to sin whose guilt has already been forgiven. (151)

in extremis—Latin phrase which describes someone who is dying. (168)

justification—God's gracious action that frees humans from sin and bestows his righteousness through their belief in Jesus Christ. It involves the free gift of grace and our willingness to accept this grace. In so doing, we turn away from sin and turn toward God. (48)

lex credendi—Latin expression (meaning "law of belief") that refers to the content of authentic Catholic faith. (50)

lex orandi—Latin expression (meaning "law of prayer") that refers to the Church's embodiment of her faith in the official prayer of the Liturgy. (50)

liturgy—The Church's public worship of God through which Christ our High Priest continues the work of our redemption by means of the Church's celebration of the Paschal Mystery in which he accomplished our salvation. (19)

Liturgy of the Hours—The official daily prayer of the Church, divided up into segments to be said throughout the day. It consists primarily of Psalms, with other readings from Scripture and various sacred writings, as well as certain hymns and prayers of intercession. (23)

magisterium—The living, teaching office of the Church that gives authentic interpretation of the word of God, whether in Sacred Scripture or Sacred Tradition. (57)

major orders—Prior to Vatican II these included subdeaconate (now suppressed), diaconate, and priesthood. (*193*)

ministerial priesthood of the ordained—Expression used to refer to men who receive a special sacramental sharing in the one priesthood of Jesus Christ at the hands of the bishop, and who are thereby committed to a life of service to the Church and the priesthood of the faithful. They are ordained to guide, lead, and build up the Body of Christ in the name of Jesus, the head of the Church. (*53*)

minor orders—Non-sacramental steps on the way to priesthood prior to Vatican II. They included porter (doorkeeper), lector, exorcist, and acolyte. (*193*)

miter—Ceremonial headdress worn by bishops: a tall, folding cap with similar parts front and back that rise to a peak on top, and with two lappets hanging down the back. (*190*)

mixed marriage—A marriage between a Catholic and a baptized non-Catholic. (*231*)

mortal sin—A serious offense against the law of God that destroys the divine life, or sanctifying grace, in the soul of the sinner. (*133*)

mystagogy—The period of time between Easter and Pentecost when the newly baptized (neophytes) receive post-baptismal instruction and are more fully integrated into the Christian community. Mystagogical catechesis initiates the neophytes more fully into the mystery of Christ. (*47*)

Mystical Body—Those who are members of the Church, united with Christ as Head of the Body. (*122*)

Original Sin—The decision by the first humans to disobey God's commandment. They followed their wills rather than God, lost the grace of original holiness, and were subjected to death. Through their actions, sin entered the world. Thereafter, all people (except Jesus and Mary) begin life with a wounded human nature, drawn to selfishness and sin and in need of redemption by Christ. The term Original Sin also describes this state of fallen human nature. (*60*)

P–R

paradise—Symbolic term used to describe the original state of holiness and justice of Adam and Eve before the Fall. It involved harmony within the human person, between man and woman, and between humanity and all creation. The term paradise also refers to heaven. (*60*)

Paschal Mystery—The mystery of, and events involved in, our redemption: Jesus' suffering, death, Resurrection, and Ascension. (*20*)

penance (satisfaction)—An essential element of the Sacrament of Reconciliation, whereby the sinner, through prayer and action, makes amends for sin, especially in reparation to God for offenses against him. (*136*)

permanent deacon—A deacon who will remain a deacon lifelong without pursuing ordination to the priesthood. (*207*)

presbyterium—The college of priests who share in the ministry of the bishop as his coworkers within his diocese. (*199*)

Real Presence—Term used to describe that the whole Christ is uniquely and substantially present in the Eucharist, living and glorious, Body and Blood, soul and divinity. (*111*)

Revelation—God's self-disclosure in which he makes known his divine plan of salvation, most fully by sending his only Son. Revelation is passed on in the Church through both Scripture and Tradition. (*83*)

S–Z

sacrament—An effective sign of grace, instituted by Christ and entrusted to the Church, by which divine life is shared with us through the work of the Holy Spirit. (*13*)

sacramentals—Sacred signs instituted by the Church that resemble in some ways the sacraments, but which unlike the sacraments do not convey their spiritual effects; These "are signified and obtained through the prayers of the Church" (*CCC*, Glossary "Sacramentals"). (*27*)

sacred chrism—The perfumed oil consecrated by the bishop on Holy Thursday and used to anoint persons who receive the sacraments of Baptism, Confirmation, and Holy Orders. (53)

sanctification—God's transforming activity whereby we are made holy through the saving graces of Christ in the power of the Holy Spirit. Through this action, we are freed from sin, enter a state of friendship with God, and receive the grace to practice Christian virtue. Through the Church, we are sanctified in Baptism and strengthened by the other sacraments. (235)

sanctifying grace—God's divine life within us which makes us his friends. (61)

secular institutes—A group of the faithful who commit themselves to the evangelical counsels by sacred bonds and observe among themselves the fellowship appropriate to their secular way of life. (202)

social sin—The cumulative effect of personal sin over time, which can affect society and its institutions. This creates "structures of sin," which by analogy we call social sin. (146)

Society of Apostolic Life—A group of the faithful without religious vows who pursue an apostolic purpose proper to their society and lead a life in common according to their proper manner of life. (202)

temporal punishment—The purification from "unhealthy attachment to creatures" resulting from sin (CCC, Glossary "punishment, temporal"). This punishment can be paid in this life or after death in purgatory. (151)

Tradition—The living and authentic transmission of the teachings of Jesus in the Church. (58)

transitional deacon—A deacon who will be ordained to the priesthood. (207)

transubstantiation—Theological concept expressing the truth that the Eucharist involves a change of the entire *substance* (essence) of bread and wine into the Body and Blood of Christ, while the *accidents* (physical properties or "appearances") of bread and wine remain unchanged. (121)

venial sin—Sin that does not destroy the divine life in the soul, as mortal sin does, though it diminishes and wounds it. (139)

Viaticum—Holy Communion given to the dying as food for the journey to heaven. (160)

virtues—Good habits, qualities, and patterns of behavior that incline us to do good and make good moral choices. (80)

worship—Adoration and honor given to God, which is the first act of the virtue of religion (CCC, 2096). (19)

INDEX

Notes

Chapter 1

1 St. Thomas Aquinas, *Summa Theologica*, I, 2, 3.

Chapter 3

1 *"Declaration of the Synod Fathers"*, 4: L'Osservatore Romano (27 October 1974), p. 6.

Chapter 4

1 Irene B. Hodgson, *Through the Year with Oscar Romero: Daily Meditations* (Cincinnati, OH: St. Anthony Messenger Press, 2005), 47.

Chapter 5

1 Council of Trent (1551): DS 1691; cf. *Phil* 4:13; *1 Cor* 1:31; *2 Cor* 10:17; *Gal* 6:14; *Lk* 3:8
2 John Paul II, RP 16.

Chapter 6

1 *General Introduction, Pastoral Care of the Sick: Rites of Anointing and Viaticum*, 8–14.

2 See also Colossians 1:24; 2 Timothy 2:11–12; 1 Peter 4:13.
3 See Council of Trent, sess. 14, De Extrema Unctione, cap. 1: Denz-Schön. 1695; Vatican Council II, Dogmatic Constitution on the Church, no. 11: AAS 57 (1965) 15.

Chapter 7

1 *LG* 29; cf. *CD* 15.
2 CIC, can. 710.
3 Cf. CIC, can. 713 § 2.
4 *LG* 29; cf. *CD* 15.

Chapter 8

1 Council of Trent (1547): DS 1600–1601.
2 Saint Leo the Great, *Sermo.* 74, 2: PL 54, 398.
3 *Jn* 16:13; cf. *Mt* 13:52; *1 Cor* 4:1.

Photo Credits